General Extenders

General extenders are phrases like "*or something,*" "*and everything,*" "*and things (like that),*" "*and stuff (like that)*" and "*and so on.*" Although they are an everyday feature of spoken language, are crucial in successful interpersonal communication, and have multiple functions in discourse, they have so far gone virtually unnoticed in linguistics. This pioneering work provides a comprehensive description of this new linguistic category. It offers new insights into ongoing changes in contemporary English, the effect of grammaticalization, novel uses as associative plural markers and indicators of intertextuality, and the metapragmatic role of extenders in interaction. The forms and functions of general extenders are presented clearly and accessibly, enabling students to understand a number of different frameworks of analysis in discourse-pragmatic studies. From an applied perspective, the book presents a description of translation equivalents, an analysis of second language variation, and practical exercises for teaching second language learners of English.

MARYANN OVERSTREET is Professor of German at the University of Hawai'i at Mānoa. Her research focuses on discourse and pragmatics. Her publications include *Whales, Candlelight and Stuff Like That: General Extenders in English Discourse* (1999) and *The Routledge Modern German Reader* (2016).

GEORGE YULE has taught Linguistics at the University of Edinburgh, the University of Hawai'i, the University of Minnesota and Louisiana State University. His publications include *The Study of Language* (2020), *Discourse Analysis* (with G. Brown, 1983) and *Puzzlings* (with M. Overstreet, 2017).

General Extenders
The Forms and Functions of a New Linguistic Category

Maryann Overstreet
University of Hawaiʻi at Mānoa

George Yule

Shaftesbury Road, Cambridge CB2 8EA, United Kingdom

One Liberty Plaza, 20th Floor, New York, NY 10006, USA

477 Williamstown Road, Port Melbourne, VIC 3207, Australia

314–321, 3rd Floor, Plot 3, Splendor Forum, Jasola District Centre, New Delhi – 110025, India

103 Penang Road, #05–06/07, Visioncrest Commercial, Singapore 238467

Cambridge University Press is part of Cambridge University Press & Assessment, a department of the University of Cambridge.

We share the University's mission to contribute to society through the pursuit of education, learning and research at the highest international levels of excellence.

www.cambridge.org
Information on this title: www.cambridge.org/9781108940450

DOI: 10.1017/9781108938655

© Maryann Overstreet and George Yule 2021

This publication is in copyright. Subject to statutory exception and to the provisions of relevant collective licensing agreements, no reproduction of any part may take place without the written permission of Cambridge University Press & Assessment.

First published 2021
First paperback edition 2025

A catalogue record for this publication is available from the British Library

Library of Congress Cataloging-in-Publication data
Names: Overstreet, Maryann, 1962– author. | Yule, George, 1947– author.
Title: General extenders : the forms and functions of a new linguistic category / Maryann E. Overstreet, George Yule.
Description: Cambridge, UK ; New York : Cambridge University Press, 2021. | Includes bibliographical references and index.
Identifiers: LCCN 2021058712 (print) | LCCN 2021058713 (ebook) | ISBN 9781108837231 (hardback) | ISBN 9781108938655 (ebook)
Subjects: LCSH: General extenders (Linguistics) | English language – Discourse analysis. | BISAC: LANGUAGE ARTS & DISCIPLINES / Linguistics / Semantics | LANGUAGE ARTS & DISCIPLINES / Linguistics / Semantics
Classification: LCC PE1442.5 .O84 2021 (print) | LCC PE1442.5 (ebook) | DDC 420.1/41–dc23
LC record available at https://lccn.loc.gov/2021058712
LC ebook record available at https://lccn.loc.gov/2021058713

ISBN   978-1-108-83723-1   Hardback
ISBN   978-1-108-94045-0   Paperback

Cambridge University Press & Assessment has no responsibility for the persistence or accuracy of URLs for external or third-party internet websites referred to in this publication and does not guarantee that any content on such websites is, or will remain, accurate or appropriate.

Contents

List of Tables		*page* viii
Acknowledgments		ix
List of Abbreviations		x

1	Introduction		1
	1.1	General Extenders	1
	1.2	The Structure of General Extenders	2
	1.3	Structures with General Extenders	4
	1.4	The Functions of General Extenders	6
		1.4.1 Referential Function	6
		1.4.2 Interpersonal Function	7
		1.4.3 Personal Function	8
	1.5	Textual Function	9
	1.6	Historical Development	10
		1.6.1 The Historical Record	10
		1.6.2 The Grammaticalization Path	11
	1.7	Social Markers	12
	1.8	In Different Languages	14
		1.8.1 In a Creole	14
		1.8.2 In French, Lithuanian and Others	14
	1.9	In Learner Language and Language Teaching	16
		1.9.1 In Learner Language	16
		1.9.2 In Language Teaching	17
		1.9.3 In English as a Lingua Franca	18
	1.10	Reflections and Projections	19
		1.10.1 Multiple Functions	19
		1.10.2 Utterance Position	20

2	Referential Function and Categorization		22
	2.1	Set-Marking Tags	22
	2.2	Terminating Tags	24
	2.3	Variable Tags	26
	2.4	Vague Tags	27
	2.5	Vague Markers	30
	2.6	List Completers	31
	2.7	Extender Tags	33
	2.8	Restricted Tags	35

v

	2.9	The SKT Tags	38
	2.10	Specific Extenders	40
	2.11	After Tags	41
3	Interpersonal Function and Intersubjectivity		43
	3.1	The Interpersonal	44
	3.2	Intersubjectivity	46
	3.3	Cooperative Fellow Speakers	47
	3.4	Solidarity	48
	3.5	Hedges	51
	3.6	Hedging Reported Speech	53
	3.7	Expressing Doubts	54
	3.8	Interpersonal Entertainment	55
	3.9	Hedging Invitations and Comments	57
4	Personal Function and Subjectivity		60
	4.1	Evaluation	61
	4.2	Subjectivity	62
	4.3	Maximizing	63
	4.4	Beyond Expectation	65
	4.5	Contrary to Expectation	67
	4.6	The Minimum Expected	69
	4.7	Formulaic Disclaimers	70
	4.8	On Being Indifferent	73
	4.9	Metapragmatic Awareness	76
5	Textual Function and Turn Construction		79
	5.1	Performance Fillers and Placeholders	79
	5.2	Punctors	81
	5.3	Brackets and Clusters	86
	5.4	Foregrounding	92
	5.5	Turn Construction	93
6	Historical Development and Change		98
	6.1	From *ant so vorth* to *and so on and so forth*	99
	6.2	From Specific to General	101
	6.3	From *or sum oþer þing* to *or something like that*	105
	6.4	From *or any other thing rounde* to *or anything like that*	108
	6.5	From *and moche other stuffe* to *and stuff like that*	110
	6.6	From *and other Thynges* to *and things like that*	112
	6.7	From *and that* to *and that sort of thing*	114
	6.8	Grammaticalization	115
	6.9	Decategorialization	116
	6.10	Morphosyntactic Reanalysis	119
	6.11	Phonological Attrition	120
	6.12	Pragmatic Shift	122
7	Social Marking and Variation		125
	7.1	The Age Factor	126
		7.1.1 Age-Grading	129

Contents	vii

	7.2	The Gender Factor	131
	7.3	The Social-Class Factor	134
	7.4	Register	137
		7.4.1 The Academic Register	138
		7.4.2 The Business Register	140
	7.5	International Variation	143
	7.6	America, Britain and Canada	144
	7.7	Australia and New Zealand	146
	7.8	Ireland and Scotland	147
	7.9	What Is the Relevant Data?	149
8	In Different Languages		151
	8.1	English Creoles	151
		8.1.1 Trinidad Creole	152
		8.1.2 Hawai'i Creole English/Pidgin	153
	8.2	Translation Equivalents	156
	8.3	Brazilian Portuguese and Spanish	157
	8.4	Lithuanian and Russian	159
	8.5	German	160
	8.6	French	166
	8.7	Swedish	171
	8.8	Persian	173
	8.9	Highlighting Differences	175
9	In Learner Language and Language Teaching		177
	9.1	Explaining Low Frequency	177
	9.2	French Learners	178
	9.3	Dutch Learners	179
	9.4	German Learners	181
	9.5	Swedish Learners	183
	9.6	Persian Learners	185
	9.7	English Learners	187
	9.8	English as a Lingua Franca	188
	9.9	In Language Teaching	192
10	Reflections and Projections		198
	10.1	Multiple Functions	198
	10.2	Utterance Position	200
	10.3	Associative Plurals	202
	10.4	An Apparent Anomaly	204
	10.5	*And/or elsewhere*	207
	10.6	Lists and the Like	211
	10.7	A New Linguistic Category	213

Notes	215
References	220
Index	235

Tables

7.1	English general extenders associated with younger and older speakers	*page* 129
7.2	English general extenders associated with male and female speakers	134
7.3	English general extenders associated with different social classes	135
7.4	Montreal French general extenders associated with social class	137
7.5	General extenders in international varieties of English	144
9.1	Disjunctive general extenders: a basic learning exercise	195
9.2	Adjunctive general extenders: a basic learning exercise	195
9.3	General extenders: a correction exercise	196
9.4	General extenders: a testing exercise	197

Acknowledgments

To fully acknowledge those who made this work possible, we would have to put the References section here to identify all our influencers, without whose scholarship we would have had much less to say. A few influencers stand out: Karin Aijmer, Jack Bilmes, Laurel Brinton, Gill Brown and Jenny Cheshire. Our thanks go to them. We would also like to thank friends (Suzy Byrd, Katinka Hammerich, Terrie Mathis) and family (Cathy Overstreet, Dorothy Jean Overstreet, Nani Overstreet) for all the data, and Helen Barton of Cambridge University Press for thinking this book was a good idea.

Abbreviations

CANBEC	*Cambridge and Nottingham Business English Corpus*
CANCAD	*Cambridge and Nottingham Corpus of Academic Discourse*
CEECS	*Corpus of Early English Correspondence Sampler*
COCA	*Corpus of Contemporary American English*
COHA	*Corpus of Historical American English*
COLT	*Bergen Corpus of London Teenage Language*
EEBO	*Early English Books Online*
ELF	English as a lingua franca
ELFA	*English as a Lingua Franca in Academic Settings*
ICE	*International Corpus of English*
L1	First language
L2	Second language
LIBEL	*Limerick-Belfast Corpus of Academic Spoken English*
LLC	*London-Lund Corpus*
MEC	*Middle English Compendium*
MED	*Middle English Dictionary*
MEMEM	*Michigan Early Modern English Materials*
MICASE	*Michigan Corpus of Academic Spoken English*
OED	*Oxford English Dictionary (Online)*
PDE	Present Day English
SKT	sort of/kind of/type of
SOV	Subject-Object-Verb
SVO	Subject-Verb-Object
VCM	vague category marker

1 Introduction

1.1 General Extenders

We first wrote about general extenders more than twenty years ago (Overstreet and Yule, 1997a, b) and since then we have witnessed an explosion of studies and articles on the topic. The term "general extender" is used as a linguistic category label for a wide range of expressions with similar positional and compositional features. These expressions are described as "general" because they are non-specific in reference and "extenders" because they extend utterances that are otherwise grammatically complete. They have a basic structure of conjunction plus noun phrase and are normally syntactically optional constituents that typically occur in phrase- or clause-final position. There are two distinct types: those beginning with *and* are described as **adjunctive general extenders** and basically signal that "there is more" (that could be said) and those beginning with *or* are **disjunctive general extenders** that signal that "there are other possibilities" (that could be mentioned). They are mostly found in everyday spoken interaction and, perhaps as a consequence, are virtually absent from older descriptive grammars.

The only grammar to document the frequency and distribution of these expressions, the *Longman Grammar of Spoken and Written English* (Biber et al., 1999: 115–17), lists the following phrases, in order of frequency: *or something, and everything, and things (like that), and stuff (like that)*. In that grammar, they are identified as "coordination tags," a label that has not been widely adopted, but the linguistic category it describes has clearly become established as part of the English language. Now more widely known as general extenders, these expressions have been documented in all varieties of English, as illustrated in the following set of examples, from southern British English in (1), (2), (6), (9) and (10); from American English in (11) and (12), from Australian English in (3), from Canadian English in (4), from Irish English in (5), from New Zealand English in (7), and from Scottish English in (8).[1]

(1) *she came in a Hackney-Coach, and some Boxes **and Things** with her*
(2) *sort of experts and psychics and wise men **and things like that***
(3) *Chaddy has lots of bargain shops downstairs **and stuff***

(4) *we used to just go to the Rouge-Valley and swim and have picnics **and stuff like that***

(5) *he'd have a swimming pool **and everything** shur they all have their houses in Mayfair Road **and everything***

(6) *the boys aren't left to do the washing-up **and that sort of thing***

(7) *they're sort of typical medieval-type baggy things – uh pantaloons **and that sort of stuff***

(8) *he was flying fae Prestwick across to Ireland **and that***

(9) *What are you doing tonight, you know, do you want to go out **or something***

(10) *if you wanted to be anonymous **or whatever**.*

(11) *Are you like planning to do that? I mean, I don't wanna step on your toes **or anything***

(12) *If you really want to hear about it, the first thing you'll probably want to know is where I was born, and what my lousy childhood was like, and how my parents were occupied **and all** before they had me, **and all that David Copperfield kind of crap***

The examples in bold represent many of the most common forms of general extenders, but they are only a small selection of the wide range of forms that have been documented.[2] From a structural point of view, we can analyze these forms as either distinctly short, with only two parts, as in most examples, or distinctly long, with four or more parts, as in (2), (4), (6), (7) and (12). Example (12) is from the first sentence in J. D. Salinger's (1951) novel *The Catcher in the Rye*, and contains a basic general extender structure (*and all that kind of crap*) with more lexical material (*David Copperfield*) included, making a much more specific reference and creating what we will describe as a "specific extender." We will investigate some of these less frequent "specific extenders" in Chapter 2.

1.2 The Structure of General Extenders

The most frequent forms are short, consisting of two parts, a conjunction and a noun phrase containing a proform, which can be a generic noun or pronoun, usually indefinite, as shown in (13). We use curly brackets to indicate that one, and only one, of the possible constituents listed is used in the construction on any occasion.

(13)   conjunction   proform
        and   {*stuff / things / everything / that*}
        or   {*something / anything / whatever*}

Other short forms include *and all (that), and others, and the like, and such, or what*.

Long forms have two different structures. In one, the comparative phrase (*like that/this*) is included as a modifier after some of the short forms, as shown in (14).

1.2 The Structure of General Extenders

(14)   conjunction   proform   modifier
             and   {stuff / things / everything}   like {that/this}
             or   {something / anything}   like {that/this}

In the other long form, normally only used as an adjunctive, one version of the "SKT-construction" is included before the generic noun as proform. The SKT-construction consists of *sort of, kind of* or *type of* (Dehé and Stathi, 2016).

(15)   conjunction   demonstrative   SKT noun   proform
            and   {that/this}   {sort / kind / type} of   {stuff / thing}

This long form can be used in the plural, as in *and those kinds of things*. The quantifier *all* is sometimes included, and a large number of other nouns can be used instead of *stuff* or *thing*, as in *and all that kind of nonsense/mess/crap/shit / jazz*. Each of the long forms in (14) and (15) can be used with a pause instead of a conjunction.[3]

The structures analyzed in (13)–(15) have some variation in their components and hence flexibility in terms of which elements can be used in a particular expression on a particular occasion. In addition to those, there are some fairly fixed expressions with a variety of different components that also fill the structural slot of general extender. Some forms are more often found in formal speech and writing: *et cetera/etc., and so on, and so forth, or so, or thereabouts*. Other fixed expressions are used with variable frequency in token counts from different corpora: (*and*) *blah, blah, blah, and (all) the rest of it, and (all) that stuff, and/or what not, and/or what have you* (cf. Aijmer, 2002: 221–23; Pichler and Levey, 2011: 469–71; Tagliamonte and Denis, 2010: 362–63). In studies of corpora of spoken discourse, there is an enormous range of forms identifiable as general extenders, many found only once in a corpus, some only used in certain contexts (*and this, that and the other*) and some restricted to a particular dialect (e.g. *or summat, or owt like that*). We will explore some aspects of sociolinguistic variation in Chapter 7.

It is tempting to see the short forms (e.g. *and things*) as a "reduced" version of the longer form (e.g. *and things like that*), following a general pattern of linguistic change, where frequency of use results in reduction in form, but there is little evidence to support this idea in the case of general extender variants, as Aijmer (1985: 373) pointed out and Tagliamonte (2016: 130) has more recently confirmed using archival data. In the historical record, as we will see in Chapter 6, some short forms came into use before the associated longer forms in the contemporary language. Moreover, short forms (*and stuff*) are not used in quite the same way as their long-form counterparts (*and stuff like that*). Short forms are often reduced in speech ('*nstu*) and are typically used inside a tone unit with a preceding constituent, whereas longer forms are much more likely to be in a separate tone unit by themselves. The short forms are also used much more frequently. This aspect of general extender use suggests that the short forms have become more integrated into the rhythmic structure of utterances, making them less salient in phonological terms (cf. Aijmer, 1985, 2002; Channell, 1994; Warren, 2007).

1.3 Structures with General Extenders

The basic syntactic structure of general extenders is conjunction (*and/or*) plus noun phrase (NP). We would expect that a structure of this type would normally combine with another preceding noun phrase to form a basic NP *and/or* NP structural context for general extenders in use. This is illustrated in *some Boxes and Things* in example (1) earlier. This example, from the year 1739, cited in the *Corpus of English Dialogues 1560–1760* (Kytö and Culpeper, 2006), comes from a time when nouns in English were written with initial capital letters and the *Things* referenced were almost certainly real physical "things." Looking at historical examples, we can see that general extenders may have originally been used with referential meaning, identifying objects in the real world, a conclusion supported by the grammatical agreement between *Boxes* and *Things*, both having non-animate [− animate] and countable [+ plural] as features. This grammatical agreement relationship continues to be very common, as illustrated in example (6) presented earlier, connecting a singular non-animate in *the washing-up* with *sort of thing* in the general extender.

Other structures incorporating general extenders can be found without strict grammatical agreement between the two noun phrases. In example (2), there are NPs with the feature [+ human], as in *wise men*, attached to an NP (*things*) with the feature [− human] in *and things like that*. In (3), the combination involves an NP (*shops*) with the feature [+ countable] and an NP (*stuff*) with the feature [− countable] in the general extender. Similarly in (7), a plural noun *pantaloons* is connected to the non-plural *stuff*. A further erosion of the expected grammatical agreement can be identified in (10), where an adjective (*anonymous*) is combined with the general extender (*or whatever*). In (4), (9) and (12), the expected NP *and/or* NP structure has been replaced by a VP *and/or* NP structure where verb phrases such as *have picnics*, *go out* and *were occupied*, combine with *and stuff like that*, *or something* and *and all* respectively. Perhaps more radical is a development whereby whole clauses or sentences, as in (8) and (11) seem to be used in combination with the noun phrase elements (*that, anything*) in the general extenders. To understand this phenomenon, consider example (11) where there is an NP *or* NP structure (*your toes or anything*) at the end, potentially indicating that *your toes*

1.3 Structures with General Extenders

could be what *or anything* is attached to. In that interpretation, the general extender would potentially be implicating "or any other possible part of you, as an alternative to *toes*, such as one or both of your feet or your ankles." Familiarity with the idiom, however, prevents us from going along with this misinterpretation (since it really doesn't have anything to do with actual "toes") and leads us to see that the general extender is actually attached to the whole idiom. We will investigate this aspect of general extender use in greater detail in Chapter 4.

At this point, it is worth noting that general extenders are best classified as examples of pragmatic markers rather than discourse markers in terms of their syntactic role, though both share the feature of being normally syntactically optional (Aijmer, 2013; Beeching, 2016; Brinton, 2017). Generally, we can distinguish between the role of pragmatic markers as establishing and maintaining "social cohesion" through the marking of shared background knowledge and experience, interpersonal relationships and the interpretation of social action while discourse markers are used in establishing and maintaining "textual cohesion," that is, marking formal connections between parts of text (spoken and written) and their information status within the larger discourse. Discourse markers (e.g. *Oh, Well, So*), as characterized by Schiffrin (1987: 40), are a disparate group of linguistic items, belonging to different word classes, most of which are used at the beginning of utterances, though utterance-final uses have also been explored (cf. Beeching and Detges, 2014). Unlike discourse markers, general extenders are not used utterance-initially and are typically in phrase- or clause-final position, with a limited range of structural components, as shown in (13)–(15). However, these are basically formal differences. When it comes to function, there is less of a dichotomy, and general extenders can be used with textual functions, such as topic- and turn-completion, for example, as we will document in Chapter 5. Attempts to list and analyze pragmatic markers (Brinton, 1996, 2017) include parenthetical forms such as *you know* and *I mean*, which are also considered to be discourse markers (cf. Schiffrin, 1987). We will also treat *you know* and *I mean* as pragmatic markers which often accompany general extenders and, like them, can be analyzed as "simultaneously serving textual and interpersonal functions" (Brinton, 2017: 7). As Aijmer and Simon-Vandenbergen point out as a general observation, pragmatic markers "can overlap with other markers in some of their meanings. Describing and constraining the multifunctionality of pragmatic markers is therefore a challenging task" (2011: 229). Accepting that challenge, at least with regard to general extenders, we will try to tease apart some of the factors involved in that multifunctionality.

1.4 The Functions of General Extenders

1.4.1 Referential Function

As we noted earlier, the longer forms of general extenders are less integrated into the stream of speech and contain an indexical form, typically *that*, which points to a connection with an element in an earlier part of the utterance, suggesting an antecedent–anaphor type of cohesive relationship. This type of connection has led a number of scholars to view general extenders as a means of indicating that, combined with the referent of the antecedent expression, there is a set or category being implicated by the speaker. Interpreting general extenders in this way assumes that they have a referential function and a role in the propositional information contained in utterances. In clear cases like example (4) earlier, this approach would identify *swim and have picnics* as two examples of a set of activities, of which there are more (*and stuff like that*), and which the speaker expects the hearer to be able to recognize based on pre-existing knowledge, and probably identify as a category of some kind, such as "outdoor activities." Similarly in (6), with a single antecedent (*the washing-up*) and a long general extender already indicating other similar activities (*and that sort of thing*), we find it easy to think of the category of "housework" or "household chores." In much of the early research on general extenders, the set-marking or category-identifying function was virtually the only one recognized and, for some researchers, remains the only one that they discuss. We will explore this (referential) interpretation of the role of general extenders in more detail in Chapter 2.

In addition, general extenders can be interpreted in terms of another referential function involved in the creation of lists. Because they are phrase-final and clause-final, general extenders are frequently at the end of utterances and, in many cases, signal that something is finished or complete. This is also illustrated in example (4), where the speaker begins a list with one item *swim*, then gives a second item *have picnics* and completes it, not with a third item, but with *and stuff like that*. This function of general extenders can be described as list-completion, explored in detail in Chapter 2. The signaling of a completion point can also serve a textual function when it marks the end of the speaker's turn in the course of an interaction. That is, the use of *and stuff like that*, as exemplified in (4), can simultaneously serve more than one function, marking a referential function ("outdoor activities") as well as both list-completion and turn-completion, with a textual function. Although we will be attempting to isolate and identify each of the key functions of general extenders, we shouldn't forget that their use may be multifunctional on any occasion, as illustrated in Overstreet (1999: 148).

1.4 The Functions of General Extenders

1.4.2 Interpersonal Function

General extenders have also been identified as having a role in social aspects of language use in spoken interaction, where their use can be described in terms of an interpersonal function. When one speaker says to another, as in example (9) earlier, *do you want to go out or something*, the function of *or something* doesn't necessarily involve alternatives in referential terms, but may be indicating the possibility of alternatives as a way of softening a potential imposition on the other speaker. In example (11), the idiomatic use of "(not) step on your toes" actually announces a possible imposition that is given wide range via *or anything*, signaling a strong desire not to impose. In these examples, the general extenders would seem to have little referential function, and more of a politeness function based on a social expectation that can be stated simply as "avoid imposing." Viewed in this way, general extenders seem to be functioning like pragmatic markers, which, along with others such as *you know* and *sort of*, are linguistic mechanisms speakers use "to create and maintain relationships with each other and to mitigate the strength of their assertions" (Beeching, 2016: 1).

The uses of *or something* and *not . . . or anything* in examples (9) and (11) earlier are both examples of negative politeness strategies in spoken interaction, based on the idea inherent in "avoid imposing." By including the general extenders, the speakers are trying to mitigate the kind of imposition inherent in asking about another person's projected behavior. In interpersonal terms, the speaker in (9) is using *or something* as a hedge to reduce the potential threat to the other's independence and freedom of action. In (11), in an utterance including *I mean*, the speaker is clarifying her intention not to do "anything" to upset the other and is essentially marking deference in interpersonal terms.

We can also use adjunctive forms in interaction as part of a positive politeness strategy that indicates the two speakers are socially similar and have certain things in common. Adjunctive extenders can be used by speakers to mark an assumed "co-conception of the world" (Aijmer, 2002: 240) and to signal invited solidarity in interpreting what is being said. Often accompanied by *you know*, another form marking an assumption of shared experience, adjunctive extenders appeal to intersubjectivity, the sense in which our backgrounds are so similar that we share mutual understanding of the world. A very clear example of these assumptions in play is illustrated in (16), from Overstreet and Yule (1997b: 254).

(16)   *y'know back when we were buddies and we used to ride our bikes together* **and stuff**

Not all interpersonal uses of general extenders are as transparent as example (16), but we can use such clear instances as a guide to the interpretation of more complex structures as we expand the discussion of intersubjectivity, politeness strategies and other instantiations of the interpersonal function in Chapter 3.

1.4.3 Personal Function

Another aspect of general extender use is the capacity to indicate how the speaker feels about what is being said. This personal type of expressive function is apparent in example (12) earlier, where the inclusion of a pejorative term *crap* in the general extender structure indicates a negative, or at least downgrading, attitude to the idea being articulated. Other pejorative terms (e.g. *nonsense, junk, shit, rubbish*) can be found in general extenders used to downgrade the nature of the information attached. Not quite as negative, but also capable of sending a signal that the speaker isn't too concerned about accuracy is the typical use of *or whatever*, as in example (10) earlier. Depending on the intonation (and possibly an accompanying gesture), this general extender can simply indicate a lack of commitment to the appropriateness or accuracy of what is being said or "can convey a stronger dismissive attitude of 'I don't care'" (Overstreet, 1999: 147). This evaluative element may not be immediately obvious to second language learners of English, who may inadvertently send an "I don't care" signal by mistake while thinking that *or something* and *or whatever* are interchangeable. What disjunctive general extenders do seem to have in common is a "subjective alternativity" feature described for the discourse (i.e. non-truth conditional) uses of *or* in Ariel and Mauri (2019: 40). We will look at the challenges facing learners in the use and interpretation of general extenders in Chapter 9.

In contrast, a speaker can signal that something has high value, as in the use of *and everything* twice in example (5) earlier. The implication here is that the speaker is referring to individuals whose wealth enables them to have extremely expensive things, exemplified by *a swimming pool* and houses in an expensive neighborhood. In this case, the phrase *and everything* doesn't just communicate that "there is more," but acts as an intensifier, emphasizing an evaluation of the preceding information as something extreme or remarkable. What is interesting about *and everything* is that the evaluation it conveys has to do with something being extreme, not just extremely good, but also extremely bad, as in (17), transcribed as it is presented in Evison *et al*. (2007: 151). The speaker had earlier talked about a trip from Birmingham to Nottingham in "the most crappy train" and in (17) provides more details to support that opinion.

(17)   *The seats were dirty and ripped. And the floor was dirty. And everything.*

Clearly this speaker had an extremely negative evaluation of the train trip. We will return to the analysis of the personal function of general extenders in Chapter 4.

1.5 Textual Function

Although they have not typically been analyzed as such, general extenders can be used with a textual function in the organization of discourse. We have already noted in connection with example (4) that speakers can use general extenders to signal that they are completing their turn at that point in the interaction, a procedural use further exemplified in Overstreet (2014: 111). General extenders have also been identified as having a role in co-constructed turn taking, where their use "supports the co-construction by projecting a bond of shared knowledge with the speaker and other participants" (Clancy and McCarthy, 2014: 440). We will look more closely at the structural role general extenders can play in conversational turn construction in Chapter 5.

Within their turns, speakers can also use a general extender as a "bracket" around a phrase or clause, with other pragmatic markers in the position of the other bracket. The general extender is naturally a right-hand bracket, with other markers forming the left-hand bracket. One effect of "bracketing" is to mark off smaller chunks within a longer utterance, a process that allows general extenders to assume a role that Secova (2014) describes as "a segmentation signal dividing discourse into smaller, more easily processed units" (2014: 290). The pattern in examples (2) and (7) is for *sort of* to fill the left bracket before a description, and for a general extender (*and things like that, and that sort of stuff*) to occur in the right bracket. Other left-bracket pragmatic markers are illustrated in (9) with *you know*, indicating the speaker's appeal to a shared perspective on things, and in (11), with *I mean*, indicating a clarification attempt, both ending with the disjunctive general extenders (*or something, or anything*) as right brackets. We will look in greater detail at this type of internal structure in utterances in Chapter 5.

One other aspect of the textual function of general extenders that may only be characteristic of the speech style of some individuals and not others was highlighted by Macaulay (1985) in his study of an individual who used the general extender *and that* with very high frequency. Example (8) from earlier is reproduced here in (18) as it was originally published, with Macaulay's (1985: 114) commentary in parentheses.

(18) *he was flying fae Prestwick across to Ireland* **and that** (i.e. to Ireland and nowhere else)

With this and a number of other examples, Macaulay (1985) argues that, far from having a referential function, many general extenders in his data were being used more like punctuation, that is, having a relatively simple rhythmic function in the structure of this individual's way of talking. If they can indeed be used as oral punctuation marks when speakers are organizing what they are trying to say, then general extenders can be seen as fulfilling another textual function that will be the subject of further analysis in Chapter 5.

1.6 Historical Development

After looking at the various functions of general extenders in the contemporary language, we will take a step back in Chapter 6 and try to discover where these current forms come from. Some researchers have looked at variation in the contemporary language as a possible window into historical processes. Others have searched older texts, and the *Oxford English Dictionary (OED) Online* (3rd edition online, www.oed.com/) in particular, to find versions of general extenders in use at earlier periods. These two approaches can be characterized in terms of their main concerns. One is concerned with the grammaticalization of general extenders, the process whereby lexical items and constructions go through formal changes and develop grammatical functions, as evidenced in the contemporary language. The other approach attempts to document the history of general extender development using diachronic data. Let's begin with the latter, and an examination of historical record.

1.6.1 The Historical Record

We have already noted that a novel published over seventy years ago, *The Catcher in the Rye*, made use of general extenders from the very first sentence. The frequent use of general extenders, particularly *and all*, is a salient feature in the speech of the main character, in many ways representing the vernacular of the era. However, finding illustrations of the vernacular from much earlier periods can prove to be a challenge. This may be, as Tagliamonte and Denis (2010: 339) point out, because the historical record mostly consists of written, typically published, material and rarely includes examples of everyday interactive spoken language use where general extenders might have been flourishing.

Tagliamonte and Denis (2010) made use of one of the few historical records of spoken English in Kytö and Culpeper's (2006) *Corpus of English Dialogues 1560–1760* in their attempt to identify earlier forms, several of which will be included in Chapter 6, with the dates of their appearance. A much more thorough search through a wide range of historical records is evidenced in the work of Carroll (2007, 2008), whose examples (with dates) will also be included in our study. One of Carroll's (2008: 13) earliest recorded examples has the form *ant so vorth*, as in (19), which has the word *vorth*, with an earlier meaning involving physical motion (cf. De Smet, 2010), that had already developed into an abstract marker of continuation in this Middle English usage from the year 1325.

1.6 Historical Development

(19)   *Tac a lutel radel ant grynt to thin asise . . . **ant so vorth**, as I seyde er*
("Take a little red ochre and grind into thin sizing . . . and so forth, as I said earlier")

[c1325 Recipe Painting (1), s. v sō (adv.) 5(c) MED]

This general extender (*and so forth*) has stayed virtually unchanged for almost seven hundred years, but others have more varied histories. We will look at the origins and development of all the most frequent general extenders in Chapter 6. One analysis follows the word *stuff*, recorded in the late Middle English period referring to "personal property," as in (20) from a will written in 1439, and "materials for an army or war," as in (21) from the year 1500.

(20)   *All his other godes **and stuffes** meveable that he leveth vnto hem*

[1439 F.J. FURNIVAL Fifty Earliest Eng. Wills (1882) 126 OED]

(21)   *with a grete power ordenance **and stuff***

[a1500 (>1461) Bale's Chron. in R. Fenley Six Town Chron. (1911) 116 OED]

(22)   *it would have taken its lead from playwrights like Brecht but also from people like Paulo Freire **and stuff like that***

[2007 O'Keeffe *et al.* p. 180]

Five hundred years later, the effect of "semantic bleaching" (Sweetser, 1988) and other long-term processes have dissolved any referential value in the word *stuff* when it is used as part of a general extender, as in (22), from O'Keeffe *et al.* (2007: 180), where its interpretation is contextually determined. We will describe how *and stuff (like that)* and other general extenders were forged through those long-term processes, collectively known as grammaticalization.

1.6.2   The Grammaticalization Path

When scholars investigate how aspects of the contemporary language came to have their modern form and function, they often appeal to several processes associated with grammaticalization, which has been defined as "the change whereby lexical items and constructions come in certain linguistic contexts to serve grammatical functions, and once grammaticalized, continue to develop new grammatical functions" (Hopper and Traugott, 2003: 18). For these scholars, it is not just grammatical morphemes that have a function in the grammar because the mechanisms of change they describe can be found in the development of pragmatic markers, such as general extenders, as well as grammatical markers (Traugott, 1995, 2016). The study of historical development using the grammaticalization framework allows us to identify specific mechanisms that lead to regular types of change. As we investigate how a linguistic item moves from a fully explicit form, with lexical status, to a new and typically reduced form, with a role in the structural organization of utterances, we can identify three related processes of change: decategorialization, morphosyntactic reanalysis and phonological attrition.

One of the indications that decategorialization has taken place in a general extender is the loss of constraints on coordination, as illustrated in (23), from Cheshire (2007: 169), where *things*, originally [non-human], is attached to *children* [human]. In this case, the word *things* is no longer being used to represent a referential category with the semantic feature [non-human] and has disappeared into a fixed phrase. A related change is described as morphological reanalysis, or fusion (Hopper and Traugott, 2003: 44), which typically involves the reduction of longer phrases with separate elements such as *or* + *some* + *thing* becoming fused together as a single unit in which the word *thing* again loses its lexical status, as in (24) from Drew (2014: 232).

(23)   *they take disabled children **and things** around*

(24)   *I'll give you a call then tomorrow when I get in 'rsumn*

Example (24) can also serve to illustrate phonological attrition, a process that is often based on a frequency effect through which expressions that we use a lot tend to become phonetically much reduced in our speech. In (24) the general extender was transcribed in the original in a way that suggests a pronunciation with much less phonological substance than would be present in the articulation of the fuller written form. We will document this type of change in more detail and take a closer look at the other effects of grammaticalization on the contemporary forms and functions of general extenders in Chapter 6.

1.7   Social Markers

Earlier, we reported on Macaulay's (1985) description of one speaker's use of *and that* which was consistent, we now know, with that individual's age, gender, social class and geographical location or region (older, male, working class, Scottish), giving it status as a social marker. There is a social marking function served by general extenders that may allow us to make sense of some of the variation in their forms and uses by distinguishing among groups of speakers along social parameters. Indeed, in the opinion of Pichler and Levey,

1.7 Social Markers

"general extenders are prime candidates for the marking of social differentiation" (2011: 463).

Social differentiation in general extender use has been studied from a regional perspective, comparing frequency and type across national varieties, such as American and British English (Aijmer, 2013), and within varieties, such as southern versus northern British English (Cheshire, 2007). Aijmer notes that a frequent variant favored by one group "can acquire social significance as a marker of ethnic identity" (2013: 146). She points out that in Singapore the form *and all that* is very frequent, yet in the United States, it is relatively rare, with *and stuff* being the most favored adjunctive form (2013: 133–37). This finding is supported by other studies of North American English by Overstreet and Yule (1997b) and Tagliamonte and Denis (2010). In British English, the form *and that* is most widespread, but it has a strong association with both social class and location, according to Cheshire (2007). Perhaps the most consistent finding in this domain is the difference between older and younger speakers. Overall, younger speakers use general extenders with higher frequency, but older speakers employ "a broader inventory of general extender variants," as Pichler and Levey (2011: 461) report. They also note that, in their data from the north of England, young speakers tend to use more short forms and older speakers use more long forms, with greater variety of infrequently used versions of general extenders among the older group. Similar findings have been reported by Stubbe and Holmes (1995), describing New Zealand English, Stenström *et al.* (2002), describing the British English of London, and Denis (2017) describing the Canadian English of Toronto. We will look in greater detail at the relationship between social parameters and general extender use in Chapter 7.

There is also some evidence that variation in register can be aligned with variation in general extender selection. A basic distinction can be made between informal talk among familiars and formal talk that is more in the public domain, as found in news radio interviews, political debates and academic discussions. This distinction is sometimes characterized as a difference between casual and careful styles of talking. In Overstreet and Yule's (1997b) study, that distinction had very clear consequences for the number and type of general extenders in use. In their report, Overstreet and Yule (1997b: 252–53) show that *or something* and *and stuff* have high frequency in the informal register, from which the forms *and so on* and *et cetera* (*etc.*) are totally absent, yet this latter pair are the most frequently used in the formal register, a finding echoed by Biber *et al.* (1999: 116), contrasting conversational and academic discourse. Other general extender-type expressions are more typical of discourse in the business register (Malyuga and McCarthy, 2018), also analyzed in Chapter 7. We will return to this and other aspects of the social marking effect of general extenders in terms of age, gender, social class, register and regional variety in Chapter 7.

1.8 In Different Languages

In recent years, there has been a lot of interest in the extent to which general extenders are used in other languages in similar ways and with some of the same functions (or not) that we have already identified. In their study of Persian, Parvaresh *et al.* (2012) provided data to show that the common assumption of utterance-final position for general extenders is probably based on the Subject-Verb-Object (SVO) word order of English where objects incorporating general extenders typically appear at the end of utterances. When the language has SOV word order, like Persian, objects with general extenders are frequently in the middle of utterances. These, and a range of other illuminating observations from the study of general extenders in different languages will be explored in Chapter 8.

1.8.1 In a Creole

We will also look in detail at how specific examples of general extenders are used in other less-studied varieties. For example, in Trinidad Creole, the expression *an ting* is reported to have a function "first as a Creole marker and second as a discourse feature entailing implicit shared knowledge" (Youssef, 1993: 291). As illustrated in (25), *an ting* is clearly being used as a general extender by the medical personnel in recordings of AIDS counseling sessions.

(25) *you know well – the AIDS virus could only spread – through sex **an ting** – it can't spread by just touching somebody you know*

As Youssef (1993: 303) notes, the general extender isn't adding anything to the propositional content of the utterance (it's not referential), but is serving to break down the power differential in the professional setting by appealing to shared knowledge and experience, giving it a clear interpersonal function. The brackets with *you know* at the beginning and end of the utterance provide support for this analysis. We will return to this study in Chapter 8 and expand the discussion of general extenders in Creoles, with examples from our own study of Hawai'i Creole English (Overstreet, 2012a).

1.8.2 In French, Lithuanian and Others

When we turn to the expanding research literature on other languages, we find a lot of variation in how general extenders are realized. In Parisian French, according to Secova (2014, 2017), disjunctive forms are much rarer than adjunctive forms which have the form *et tout* (literally "and all") in about two-thirds of all general extenders recorded. Example (26), from Secova (2017: 10), with her translation, illustrates the frequent occurrence of *et tout* in the speech of a teenager, not unlike the punctuating use of *and that* in English discussed

1.8 In Different Languages

earlier. We will review Secova's work in more detail in Chapter 8, as well as Dubois' (1993) earlier analysis of general extender-type expressions in Montreal French.

(26) *elle était souvent avec eux **et tout** elle s'asseyait sur leurs genoux tout ça **et tout** elle les calculait elle leur courait après **et tout** donc eux ils avaient l'habitude ils se sentaient ils se sentaient beaux frais **et tout***
("she'd hang out with them and stuff she'd sit on their knees all that and everything she was always after them and everything so they were used to it they felt- they felt handsome hot and everything")

It is interesting that in translating the extract in (26), Secova (2017) translates three examples of *et tout* as *and everything* and one example as *and stuff*, without explanation. The analyst must have sensed a difference in the uses, which might signal a difference from the initial general statement of the girl's behavior of which "there is more," signaled by *and stuff*, then goes on to describe examples of the "more" that are treated as surprising or extreme, an implication of the English general extender *and everything* already discussed in section 1.4.3. This type of analysis is speculative and potentially inaccurate, reminding us that we should be extra cautious when trying to identify English general extender functions in other languages.

One concern with the reliability of data in other languages is raised by Ruzaité (2010) in a study investigating general extenders in Lithuanian. In that study, a corpus of contemporary Lithuanian and a parallel corpus of English and Lithuanian were investigated in search of translation equivalents for general extenders. Whereas general extenders "are of extensive use" in the monolingual Lithuanian corpus, there are "frequent omissions of general extenders" in translated material from English to Lithuanian (2010: 37). As Ruzaité points out, the omissions are not the result of there being no translation equivalents of English general extenders in Lithuanian, but because of the attitude of the translators: "omissions in translations most probably occur not due to cross-linguistic differences, but because of the general attitude to vague language items, which are often treated as unnecessary linguistic items that are optional and can be easily excluded from a proposition" (2010: 37). We should bear this caveat in mind when working with translated material in other languages.

We will return to aspects of general extender use in Lithuanian in Chapter 8, along with reports from their use in a number of other languages, including Brazilian Portuguese, Dutch, German, Persian, Russian, Spanish, and Swedish. Part of the goal will be to try to reliably identify translation equivalents in pragmatic terms and to record previously unrecognized forms and their functions where possible.

1.9 In Learner Language and Language Teaching

In recent years, there has been a surge in studies investigating the use of pragmatic expressions, including general extenders, in the output of second and foreign language learners of English and a concomitant interest in how teachers might best go about creating pedagogical activities and materials to foster greater pragmatic awareness among learners. The main impression from earlier research is that English L2 speakers use fewer pragmatic expressions overall and a more limited range of expressions than comparable groups of English L1 speakers (Murray, 2012; Overstreet, 2012b). A similar finding was reported in a study of the output of English L1 speakers learning German (Dippold, 2008). A simple explanation may be that many learners may see no need to acquire small details of conversational usage when their goals are primarily instrumental, not integrative. For a lot of speakers of English as an L2, their most common interactions may involve the use of English as a lingua franca, details of which we will consider later in section 1.9.3 and in Chapter 9.

However, it is hard to imagine that those learners would have absolutely no need (or desire) to develop some pragmatic awareness regarding their L2 interactions. There is certainly increasing interest in the language teaching field in developing not only more knowledge about pragmatics, but also more particularly in how pragmatic expressions such as general extenders can be included in the pedagogical program. From a research perspective on that program, it has seemed important to describe what aspects of general extender use learners had already acquired in the absence of any overt pedagogical focus on those forms.

1.9.1 In Learner Language

One of the most regular findings from research on general extenders in learner language is the very limited number of phrases in use and the frequently formal nature of those phrases. In a study comparing general extenders in the spoken English of two groups of university students, one consisting of French L1, advanced-level learners of English and the other of English L1 native speakers in Britain, De Cock (2004) found a systematic, and quite revealing, pattern of usage. The French L1 group overwhelmingly relied on the expressions *and so on* and *et cetera*, whereas the English L1 group hardly used these forms at all. Their most frequent adjunctive general extenders were *and things (like that)*, *and everything* and *and stuff*. When the French speakers occasionally chose a different form, they preferred the long form *and things like that* and almost never used the short form *and things*. They didn't use *and stuff* at all. This divergence in preferred forms mirrors a difference between those expressions found mostly in formal and academic discourse or written English and others more typical of informal casual discourse, as documented in Overstreet and Yule (1997b) and Biber *et al.* (1999). Those learners would seem to be using general extenders in their spoken English that they had acquired mainly through written input. A similar pattern of use, with a similar suggested cause (formal education), is reported by Cheng (2007) in a study of Hong Kong speakers of English.

There is also a potential L1 effect to keep in mind. In a study of Persian L1 speakers' use of general extenders in English, Parvaresh *et al.* (2012) recorded a number of forms that are not typical of English L1 usage. The repeated use of the translation equivalent of *and* (*væ*) is a common type of general extender in Persian (*væ, væ, væ*), transferred into English, as in (27), from Parvaresh *et al.* (2012: 266).

(27)   *I have to study, I mean – memorize things* **and, and, and**

Finding ways to help English L2 learners make better general extender choices has been a goal of those advocating explicit teaching of pragmatic expressions used by English L1 speakers.

1.9.2   In Language Teaching

Interest in the development of pragmatic awareness among learners is not new, as evidenced in a number of articles from the 1990s (Bouton, 1994; Bardovi-Harlig, 1996; Kasper, 1997; Overstreet and Yule, 1999), as well as edited collections from the early 2000s addressing the need for pragmatics instruction (e.g. Rose and Kasper, 2001). One of the persistent problems facing those who advocated pragmatics instruction was the absence of relevant information in textbooks for classroom learners (cf. Bardovi-Harlig, 2001; Ediger, 1995; Cheng, 2007). In addition, there was an early realization that exposure to an L2 in a pedagogical context by itself was insufficient for the acquisition of pragmatic competence (Rose, 2005). As a consequence, there has been almost universal acknowledgment that information about the pragmatics of a language has to be presented explicitly and actively taught (Kasper, 2001). The earliest attempts involved speech acts, an area where success continues to be reported, as in Takimoto's (2009) report of Japanese L1 students learning, through explicit instruction, to improve their performance of polite requests. Attention to aspects of politeness and other pragmatic features of English has become a more common feature in instruction, supported by the inclusion of more information and exemplification in reference works such as Carter and McCarthy (2006), and resource books for teachers such as O'Keeffe *et al.* (2011), Archer *et al.* (2012) and LoCastro (2012).

As a result of our improved understanding of what can and cannot be taught in the classroom, there has been a general consensus that increasing pragmatic awareness among L2 learners represents an attainable goal. It has also become apparent that forms and structures used regularly for fairly conventional pragmatic functions may be the best material to focus on while raising that awareness. Carter and McCarthy (2006) devote a lot of attention to discourse markers and their role in organizing both written and spoken English. Evison *et al.* (2007), Overstreet (2012b) and Overstreet and Yule (1999) focus on pragmatic markers, with special attention to general extenders. For Evison et al., these forms are "highly patterned and eminently 'learnable'; they are chunks, and fit in well with the lexical approach to language teaching" (2007: 154). They propose including VCMs ("vague category markers" = general extenders) in pedagogical tasks designed to create "comparisons between native speaker VCM usage and that by non-native expert users" (2007: 155) in order to focus learners' attention on salient details and differences.

We will revisit these issues, along with examples of exercise materials for the teaching of general extenders, in Chapter 9.

1.9.3   In English as a Lingua Franca

Quite distinct from the language produced by L2 learners in ESL/EFL settings, where accuracy and attaining general proficiency in the target are essential goals, the language produced by speakers of English as a lingua franca (ELF) is less constrained by a need for accuracy in matching native speaker models and more concerned with effective self-expression and successful communicative events (cf. Seidlhofer, 2011). They are creating their own norms. For example, ELF speakers in Europe seem to have adopted *or so* as their preferred disjunctive general extender. Terraschke (2007a) described the relatively high frequency of *or so* among German L1 speakers of English, used even more often than *or something*, as illustrated in (28), from Terraschke (2007a: 111). More recently, Buysse (2014: 233) reported a similar phenomenon in the English of Dutch L1 speakers, an example of which is presented in (29).

(28)   it's not the it's not it doesn't cover the highest special high-speed trains ***or so***

(29)   it seems like they don't have any stress ***or so***

In both these cases, there are L1 cognates, *oder so* in German, *of zo* in Dutch, that may have been the source, via transfer, of the original uses of *or so*. Yet, in these uses, the speakers have moved beyond the restrictions that exist for English L1 speakers and no longer limit the use of the phrase to collocations with approximate measurement, number and time expressions (cf. Quirk *et al.*, 1972: 928–30; Channell, 1994: 59–61). A similar use of *or so*, illustrated in (30), is reported

1.10 Reflections and Projections   19

from an *English as a Lingua Franca in Academic Settings (ELFA)* database, collected in Finland (Mauranen, 2008, 2012), with a focus on interactions in an academic setting involving speakers from a wide range of L1s.

(30)   *despite it's maybe bit of confusion not so much, well, really hard to, collect any of the ideas of the text **or so***

Extract (30), from a study by Metsä-Ketelä (2016: 337), not only provides a clear example of the new use of *or so*, it illustrates one context of occurrence, that is, a situation where speakers are dealing with some uncertainty in expressing what they want to say. In fact, in Mauranen's (2012) Lingua Franca study, the highest-frequency three-word phrase was *I don't know* and, in Aijmer's (2004) study of Swedish L1 speakers, the phrase was not only frequent, it "functioned only as an uncertainty device or filler" (2004: 188). The accumulation of markers of uncertainty in (e.g. *maybe bit of confusion not so much*) and fragmented syntax in (30) often co-occur with the use of general extenders in ELF, as reported by both Buysse (2014) and Metsä-Ketelä (2016). We will explore other aspects of general extender use in ELF in Chapter 9, paying particular attention to how they are used in innovative ways.

1.10   Reflections and Projections

Throughout this book we will be identifying the different individual forms of general extenders and analyzing their uses to demonstrate their wide range of instantiations and functions. One victim of this dissection into separate functions is the common observation that a general extender may be used with more than one function on a particular occasion. In Chapter 10, we will try to describe this multifunctionality in action with examples from English and French.

1.10.1   Multiple Functions

An example of the way in which combined functions can be performed with general extenders is evident in (31), where two students are working out what areas will be tested in a final exam. This extract is from Jucker *et al.* (2003: 1748).

(31)   A: *and then ... the other ... <u>you know for the final</u>,*
              *it's erm ... the different religions ... **and stuff***
          B: *mh hm ... mh*
          A: *say something [about] different religions and ... psychological ...*
              aspects of it
          B: *[yeah]*
              *psychology an religion **and [all that stuff]***
          A: ***[all that stuff]** <u>yeah</u>*
          B: *sociology [... re]ligion*
          A: *[uh huh] sounds real great*

Speaker A's first turn contains a double bracket involving *you know . . . and stuff*, which organizes the text around the first piece of information. At the same time as they are performing this textual function, the two pragmatic markers combine to perform an interpersonal function, signaling that there is an assumption of shared knowledge. As speaker A adds another detail, speaker B indicates understanding with *yeah*, and repeats the details with a concluding general extender *and all that stuff*. Simultaneously, speaker A produces exactly the same expression, with the result that both speakers mark that they are not only in harmony in expression, but also in understanding, very much an interpersonal function being performed. Speaker B's initial *yeah* is echoed at the end of speaker A's response, confirming that they are "on the same page," both structurally within the interaction and conceptually in terms of sharing the same information. According to Jucker *et al.* (2003), that information state is co-constructed and indicates a close connection between these cooperative fellow speakers. Extract (31) provides a good example of an aspect of interaction (and general extender use), as described by Clancy and McCarthy (2014) in their observation that "the creation of rapport and empathy is often displayed in acts of symmetrical accommodation and co-construction" (2014: 431).

1.10.2 Utterance Position

Another aspect of general extender use that tends to be neglected is their positioning inside utterances. They were originally considered to be "utterance-final" (Aijmer, 1985: 366), yet that position may simply reflect the fact that they are used for list-, topic-, text- or turn-completion on occasion, rather than representing a general structural requirement. In Chapter 10, we will investigate alternative positions where general extenders can be found, with a focus on the subject noun phrase. Example (32), from Aijmer (2002: 245), illustrates the use of one general extender (*and everything*) as part of an object noun phrase and another (*or something*) as part of a subject noun phrase, and neither of them in utterance-final position.

(32)   *I got my coat **and everything** caught under me and a young postman **or something** got up and I thought ooh this is grand*

Examples of general extender-type phrases in subject position date back to 1400, as in (33), from the *Middle English Dictionary* (Kurath *et al.*, 1952–2001), cited in Carroll (2008: 15). Extracts (34) and (35), from Aijmer (2002) and Levey (2007) respectively, in very different data sets, both illustrate the use of the adjunctive form as part of the grammatical subject.

(33)   *Iob, Iosep, **and mony opere such** weren riche of pite*

[c1400 Bk. Mother s. v. riche (adj.) 1(c) MED]

1.10 Reflections and Projections

(34) *I mean nuclear disarmament **and all that kind of thing** really fades into the background*

(35) *well normally like boys think football's a boy game cause David Beckham **and all that** are boys.*

Example (35) is particularly noteworthy because it exemplifies not only an adjunctive form as part of the subject noun phrase, but it also represents a counter-example to our own earlier claim (Overstreet and Yule, 1997a) that these expressions are syntactically optional. (We have since added "normally," as in section 1.1 earlier.) If the adjunctive phrase (*and all that*) is removed from (35), an ungrammatical structure, **David Beckham are boys* is the result, so in this case it is clearly not optional. We suspect that this example, from a young speaker in London, may represent an interesting new function for adjunctive extenders. Here the phrase *and all that* seems to be used like an associative plural marker to convey group membership with the focal referent (Corbett, 2000; Corbett and Mithun, 1996; Moravcsik, 2003). The meaning of a noun phrase with an associative plural is "X and other people associated with X," where X is mostly a definite human referent. Note that this is different from a grammatically plural marker, which would signal a reference to multiple David Beckhams. Instead, *and all that* in (35) seems to be functioning like an enclitic, forming a grammatical unit with the name of the focal referent, as an associative plural. This is a grammatical function not normally believed to exist in English, or other European languages, but well documented in the languages of Asia, Africa, Australia and the Pacific (Daniel and Moravcsik, 2000). In Chapter 10, we will present more examples and discussion of further research on this intriguing new development, along with others, in the ongoing study of general extenders.

2 Referential Function and Categorization

As we noted in Chapter 1, general extenders are frequently analyzed as having a referential function, meaning that they make a contribution to the propositional content of utterances in which they are used. In this chapter, we will take a closer look at the typical forms used with this function and review the substantial literature on this aspect of general extender use.

2.1 Set-Marking Tags

In most of the early attempts to describe and analyze general extenders, the focus was first on their position as "tags" and secondly on their function as referencing a "set" through their attachment to a preceding element. In their discussion of the use of *or something*, Ball and Ariel (1978: 38) analyze the "vague set" that can be inferred from (1) as potentially containing the following group of alternatives in the referential set of the expression *daughter or something*: cousin, daughter, daughter-in-law, niece, sister.

(1)   *It turns out she's the daughter **or something** of the late Benveniste.*

The set of alternatives offered here might be generalized as "younger female family member," and for many researchers this type of analysis became the preferred way to describe the function of these tags, that is, that they "evoke the unifying property of a class of alternatives" (Ball and Ariel, 1978: 41). In this chapter, we will talk about general extenders as "tags," in line with the terminology used by the early researchers, and investigate the extent to which they serve a function tied to a process of identifying a set, class or category, originally described as "set-marking."

Dines (1980) produced the first major study of what she described as "set-marking tags," initially identifying the group of expressions in terms of their position in an utterance as "clause-terminal tags" (1980: 18). What also unified this group was their common function.

[T]he tags serve a very definite function in the discourse and it is by virtue of their common function that they are seen to be related. In every case their function is to *cue*

2.1 Set-Marking Tags

the listener to interpret the preceding element as an illustrative example of some more general case. Tags, then, operate on "parts" to relate them to "wholes". (Dines, 1980: 22, italics in the original)

Dines argues that the addition of the tag triggers a particular processing effect and this determines their function as "set-marking tags" (1980: 23).

The presence of a clause-terminal tag indicates that an underlying general notion has been realized by a specific example. (1980: 22)

Throughout the corpus, the tags demonstrate the common function of marking the preceding element as a member of a set. This precludes the possibility of the alternative variant being null. (1980: 23)

The following example is used as illustration of the process at work (1980: 22).

(2)   B: *Does your husband drink much?*
       A: *Not much. He'll have a drink at <u>a party</u> **an' that**.*

In this case, according to Dines, the addition of the tag (*an' that*) cues the listener to extract not only the specific meaning of *party*, but also the more general meanings of "He's a social drinker" or "He's an occasional drinker." To arrive at this interpretation, the listener presumably identifies *a party* as a member of a set of social events where the husband has a drink. Note that there has to be an additional inference, based on social knowledge, that the location of the set of events can be interpreted in terms of a characterization of the type of person the husband is. The implication that there is a recognizable and relevant set of social events depends not only on the use of the tag in referential terms, but also on its function in interpersonal terms as signaling "you know what I mean" (without the necessity of having a detailed description or explanation). Although the focus in this chapter will be on how "set-marking" can be signaled and interpreted, we must not forget that this process inevitably depends on an assumption of shared knowledge and/or experience.

In other examples such as (3), Dines (1980: 28) illustrates the flexibility of tags in their co-occurrence not only with noun phrase antecedents, as in (2), but with verb phrases as antecedents as well.

(3)   *she's sort of a child who swings and does somersaults **and things like that***

In (3), the tag (*and things like that*) is attached to two verb phrases describing actions involving physical exertion, of which there may be more, used to identify a set of behaviors that characterize the *sort of a child* being referenced. As in (2), a behavior set is employed in the characterization of a type of person.

For Dines, the analyses of the utterances in (2) and (3) are used to argue against the idea that tags only serve as "vague and inexplicit speech" by showing how "general ideas are expressed through specific examples" (1980:

30). In this approach, the set being marked is based on exemplification via members of the set rather than by specifying characteristics of the set. That is, rather than specifying explicitly that "she's a physically active child," the speaker gives examples of behaviors to implicitly convey essentially the same characterization. Similarly, returning to example (1), the speaker doesn't identify the individual by specifying "younger female family member," but uses one exemplar plus a tag, as in *the daughter or something*. This does raise the question: if a more precise specification is possible, why would a less explicit means be chosen?

One way to go about answering that question is by thinking about the data in a different way. For example, in (1), we might say that "daughter" is the speaker's best guess (with no thought of "a class of alternatives") to accomplish adequate reference in this situation and avoids any part of the semantically more explicit "younger female family member." In this case, the use of *or something* can be viewed as having a hedging effect, signaling approximation, just in case the speaker is mistaken, in accordance with a conversational convention not to overstate your knowledge. Without more information about the context of the utterance, it is difficult to be sure that *or something* is being employed in (1) with a set-marking function. The more general issue of why a less specific form of reference would be chosen over a more specific expression will be explored in Chapter 3.

2.2 Terminating Tags

Aijmer (1985) continues Dines' focus on these forms as tags, using position in the utterance to describe them as "terminating tags" and also "utterance-final tags." Like Dines, she also bases her analysis on the set-marking function, as in this description:.

the speaker instructs the listener to pick out all the members of the set on the basis of the member (or members) which has been produced as an example. (1985: 374)

To illustrate this process, Aijmer (1985) presents a number of examples where the set in question can be accessed on the basis of similar semantic features. In (4), describing Gothic architecture, the semantic features [+plural, −animate] of *and things* match those of the preceding noun phrases (*pinnacles, nodules*). In (5), part of a discussion of house decorating, the semantic features [+mass, −animate] of the specific noun (*paint*) are matched by the general noun (*stuff*), creating cohesion and allowing the listener to "reconstruct the set on the basis of the semantic properties of the members of the set" (1985: 375).

(4)   *it's all full of little pinnacles and nodules **and things***

(5)   *but there's no money and they need paint **and stuff***

2.2 Terminating Tags

It may be that when semantic features are shared there is a stronger cohesive tie between the tag and the "member," as in (4) and (5). However, Aijmer goes on to describe the frequent use of tags without a semantic feature connection, as in (6). In this example, the tag (*and things*) is [+plural, −human] and is tied to either *people* [−plural, +human] or *third world* [−plural, −human]. In either case, there is no semantic feature match.

(6)   *in the way they talk about people out in the sort of wild third world **and things***

Aijmer argues that the existence of the set cannot always be objectively determined by the expressions used and goes on to draw attention to the need for some cooperation between the speaker and listener in order to arrive at an appropriate interpretation. While Dines focuses almost exclusively on what the speaker is doing with a terminating tag, Aijmer points out that using these forms depends on the assumption of some kind of shared understanding between the participants.

It is not possible for the listener to reconstruct the set on the basis only of a member of the set. The speaker and listener must cooperate to come to an agreement on what the set is. (1985: 377)

Acknowledging this need for cooperation leads Aijmer to recognize that functions other than set-marking seem to be involved. In the course of her analysis, Aijmer points out that "in addition to the basic set-marking function we can distinguish a number of 'special' conversational functions" (1985: 377). These are all pragmatic functions that "fill a number of conversational needs" and give the tags a role in interpersonal interaction, an idea that we will investigate further in Chapter 3. To illustrate one of these special functions, Aijmer offers an insightful analysis of *and everything* as adding the feature [+remarkable] to the information in the utterance of (7).

(7)   *but I mean the women – the women wear veils **and everything** don't they*

Aijmer argues that, in a context where women don't normally wear veils, this speaker's assertion is marked as "special or surprising by means of the tag" (1985: 383), rather than implicating other things the women might wear or do. This type of observation takes us away from a concentration on how the tags are to be interpreted in objective terms, via set membership, and invites us to see the tags functioning much more in pragmatic terms, via assumptions of ideas and attitudes shared by the participants in the interaction. Aijmer's (1985) study introduces a more pragmatic perspective, that, when later taken up by others, leads to many other revelations about the use of these tags beyond set-marking. We will return to these points in Chapters 3 and 4 in our investigation of other functions, but first we have to take account of the work of Ward and Birner (1993), who present an analysis of *and everything* as definitively set-marking.

2.3 Variable Tags

In contrast to Aijmer's (1985) more wide-ranging analysis, Ward and Birner (1993) take a strong deterministic approach to the effect of the inclusion of a tag, focusing on the use of *and everything*. When they look at Dines' (1980) analysis of set-marking tags, they argue that different versions (e.g. *and stuff like that* versus *and everything*) are not interchangeable and hence should not be treated "as sociolinguistically conditioned realizations of a single underlying discourse function" (Ward and Birner, 1993: 207). They argue that *and everything* has a distinct meaning which is "straightforwardly compositional, i.e. determined by the semantics of the lexical items *and* plus *everything*" (1993: 206). To describe the specific function of this composition, they treat the "anchoring constituent" (in their examples, the phrase before the tag) plus *and everything* as a variable which is to be instantiated by at least one other of some inferable set. This leads to the following claim (Ward and Birner, 1993: 209) about the use of *and everything*.

Of course, there may be any number of other motivations for a speaker to avoid specifying alternative instantiations of the variable; however, in all cases felicitous use of *and everything* requires that such instantiations exist and constitute members of a well-defined (and in principle enumerable) set.

In their analysis of the following example, Ward and Birner propose that "*and everything* instantiates a type of open proposition, obtained by replacing the entire conjunction (i.e. *and everything* plus the anchoring constituent) with a variable" (1993: 208). The anchoring constituent in (8) is *steam-cleaned it* and our interpretation of *and everything* here would be based on a recognition that "the anchoring VP is not an arbitrary member of a set of carpet cleaning methods. Rather 'steam-cleaned' exemplifies a high value on some inferable scale" (1993: 213).

(8)   *They cleaned it up that night. They steam-cleaned it **and everything**!*

Ward and Birner's analysis makes it clear that there is a set ("carpet cleaning methods") being evoked, but also that there is something special about the information in the anchoring constituent. Although the technical terminology is different, this analysis matches Aijmer's earlier observation that the use of *and everything* frequently goes beyond set-marking and evokes a distinct function tied to the speaker's evaluation of the information as "special or surprising" (Aijmer, 1985: 383).

To take another of Ward and Birner's (1993: 213) examples, in (9), we might find it much harder to think of other "instantiations" that would constitute members of a set evoked by *a Rhodes scholar*.

(9)   *We just knew he was up for it because of how good he was. He's going to be a Rhodes scholar **and everything**!*

2.4 Vague Tags

Rather than require that *and everything* must necessarily evoke "a well-defined (and in principle enumerable) set," we might acknowledge the possibility of a set-marking role, but recognize that the frequency with which the phrase is used with another function may constrain the need to search for other instantiations, especially when that might seem like a difficult task. In the case of (9), we might be quite satisfied with the invited interpretation that *to be a Rhodes scholar* is, by itself, something remarkable and no other instantiations need exist. We will return to the analysis of *and everything* in Chapter 4.

2.4 Vague Tags

Channell (1994) doesn't include an analysis of *and everything* among the examples of "vague tags" investigated in her book *Vague Language*, but she continues the tradition of describing the function of tags in terms of set-marking. She identifies two parts, the "vague tag" (*or something*) and the "exemplar" (*bread*), that combine to create the "vague category," identified as "the set of edible things" (*anything edible*), as illustrated in (10) from Channell (1994: 121).

(10)   A: *So you'd like some bread?*
        B: ***Or something**. Anything edible will do*

This example is quite unusual because it is co-constructed, indicating that the second speaker (B) knows how *or something* functions, not as a performance "filler," as Channell points out, but as a way of modifying the reference in speaker A's question. This example is also noteworthy for the articulation of the "category" by speaker (B) as *anything edible*, providing the analyst with an indication of what the speaker had in mind. This is not very common, but in such cases we have evidence in the utterance (i.e. what is said) to support how what is said should be interpreted. Later in this chapter, we will look at some other examples with similar effects in terms of a set- or category-based analysis.

Channell describes the combination of exemplar + tag as a "vague category identifier," and echoes Dines in her analysis.

[T]he whole expression directs the hearer to access a set, of which the given item is a member whose characteristics will enable the hearer to identify the set. (1994: 122)

Although she talks about this process initially in terms of a set-marking analysis, Channell prefers to describe the interpretation mechanism in the following way.

The exemplar + tag construction is understood as an instruction to access a category, whose characteristics are defined for the hearer by the exemplar provided, taken in conjunction with relevant pragmatic information. (1994: 131)

Channell differs from previous set-marking studies by explicitly introducing the existence of "characteristics" as part of the processing load in accessing a category. It may have been a desire to unpack those characteristics that led Channell to create an experiment asking British university students to list items they thought the speakers of some short written sentences, with tags underlined, "could reasonably have been thinking of" (1994: 124). This is not a typical way of investigating language use and interpretation, but it does present a certain kind of evidence. Two of the sentences are shown in (11) and (12). In Channell's description of the form and function of these sentences, the vague tag (*and that, or something*) is attached to an "exemplar" (*a car*) to create a "vague category identifier" in each of the examples (1994: 146, 150).

(11)   *They've got a car **and that***

(12)   *a car **or something** came by*

For (11), the top three items in the responses were *caravan, washing-machine* and *TV*. Channell analyzes these responses as indicating that the vague category identifier in *a car and that* is interpreted in terms of the category "possessions of affluent persons" (1994: 128). For (12), the top three items provided were *lorry, van* and *bus*, suggesting that the vague category identifier in *a car or something* is interpreted in terms of "vehicle." Initially, this seems to be good empirical proof that the respondents were thinking in terms of the categories identified, and indeed this may have been the case. However, it is hard to believe that the really different interpretations are the result of using the vague tags *and that* and *or something*. By themselves, these vague expressions couldn't possibly have been the source of such distinct meanings. Surely the difference is in the verbs used, with *They've got X* signaling possession and *X came by* signaling something that moves. But those interpretations are neither necessary nor categorical, with *dog* being offered by one respondent for (11) and *horse* by another for (12), among an extremely large range of other words. None of this helps to clarify whether vague tags might be used to implicate categories, but it does show that the linguistic context in which a vague category identifier is used has a strong impact on how the form is interpreted. The absence of a larger conversational context may have been responsible for the high number of different individual responses, with fifty-six different items produced in response to example (11). If this wide range of responses is an indication of category identification via members, then the finding would indicate that people mostly seem to have non-equivalent category membership, or that they rely on different "characteristics" to identify categories. Rather than focus on how tags are being interpreted in these types of examples, we suspect that the results were an effect of the experimental procedure rather than any categorization processes.

2.4 Vague Tags

Channell's discussion of categories includes a distinction based on Barsalou (1983) between common categories, such as *vehicle*, with subcategories of *car* and *bus*, as in (12), and "ad hoc categories," such as *things to save in case of fire*, which have no general term, and are typically temporary and "often created spontaneously for use in specialized contexts" (Barsalou, 1983: 211). (Mauri and Sansò (2018) present a recent review of this topic.) For Overstreet (1999: 42), this dichotomy is reanalyzed in linguistic terms as a distinction between "lexicalized categories," encoded as a single lexical item, and "non-lexicalized categories," for which no single lexical item is readily available. The traditional interest in psycholinguistic studies of categorization (e.g. Rosch, 1975) has mostly been devoted to lexicalized categories and their semantics, involving our understanding of the relationship between a word like *bird*, and other words such as *canary, owl, parrot, peacock, penguin* and *robin* in terms of how "birdy" people judge them to be. However, the interpretation of non-lexicalized categories has a pragmatic basis, dependent on shared background knowledge assumed by a speaker in a local context. When vague category identification is expressed with phrases such as *or something*, it is typically non-lexicalized categorization that is involved. Conceptually, the presentation of non-lexicalized categories is often achieved through contrast. Indeed, as Bilmes (2015: 87–105) notes, contrast is often a vehicle for categorization in spoken interaction. In (13), from a newspaper report (*Honolulu Advertiser*, December 24, 1995), the speaker is talking about a friend who had died while surfing in large waves.

(13) *I'm glad for him. I'm sure all surfers would rather go this way than in a car accident **or something***

If the speaker of (13) had stopped at the word *accident*, there would be a straightforward contrast. However, the addition of *or something* implies that *in a car accident* is only one example of some type of implied category that might be assigned an interpretation like "other ways to die that aren't cool." This, of course, represents only one interpretation and, given the vagueness created by *or something*, may be a more explicitly defined categorization than the speaker was thinking of. The speaker may not have had any additional instantiations of the potential category in mind when adding the vague tag (*or something*) and was simply creating a contrast between "dying while surfing" and "any other way of dying." In such cases, we have no way of determining whether category implication was involved at all. Rather than view all cases of the use of vague tags as an indication of categorization taking place, we should really restrict such an interpretation to those situations where there is clear evidence in the data that some type of category is being evoked.

2.5 Vague Markers

The tendency among researchers to treat tags as contributing to category implication continues to be found in the work of other scholars who use similar terminology to Channell (1994), but with "identifier" being replaced by "marker" in the label "vague category marker" (O'Keeffe, 2004; O'Keeffe *et al.*, 2007). Vague category markers are included in the list of expressions with "approximately" as their meaning, as in (14) from Carter and McCarthy (2006: 205).

(14) *The room will take up to two hundred **or so** people, won't it, **or something like that***

In related studies, what is being (approximately) marked by these vague category markers is described in very broad terms as connecting to, for example, "global, societal or local frames of knowledge" (Evison *et al.*, 2007: 149). This type of analysis makes the reference to categories much more general and culturally defined, and less concerned with the interpretation of the markers as linguistic items in their discourse context. Most of the discussion centers on what are the relevant cultural domains of reference in a particular corpus, such as data from "an Irish radio phone-in show" (O'Keeffe, 2004), where the categorization process is analyzed exclusively in terms of very general sociocultural categories like "social practices and attitudes" (2004: 12). A good example of an assumption of a "local" (not "global" or "societal") frame of knowledge is the reference in (15) to *Gaeltacht*, which the analyst has to explain to the general reader as "areas of Ireland where Irish is the first language" (O'Keeffe, 2004: 15).

(15) *Didn't get a Gaeltacht grant **or anything like that**?*

The very general culturally focused perspective taken in some of these studies is reflected in no differentiation being made in token counts for adjunctive versus disjunctive forms or for particular markers such as *or something* versus *or something like that*, and *and everything* versus *and everything like that* (Evison *et al.*, 2007: 143). In each case, they are counted as the same. We have already noted a very specific interpretation implicated for one of these phrases, *and everything* in examples (7)–(9), that is not shared with the longer version. Substantial differences in the functions of short forms and long forms (*and stuff* versus *and stuff like that*) have been noted in a number of studies (Aijmer, 2002: 231; Palacios Martínez, 2011: 2466). Since many of the studies devoted to analyzing the role of vague category markers are concerned with culture and regional varieties, such as Irish English (Vaughan *et al.*, 2017; Murphy, 2010; Walsh *et al.*, 2008), or with cross-linguistic differences, for example English versus Russian in the business world (Malyuga and McCarthy, 2018; McCarthy, 2020), we will review these studies in Chapter 8.

2.6   List Completers

Returning to the analysis of tags from a linguistic perspective, we should consider the proposal that expressions such as *or something (like that)* and *and stuff (like that)* are examples, as in (16) and (17), of "generalized list completers" (Jefferson, 1990: 66, 71). For Jefferson, the type of structure found in lists consists of two items followed by a tag that indicates there may be more or other examples, but which completes that list for current purposes.

(16)   *I said no I know his name is something else. Teddy'r Tom'r **something***

(17)   *I brought th'pie en the whip cream **en stuff** en they gonna deliver the turkey*

The two items in (16) are examples of names and the tag (*'r something*) indicates that there may be an alternative, but the speaker isn't going to try to continue the list. Similarly, the list of items in (17) that the speaker brought has two examples plus a tag (*en stuff*) that completes the list. Since the preceding discourse context involves a discussion of Thanksgiving, the category being evoked can be tentatively identified as "food items (but not turkey) associated with Thanksgiving dinner."

The role of general extenders in list creation is particularly transparent when the list is used to exemplify a general description, introduced by *such as* with particular instantiations, as in (18) from COCA, the *Corpus of Contemporary American English* (www.english-corpora.org/coca/, see Davies, 2008, 2010). In this case, the indication from the general extender that "there is more" is supported by the addition of other examples following it.

(18)   *a deficiency that causes disease, side diseases, such as pneumonias and bronchitis, **and things like that,** also chronic diarrhea and bleeds*

[1990 *CNN King* spok COCA]

In many of Jefferson's examples, it is quite transparent that the speaker is not only creating a list, but also, by giving more than one example, increases the likelihood that a category or set of items is being evoked. However, Jefferson is more focused on the nature of lists and their strong tendency to exhibit what she describes as "three-partedness."

Three-partedness, then, is not only an empirically observable, recurrent phenomenon which occurs in drastically simple and enormously elaborate structures, but appears to be the product of an oriented-to-procedure by which lists are properly constructed. (1990: 68)

The function of tags in this approach is not explored in terms of content such as category implication, but is treated as procedural in the sense of solving a need for a "properly constructed" list, as in this explanation.

Sometimes a projected third list item is not produced. In that case, a methodic solution to the problem of three-partedness is available and used. The search for a third *item* is terminated, and the list is closed with a generalized list completer. (1990: 67)

The "methodic solution" proposed here for the use of tags is tied to a very specific structural concept, but no rationale is offered to explain why speakers would be oriented to "the problem of three-partedness." It is also empirically observable that tags do not normally occur with two items and complete a list. Channell (1994: 134) comments that her corpus contained few three-parted lists with tags. In Overstreet's (1999: 27) study, tags only occurred as third parts in about one-fifth of their uses, and Aijmer (2002: 237) reported even fewer instances (18%) in her corpus. It may be, as Aijmer (2002: 239) has noted, that only some general extenders (e.g. *and things (like that)*) are typically found as list completers or that it is only with a particular function at the end of lists that a particular general extender is included, as we will see with *or whatever* in Chapter 4.

In some uses, the tags can feature in extended lists. In extract (19), from Schiffrin (1994), the speaker lists items sold in "corners" (i.e. corner stores in the United States) that identify the type/category of store, which is also negatively defined (*Not a grocery store*). The lineation in (19) follows Schiffrin (1994: 401).

(19) *Now we- see, all these corners were uh a-*
course, this one store, that's a hold out.
Like he has candy
And ice cream,
And uh a little milk maybe
And bread
Stuff like that.
Not a grocery store.
Odds and ends.
Cigars,
Cigarettes

This is certainly a list and the tag in the middle does seem to be an attempt to complete the list, but the speaker's need to effectively describe and categorize the store is obviously not yet considered complete at that point.

One expression that appears to be oriented to list-completion is *et cetera*, as in (20) from Denis (2017: 160), which is sometimes repeated, as in (21) from O'Keeffe (2004: 2), but not necessarily constrained by the limitation of three-partedness. In (21), the list consists of body parts, which the speaker presents as a potentially even longer list, but is sufficiently complete at that point.

(20) *I generally played on all the teams that went out of high school. Uh the basketball, baseball, hockey,* ***et cetera***

(21)   *those men were tattooed all that I could see okay so starting with the forehead face ears neck hands **et cetera et cetera***

From this brief review, we can certainly say that tags can sometimes be used as part of a listing structure, but that is clearly not their primary function. An exception may be the structures covered by the pattern *and (all) the rest (of it)*, which were always used in list-completion in the data analyzed by Aijmer (2002: 239). The inclusion of general extenders in list construction has been investigated by others (e.g. Lerner, 1994; Masini *et al.*, 2018), but there has not been any general uptake of the idea that tags are best analyzed as "generalized list completers."

2.7 Extender Tags

There is a particular use of *et cetera* to indicate that there is "more" in the sense of a "continuation" of the preceding text. In list construction, the signal in *et cetera* is that the list could continue with other items, but is sufficiently complete at that point. Speakers, or more often writers, can use *et cetera* for a different type of continuation that the hearer is expected to be able to follow and make complete. According to Carroll (2008), this use of *et cetera* is among the earliest documented, as illustrated in (22), from (approximately) the year 1450, with Carroll's translation (2008: 31).

(22)   *A charme for to stawnchyn blood . . . "In nomine patris **et cetera** . . . I conjure the, blood*
("A charm for staunching blood . . . In nomine patris et cetera . . . I conjure thee, blood")

[c1450 Stockb. Recipes MED]

In the case of (22), the writer uses *et cetera* to indicate both that the text continues and that the reader knows what piece of text comes next, following "In the name of the father . . ." Carroll (2008) describes *et cetera* in this function as an extender tag and provides another early historical example of a similar function being fulfilled by *and so forthe*, as in (23) from (approximately) the year 1430 (2008: 31).

(23)   *saienge to ham: "Dredeth nouȝt! ȝe secheth Jesu!" **and so forthe**, as the gospel telleth*
("saying to them, 'Fear not! You seek Jesus!' and so forth, as the Gospel tells")

[c1430 (a1410) *Love Mirror* MED]

In (23), the addition of "as the gospel telleth," indicates to the reader where the rest of this text is recorded, but the clear assumption is that the readers are expected to be sufficiently familiar with the source that they can provide it themselves. In both (22) and (23), the assumed textual knowledge is from a religious source, presumably the most widely known type of text in the medieval period and also the type most likely to be cited with the assumption of general familiarity.

We should note that in neither (22) nor (23) is the extender implicating a set or category. Instead, what we have are examples of intertextuality, where the interpretation of one text is based on knowledge of another. First identified and exemplified in the study of literature (Kristeva, 1966/82) and originally considered to be "a literary device," intertextuality is now recognized as a general-purpose device for evoking already existing textual knowledge (spoken as well as written) as a way of interpreting the current text. As Fairclough (1992: 104) has pointed out, we are constantly interpreting new text on the basis of our experience with earlier texts (though we may not always be aware of the process). The extender tag use of *et cetera* continues to be a device, especially favored by writers, to evoke intertextuality in the process of involving the reader in the joint construction of textual meaning, as in (24), from R. Lakoff (1990: 211).

(24)   *If we assimilate to men's ways ("when in Rome, **etc.**"), we risk discrimination as too aggressive*

In the case of (24), the writer uses part of a well-known saying and invites the reader to continue and complete it as a way of supporting the interpretation of the current text. In (25), the writer (Ephron, 1983: 70–71) uses *et cetera* with an allusion to a type of idiom, inviting the reader to see the similarity between what is currently being described and the sentiment inherent in the idiom.

(25)   *I've always liked odd and interesting-looking men because I'm odd and interesting-looking myself, and I always figured I had a better shot at them than at the conventionally good-looking ones. (Water seeks its own level, **et cetera**.)*

These past two examples, (24) and (25), are from accomplished writers and have a creative-writing feel to them. However, the intertextual appeal that they incorporate in their use of *et cetera* is whimsical compared to the forceful multiple use of the form in (26), from an Irish radio phone-in program where the topic concerns the police response to small crimes such as petty theft, a broadcast media focus at the time (O'Keeffe, 2004: 18).

(26)   *I don't know ho- how the decision is made ... in the order of things the people weren't that offended **et cetera et cetera et cetera** and there are drug barons **et cetera** out there you know yourself how the argument goes*

In (26), the speaker is appealing to the audience's familiarity with what reasons or excuses are given when the police are unable to devote time and energy to investigating minor crimes. The interpretation of *et cetera* here must involve a recognition via intertextuality of the known elements and type of talk that would be presented on the topic. We know that the reference is to a type of talk because the speaker goes on to explicitly lexicalize that known talk as *the argument*, with a very obvious appeal to shared knowledge in *you know yourself*.

The type of shared knowledge being evoked in (26) would easily fit into a referential domain analysis described in Evison *et al*. (2007), another study that included some of the same data. In that analysis, examples like (26) evoke a referential domain that is "societal" (not "local" or "global"), meaning that the text should be "interpretable by all members of a speech community or sociopolitical entity who share a common culture and history" (2007: 149). The uses of *et cetera* in all these examples of extender tags illustrate a quite distinct referential function that signals to the addressee that there is a textual referent to be recovered from shared knowledge, a referential function quite distinct from set- or category-marking. While Carroll's (2008) analysis of early uses of *et cetera* and *and so forthe* revealed quite distinct functions for these forms as markers inviting an interpretation based on intertextuality, more recent studies have tended to focus on other functions.

2.8 Restricted Tags

Returning to the task of identifying referential function in terms of categories, we can try to determine the conditions under which categorization seems most transparent. As we noted earlier, the three-part lists identified by Jefferson (1990) often support a categorization interpretation because they provide more than one member of what might be the potential category. Those lists often end with a short form of the tag when the referenced category is relatively easy to identify from the examples, as in (27), where the activities may be taken as representing a category of "housework." Aijmer (2002: 237) presents example (27), as well as (28), transcribed with separate lines for the tone units involved.

(27)   *and I'd have a day at home and*
        get on and do a bit of ironing
        *or washing **or something***

Aijmer (2002) also notes that large numbers of examples with *and things* are used in this way, and with even longer lists, as in (28). In this example, the speaker has provided a general term (*reproductions*) that helps with the categorization of what the list ending in *and things* is referencing.

(28)   *oh they've got absolutely super*
       reproductions
       of all his
       sketches and drawings and water colours ***and things***

As we noted in Chapter 1, the short forms tend to occur inside tone units with the forms to which they are attached, as illustrated in both (27) and (28). Aijmer provides a more detailed analysis of this pattern.

> The short, unrestricted tag (*and things, or something*) is unstressed or carries weak stress and is attached to the preceding utterance as a "tail." The "tail" is pronounced less loudly and more quickly than the rest of the utterance. (2002: 231)

From this description, we would expect that the short forms would be less salient in the stream of speech. When they are not attached to two or more members that indicate a likely category, these weakly stressed forms may not have a categorization role as their primary function. Some other functions for short forms will be explored in later chapters, but an obvious question arises: are long forms more likely to signal a categorization function? Palacios Martínez would seem to be answering in the affirmative when he concludes: "the set-marking function is easier to identify when general extenders are found in their full form" (2011: 2466). Aijmer comes to the same conclusion: "longer forms appear to be more frequently used for categorization" (2002: 224). Aijmer (2002: 231) goes on to create a distinction in referential terms between longer forms as "restricted" and shorter forms as "unrestricted." Restricted tags have an indexical element (e.g. *that*) that can be included in a comparative phrase, as in *and things like that*, which has the potential to create an antecedent–anaphor relationship between the member(s) and the tag, resulting in a cohesive effect, as in (29), from Overstreet (1999: 23). In this situation, with the speakers in a kitchen talking about making dinner, the interpretation here is not just about recognizing a list, but knowing that there's a category of "flavoring items used in cooking" being identified. The restriction in terms of reference can be even more specific when the speaker gives a name to the category (*English food*), before an example (*roasts*), plus a tag indicating other examples with an anaphoric form (*that*) connecting to the antecedent category label, as in (30) from Cheshire (2007: 167). In (31), from COCA, the speaker establishes an activity category *being outdoors*, then exemplifies it with *camping* and *hiking* before the tag indicating more of the same kind.

(29)   *There's garlic salt an' onion powder* ***an' things like that***

(30)   *I quite like English food actually I love roasts* ***and things like that***

(31)   *I love being outdoors. I'm big into camping and hiking* ***and things like that***

2.8 Restricted Tags

As illustrated in (30) and (31), speakers can explicitly identify the category (*English food, being outdoors*) that they are referring to, prior to the exemplification with a general extender. This form of restriction in terms of set reference involving concrete/physical entities is frequently associated with the long form *and things like that*, as in (32) and (33), from COCA. In (32), speaker B is talking about ways to produce biofuel and speaker A references a set (*woody plants*), then asks about some possible members with a general extender and receives a positive response, with the provision of another possible member of the set to confirm successful reference. In this case, the set is essentially co-constructed by the two participants.

(32) A: *Could you possibly engineer it into other woody plants?*
      B: *Absolutely*
      A: *You know, like willow and poplar **and things like that**?*
      B: *Sure. Poplar, sugar cane*

(33) *what about the disruptions in the world that are going on now, the wars **and things like that**, the famine?*

An interesting aspect of (32) and (33) is the way in which one of the speakers provides another member (*sugar cane, famine*) of the set (*woody plants, disruptions*) after the general extender, showing that the implication in the adjunctive general extender that "there is more" can sometimes be instantiated by further members of the set.

The set that is being referenced need not simply be "things," in the sense of physical objects, but can also include actions, as in (31) earlier, and in (34), with *pushing, shoving* and *punching*, and (35) with *riding* and *roping*, both from COCA.

(34) *the worst that would have happened maybe would have been a fight, some pushing and shoving, some punching **and stuff like that***

(35) A: *Have you ever actually spent some time with or around actual cowboys doing cowboy things, riding and roping **and stuff like that**?*
      B: *I forgot to mention that I direct while sitting in the saddle*

Aijmer's (2002) study of the use of long forms as having restricted reference provides a much clearer and less subjective way of identifying set-marking or category-marking as the most obvious function of some general extenders in particular contexts. That conclusion is not limited to categories identified via adjunctive forms, but, as shown in (36) from Channell (1994: 134) and (37) from Mauranen (2004: 183), the long form of a disjunctive general extender is also used with a fairly clear identification of categories (underlined).

(36) *it was some kind of <u>condiment</u> like salt or pepper **or something like that***

(37) *just pick some <u>weird herb</u> and put that in there too, some tansy **or something like that***

However, the examples in (30)–(37) we have just analyzed would not seem to warrant a characterization as "vague category marking," mainly because the categories are not vague at all. They are explicitly articulated along with some of their members.

2.9 The SKT Tags

The second long-form structure of tags discussed in Chapter 1 also typically includes *that* (and occasionally *this*), along with *sort, kind* or *type of stuff* or *thing*, and seems to have a function tied to the identification of some "kind" of category. Restricted tags of this type contain nouns that suggest the speaker is thinking in terms of a *sort, kind* or *type*, all nouns that can be used to indicate that a classification is involved (Brems and Davidse, 2010). In their study of the use of what they call the "SKT (*sort of, kind of, type of*) constructions" in British English, Dehé and Stathi (2016) found an overwhelming preference for *sort of* in general and in the SKT-*of-thing* structure in particular. Beeching (2016), Biber *et al.* (1999) and Miskovic-Lukovic (2009) report a greater use of *sort of* in British English and *kind of* in American English. Mauranen's (2004) study found a greater preference (i.e. four times as many) for *kind of* in American versus British English and, in both varieties, examples of *type of* were much less common. We should note that SKT structures used as general extenders are generally reported to be much less frequent than the other forms we have investigated so far. In Overstreet's (1999: 7) informal spoken data, only three of the seventy-six adjunctive general extenders had the structure of an SKT tag. In Aijmer's (2002: 221–22) data, there were 353 adjunctive general extenders listed, of which only 27 had the structure *and (all) {that/ this} {sort/kind/type} of {stuff/thing}*. In Tagliamonte and Denis's (2010: 362–63) report, this latter structure occurred 61 times compared to 736 examples of the most common form *and {stuff/things} (like that)*. Palacios Martínez (2011: 2461) reported that, in British English, SKT tags had been used in an earlier corpus (1960s) with more than double the frequency of a later collection (1990s), so it may be that this type of structure is simply falling out of favor among a new generation. Small token counts generally result in less attention, which is unusual in the case of SKT tags because they offer such clear evidence that certain general extenders are designed to evoke category reference.

Some of the categorization signals involving SKT-*of-thing* structures exhibit Jefferson's "three-partedness" of two examples plus a tag, as in (38), but tags with single examples, as in (39), are common. Both of these examples are from COCA and contain expressions that function like superordinates (*disease, old-fashioned country music*), providing category labels for the examples and restricted tags that follow. Notably, as in (39), the name of a person (with the

2.9 The SKT Tags

feature [+human]) can be used as an exemplar in conjunction with an SKT tag *sort of thing* ([−human]).

(38) *the thing that follows these disasters is a worry of disease, cholera, dysentery **and that sort of thing***

(39) *I'm a huge fan of old-fashioned country music, Kitty Wells **and that sort of thing***

These examples feature *sort of*, but *kind of* is used in a very similar way, as in (40), also from COCA, describing a visit to Greece of Angela Merkel, then German chancellor, where "the usual trappings of a state visit" is mentioned as an ad hoc category label, followed by three items and concluded with the restricted tag featuring *kind of*.

(40) *she arrived at the airport to the usual trappings of a state visit – smiles and handshakes and anthems **and that kind of thing***

Other similar examples feature *stuff* instead of *thing*, as in (41), from Carter and McCarthy (2006: 239), and *type* instead of *sort* or *kind* in (42), from Jefferson (1990: 66). In (41) the speaker is talking about meeting Mick Jagger and, contrary to the journalist's expectation that the topic of conversation would the Rolling Stones' latest album, reports on a different topic by first using a category label (*sport*), then producing a list of examples plus *and that sort of stuff*.

(41) *He was talking about sport, Wimbledon, the World Cup, US Open golf **and that sort of stuff***

This is about as convincing an example as we might wish for in the search for a speaker clearly categorizing, with each of the named examples instantiating the named category (*sport*), and the tag indicating that more examples could be named within the restricted category. The category may not always be expressed by means of a superordinate form, but by means of a term establishing the context in which the categorization is understood as connecting the items mentioned, as in (42). Here, mention of *a concession stand* creates the context in which *coke* and *popcorn* become members of a set of items (*type of thing*) available in that context.

(42) *And they had a concession stand like at a fair where you can buy coke and popcorn **and that type of thing***

Aijmer's (2002) analysis of the function of restricted tags provides some of the clearest examples of their role in categorization, most saliently in the case of SKT tags. It also represents the last major treatment of the phenomenon using the descriptor "tag" to identify the phrases involved. Following Overstreet (1999), the various labels incorporating "tag" are used much less and the term "general extender" becomes the most common label used to describe the forms.

2.10 Specific Extenders

Before moving on, we should recognize that there are also clear instances of categorization taking place via forms earlier identified as "specific extenders." In Chapter 1, we analyzed the phrase *and all that David Copperfield kind of crap* as having a standard long-form general extender structure, with specific referential information inserted. As the main character is introducing an autobiographical account of events, he wants to be clear about the "kind" of narrative that will follow and defines it as not being in the same category as the reader might be familiar with from the novel *David Copperfield*. This is a fairly straightforward example of creating an ad hoc category via contrast (i.e. a personal narrative, but without traditional elements), using a specific general extender for a specific intertextual effect.

The preferred position of the inserted material in adjunctive general extenders that makes them more specific seems to be before the *kind of* constituent, as with our *David Copperfield* example, in one of the long forms, and before the *stuff/thing* constituent in the other long form, as in (43), where the category being identified also appears to have low value. In disjunctive general extenders, inserted material follows *something* or *anything*, as in (44), from a news interview with a famous baseball player. The addition of the adjective *crazy* acts like an intensifier in the expression of how improbable his father's big dream must have seemed. In both (43) and (44), the inserted terms (e.g. *stupid, crazy*) make the general extender structure more specific in its evaluation of the associated material.

(43)   *We spend more time on assessment reports **and stupid bureaucratic stuff like that***

(44)   *My dad always thought I would play for the New York Yankees **or something crazy like that***

Even more specific details can come after the disjunctive form, a feature especially noticeable in older texts, as in (45), cited in McColm and Trousdale (2019: 97) from the year 1826. In this case, there are examples first, then the larger category follows *or whatever*, all very specifically identified.

(45)   *The squaws seized clubs, axes, **or whatever weapon of offense** first offered itself to their hands*

We will look more closely at the historical (and ongoing) changes associated with the disjunctive extender *or whatever* in Chapter 4.

A structural option by which extenders can be made more specific is through the addition of (appropriately named) restrictive relative clauses, as illustrated in (46), from the Bible (1611: Deuteronomy 5:2), and (47) from Overstreet

(1999: 52). In (46), the category being referenced could not really be any more specific.

(46)　*Neither shalt thou desire thy neighbour's wife, neither shalt thou covet thy neighbour's house, his field, or his manservant or his maidservant, his ox or his ass,* ***or anything that is thy neighbour's***

(47)　*my nose runs and my eyeballs ooze **an' things like that that aren't real attractive***

The addition of the final relative clause to a basic general extender structure (*and things like that*) in (47) creates a specific extender that summons up a very specific ad hoc category. The categorization taking place in examples (46) and (47) may involve very different categories, almost four hundred years apart, yet they are based on the same general extender plus restrictive relative clause construction.

One other way in which speakers can use general extender structures with restrictions on their referential range is by incorporating nouns that are more specific than *things* and *stuff* in the long form, as in (48), from O'Keeffe (2004: 8), and (49), from Aijmer (2013: 141).

(48)　*a lot of undesirables criminals **and people like that***

(49)　*The uh Park-Hyatt Coolum **and places like that***

These examples would suggest that general nouns like *people* and *places* have a more limited referential range, making them more like specific extenders. Supporting this interpretation is the fact that the two extender forms in (48) and (49) aren't used without the comparative phrase (*like that*), unlike the more common forms with *things* and *stuff*. They can only be used with an explicit cohesive connection to the referential antecedent.

Interesting though they are, specific extenders have received little attention and we know of no research reports that have investigated them in detail. Overstreet (1999) reported that there were very few specific extenders in her conversational data and, as we noted earlier, small token counts result in little attention from researchers.

2.11　After Tags

During the same period that the term "general extender" becomes the linguistic category label of choice, the idea that the use of the forms is based on a dominant referential function (i.e. set- or category-marking) comes under increasing scrutiny and researchers begin to report more often not only on other observed functions, but also on the fact that a single use of a general extender can be multifunctional. Some investigators continue to report that set-marking is the nearly exclusive function of general extenders in their data (Tagliamonte and Denis, 2010: 356), but there has been more discussion of, and a greater concern with, how to analyze the many examples of general extender use where the "set" that is supposedly "marked" is not easily identifiable and the need to account for other functions (Cheshire, 2007: 184; Overstreet and Yule, 1997b: 250; Pichler and Levey, 2011: 453). Some of these examples will be investigated in Chapter 3.

In a rather unique experiment, one group of researchers made a serious attempt to overcome the tendency to make decisions about set-marking based on researcher intuition and to bring a group-consensus approach to the process. Wagner *et al.* (2015) report on their attempt, as a group, to use "a rigorously operationalized concept of the set-marking general extender" (2015: 724) in order to quantify the referential function of general extenders. Their serious attempt to create a coding scheme, with trained coders, was designed to achieve "a high degree of certainty with respect to the general extenders that DO have a referent" (2015: 711, emphasis in the original). In their study of three distinct corpora of North American English, they reported that between 15 and 23 percent of uses of general extenders could be identified as set-marking. They also noted that "unambiguously referential general extenders are likelier to be lexically long" (2015: 727), supporting the conclusion of Aijmer (2002) presented earlier. Clearly there are other functions involved in the use of general extenders, particularly the short forms.

While many of the earlier researchers, especially Aijmer (1985) and Channell (1994), had commented on other functions of general extenders, the analytic approach was mostly concerned with referential meaning and categorization. In addition, throughout the literature describing set- or category-marking tags, there is a general sense in which these tags are, with a few exceptions, clearly assumed to be "content-oriented" within their utterances and not "speaker-oriented," like *I mean*, or "addressee-oriented," like *you know* (Stubbe and Holmes, 1995: 70). When the focus shifts to a consideration of functions beyond the content-oriented, and its tendency to favor a referential, particularly semantic, analysis, the alternative orientations involving the roles of speaker and hearer point to a need for pragmatic analysis and a consideration of interpersonal and personal expressive meanings. The exploration of these concepts in the analysis of general extenders will be the focus of Chapters 3 and 4.

3   Interpersonal Function and Intersubjectivity

In their introduction to a study of pragmatic devices, now more commonly known as pragmatic markers, Stubbe and Holmes (1995: 64) made the following observation about their uses.

> While pragmatic devices often reflect the speaker's degree of certainty in relation to the propositional content of an utterance, they also convey affective, addressee-oriented meaning, especially in informal interactions where the maintenance of social relationships takes priority over the exchange of information.

In this chapter, we will focus on the "addressee-oriented" uses of some of those pragmatic devices that we have identified as general extenders. In some approaches, this is described as the expressive function of language, which is tied to the speaker's view of the interaction and "the resources a language has for expressing personal attitudes to what is being talked about, to the text itself, and to others in the speech situation" (Traugott, 1982: 248). In later chapters, we will explore the personal and textual elements mentioned in this definition, but to begin with, we will be investigating the speaker's concern with others in the speech situation. In this chapter, we will focus on the ways in which speakers employ general extenders as resources that allow them to create and maintain their relationship(s) with other speakers, a subtype of expressive function that is widely known as the interpersonal function (Halliday, 1970). We begin with a brief consideration of the idea that there must be aspects involved in achieving referential success in interaction that are dependent on the accomplishment of an interpersonal connection. However, our main interest is in the ways in which speakers create utterances with audience-design, marking what can be assumed and what has to be mentioned on a particular occasion, being careful not to create problems for the addressee with excessive or inaccurate information, providing indications, often combined with other pragmatic markers, that the participants have a lot in common, and paying attention to the addressee's face, or self-image. It is this concept of "a public self-image" (Brown and Levinson, 1987: 61) that motivates speakers to be concerned with how their utterances might affect their addressees in psychological terms, by signaling awareness of their addressees' needs (e.g. to be connected and liked or to be free from imposition), according to the politeness conventions and social norms of the context in which the interaction takes place. In all these aspects of interpersonal communication, general extenders can be shown to have a significant role.

3.1 The Interpersonal

In Chapter 2, we reviewed the various terms and approaches that have been used in the analysis of general extenders as contributing to the interpretation of the content of utterances. In those approaches, there is a tendency to devote more attention to the cognitive connections between specific exemplars (*a car or something*) and more general concepts (*a vehicle*) based on a relationship similar to hyponymy. In the clearest cases, this type of semantic connection seems to provide a straightforward basis for analyzing how general extenders contribute to referential meaning. One effect of this relatively narrow focus is a tendency to decontextualize utterances as objects of analysis with little connection to the social circumstances of their occurrence. Given that general extenders are a characteristic feature of spoken interaction, we would expect that social aspects of interaction might be involved in motivating the use of specific forms in particular contexts.

In an attempt to illustrate the impact of different contexts, Overstreet (2014) cited two examples of the same phrase *forks and things*, heard in different circumstances. In the first (1), the speaker was in her kitchen, talking to a friend, and referencing what could be interpreted as a set of items, with *cutlery* as a possible superordinate label for the set.

(1) *there's forks **and things** in the top drawer*

(2) *Go get forks **and things***

When she uttered (2), the speaker was waiting in line in a fast-food restaurant and talking to her young son. Off he went and returned from a side area with plastic forks, paper napkins, straws and small packets of mustard and ketchup. In (2), the use of *and things* is not referencing an established set of any kind, with a lexicalized superordinate, but rather a loose collection of "items you can get from a side counter to use with food and drink ordered in a fast-food restaurant" (Overstreet, 2014: 116). We could treat this collection as an example of creating an ad hoc category, already described in Chapter 2 as a type of non-lexicalized category, which is "often created spontaneously for use in specialized contexts" (Barsalou, 1983: 211). As Barsalou (1983) points out, such categories tend not to have well-established representations in memory and typically serve to fulfill a temporary communicative goal. We should also note that they require an assumption on the part of the speaker that the

3.1 The Interpersonal

intended ad hoc grouping will be familiar to the addressee and, in the case of (2), that he won't return with just *forks* or with the logically possible, but locally improbable, *forks and chairs*.

In both examples (1) and (2), the speakers depend on assumptions of different kinds of knowledge shared with their addressees, with an additional element of "you know what I mean," signaled by the use of the general extender. This element in the study of human interaction has been described as intersubjectivity (Rommetveit, 1974) and is considered to be the crucial element in each individual's ability to make sense of what every other individual tries to communicate (Overstreet, 1999: 66; Pichler and Levey, 2011: 450). A more formal definition is provided in Traugott (2010: 33), where intersubjectivity is tied to "the locutionary agent's expression of his or her awareness of the addressee's attitudes and beliefs." We will explore the ways in which this concept helps us understand how general extenders can be used with an interpersonal function. In that undertaking, we adopt a perspective that involves a consideration of how these forms are used by speakers to establish and maintain a social orientation within interaction. We could simply describe this as a shift from a content-oriented analysis to a person-oriented analysis of general extender use. The need for this alternative perspective is motivated by the common observation that a lot of general extenders used in spoken interaction don't seem to be content-oriented at all.

If we were to limit our analysis of general extenders to only those with an identifiable referential function, then examples such as (3) would simply go unanalyzed. In this extract from Carter and McCarthy (2006: 203), it is hard to imagine any additional actions beyond what is stated (i.e. *fill in the form*), but it is possible to interpret the use of *and stuff* as an attempt to soften the sense of imposition in the requirement being expressed, followed by a reason for needing to fulfill the requirement. In rather obvious ways (*you, you, you, you*), this utterance was clearly addressee-oriented.

(3) *They give you a form. You have to fill it in **and stuff**, cos if you don't you won't get an interview.*

We can imagine that the speaker who has to convey a requirement, as in *You have to* ... in (3), that doesn't actually come from the speaker, might feel a need to add some kind of vague indication that "there is more" involved in this (e.g. as in all bureaucracy) than the speaker has control over.

When we talk about a speaker's concerns about the personal impact of what is said, we can use some existing frameworks of analysis in pragmatics that provide insight into the motivation(s) for using general extenders on particular occasions. In recent studies, Grice's (1975) Cooperative Principle, with associated maxims, and Brown and Levinson's (1987) analysis of politeness, with associated strategies, have been used to make sense of what interacting speakers are doing with general extenders when they signal to their addresses: "you know what I mean."

3.2 Intersubjectivity

The underlying assumption in the analysis of set- and category-marking is that the speaker is signaling to the addressee an intention that some kind of shared knowledge is to be accessed in order to process the utterance. If that shared knowledge is evoked with the intention of identifying a particular category, an additional assumption must be that both speakers have very similar, or even identical, worlds of reference in order that a specific match can be made in categorical terms. This is not as straightforward as it sounds, especially if we take into account Labov's (1994: 549) observation regarding the assumption of accuracy in our assessment of others' intentions.

There is no reason to think that our notions of what we intend or the intentions we attribute to others are very accurate, or that we have any way of knowing whether they are accurate.

The fact that each individual's subjective life experiences will necessarily result in separate, non-identical mental worlds has the potential to undermine any assumption of strict accuracy. There is an inherent subjectivity in each of our individual mental worlds, "each locked in our own head" in Gillian Brown's very memorable description (1998: 181), so that an overt appeal to shared knowledge is not an indication that we think we have the same knowledge or identical worlds of reference, but an acknowledgment that we are different yet can recognize clues in what is said to enable us to achieve common ground.

It was the realization that individuals necessarily come to interactions with inherently subjective mental worlds that prompted some scholars in the early twentieth century (Husserl, 1929/1977; Schutz, 1932/1967) to try to identify the underlying principle that allows us to act as if our different personal life experiences won't get in the way of understanding each other. That principle was described in terms of "a reciprocity of perspectives" (Schutz, 1962), which Cicourel would later explain in terms of an assumption by participants in an interaction that "their mutual experiences of the interaction are the same even if they were to change places" (1974: 34). This is one way to describe intersubjectivity. From a linguistic perspective on this phenomenon, we would expect that interactive talk would contain expressions that conventionally invoke intersubjectivity ("you know what I mean"). When we considered the use of general extenders in category implication in Chapter 2, we were implicitly operating with that assumption with regard to message content.

When Channell (1994: 146) analyzed the meaning conveyed by a speaker with the adjunctive extender in *They've got a car and that*, the final phrase was identified as a signal to the addressee to access shared knowledge to create a category that both understand, although both may have different aspects of that category in mind, as Channell's (1994: 151) research illustrated (with fifty-six different items elicited as possible instantiations of *and that*). What this reveals about intersubjectivity is that there is a tolerance of approximation, so that speakers do not have to spell everything out for their addressees. They can rely on certain underlying facets of cooperative action that carry expectations about the amount and accuracy of our interactive contributions.

3.3   Cooperative Fellow Speakers

A basic element involved in intersubjectivity as an underlying principle of conversational interaction is that speakers are generally collaborating with each other and not intentionally trying to confuse or withhold information (although, of course, this may not always be the case, given particular circumstances). That basic element is in line with Grice's (1975) description of conversations as "characteristically, to some degree at least, cooperative efforts" (1975: 45). This idea is formulated in terms of a Cooperative Principle, which attempts to spell out some expectations your interactive partners have that you make your "conversational contributions such as is required, at the stage at which it occurs, by the accepted purpose or direction of the talk exchange in which you are engaged" (1975: 45). You are assumed to be a cooperative fellow speaker.

More specifically, Grice describes a Quantity maxim that assumes speakers will not make their "contributions more informative than is required" (1975: 45). When a speaker wants to mark an awareness of the requirements in this maxim, adjunctive general extenders can provide a very useful instrument. As indicators of "there is more," adjunctive forms allow speakers to limit their spoken contributions, as evidenced in one young speaker's description of a film (that the addressee had not seen), in (4) from Cheshire (2007: 172).

(4)   *and there was another sister and then they find out that she's distantly related to them cos she gives a false name **and all that kind of stuff***

Recognizing that she won't be able to describe the whole plot of the film (nor would it be appropriate), the speaker in (4) gives a few details then signals "there is more," thereby avoiding being more informative than is required. Example (4) illustrates the use of an adjunctive form to limit the amount of information (unknown to the addressee) that the addressee doesn't need to hear. In (5), from Aijmer (2013: 141), the speaker uses two adjunctive phrases in what seems to be the opposite situation from (4), alluding to information the addressee already has (concerning the quality of the type of hotel mentioned) and hence doesn't need to hear.

(5)   *The uh Park-Hyatt Coolum* **and places like that** *Regency in Melbourne* **and things like that**

The circumstances in which the adjunctive forms are produced by the speakers in (4) and (5) are different, but the motivation for their use is essentially the same, that is, not being more informative than is required in those circumstances. A similar appeal to something already known, in this case reporting on how a casual telephone call to a friend might begin, is illustrated in (6), from Overstreet (1999: 132).

(6)   *an' y'know, "I was just sayin' hi, an' seeing how your first day on the job was"* **an' that kinda thing**

The combination of *y'know* at the beginning and the adjunctive general extender at the end provides a double signal that the participants are close (they are long-term friends) and familiars in a shared social world. Aijmer (2013) describes this use of adjunctive forms not only as cooperative, but as indicative of "familiarity, similarity, and solidarity" (2013: 141).

Aijmer (2013: 139) also cites extract (7) as a good illustration of how a speaker uses the general extender *and stuff like that* twice, accompanied by *you know* twice, when talking about events and places familiar to both participants. (The lineation is as in the original.)

(7)   *Uhm people who had to come back to*
        do their to do their final years **and**
        stuff like that *after working* <u>*you know*</u> *in*
        in industries which is like an an
        office with with <u>*you know*</u> *people with drawing*
        boards **and stuff like that**

With respect to extract (7), Aijmer (2013: 139) not only notes the marking of assumptions of a shared world of reference that indicates the speaker is adhering to the Quantity maxim, but also points out that the same process can signal common ground and hence solidarity in a politeness sense, more specifically in terms of positive politeness.

3.4   Solidarity

Speaking with the assumption that there is shared knowledge signals that the participants are close and have enough in common that they can understand each other without much difficulty. The sense of standing on common ground in terms of knowledge in general becomes part of a sense

3.4 Solidarity

of solidarity in terms of social knowledge. We can illustrate this in the use of adjunctive extenders as markers of politeness, specifically positive politeness, which rely on the convenient fiction that "we're the same" (or at least similar enough for current purposes). Positive politeness assumes the participants are connected, having similar ideas and a joint purpose in the event in which they're engaged (cf. Yule, 1996: 60–62). Support for this interpretation of the role of some general extenders in conversation can be found in the way participants use them when marking "similarity" in their ideas and values.

Cheshire (2007) notes that in her interview data, two of the young interviewees would occasionally collaborate on a topic, as in (8), where they are talking about the Spice Girls, "an all-female band popular in the 1990s" (2007: 182).

(8)   A: *but I admire like they've what they've done – how they've got so – far **and stuff***
            B: *the girl power=*
            A: *=the girl power thing*

Cheshire (2007) points to the co-construction of shared views by these speakers, with one using the same expression (*girl power*) as the other, almost instantaneously (as marked by = in the transcript, indicating no break or pause between the two utterances). Cheshire sees the use of *and stuff* as part of the process of "the construction of solidarity between the two friends" (2007: 182). By appealing to their shared experience and values (i.e. admiration for "girl power"), the two speakers emphasize their similarity, one of the clear indicators of positive politeness in action.

A similar interpretation is possible of the function (perhaps not the only one) of the use of *and things like that* in another interaction (9) between two other participants in Cheshire's (2007) research, where they collaborate in expressing a negative opinion of how their teachers talk to them.

(9)   C: *they ask really stupid questions like "can you bring one to school" **and things like that***
            B: *they can be a bit patronizing*
            C: *these are the sort of things that they think of sometimes*

In this interaction, as the two speakers construct a shared evaluation, "the general extender could be said to underline the two friends' overall expression of solidarity" (Cheshire, 2007: 183). We should note, along with Cheshire, that there is an effect of several elements in these interactions, such as "co-constructed turns and repetition of key lexical items" (2007: 184), as well as markers (*like, a bit, sort of*) combining with the general extenders to create the impression of having the same ideas.

Even more harmonious is the co-construction in (10), also from the teenagers in Cheshire's (2007: 176) study. The topic is the size of heels on girls' shoes at school.

(10) H: *yeah it's not allowed to be like two and a half centimeters [or something*
      S: *[yeah or something*
          it's got to be really flat

As indicated in (10) by the symbol "[" representing the start of overlapping speech, these two speakers express the same approximating element with a general extender virtually in unison, demonstrating rather transparently that, by using the same expression, they have the same voice and the same thoughts. That's close.

In other situations, we can identify more elaborate examples of cooperative interaction and also find speakers using several ways to mark closeness, as in (11), from Carter and McCarthy (2006: 203).

(11) A: *I had a big lump in my throat and I couldn't understand it. I mean there was no reason for me to cry **or anything**. Nothing really horrible happening. I guess I must be really tired though cos like+*
      B: *Oh yeah you've been working quite hard **and that***
      A: *+I've been working hard and I've been traveling all the time **and all that sort of thing***
      B: *Yeah*

In (11), speaker B sends signals of understanding and empathy with positive backchannels (*Oh yeah, Yeah*) and expressions of support including a general extender (*and that*). In this fragment of conversation, speaker B actually anticipates what speaker A is about to say, resulting in one turn echoing the previous turn. (In the transcription, the + sign is used to indicate continuous speech.) Note that speaker A is also using general extenders (*or anything, and all that sort of thing*) as well as other pragmatic markers (*I mean, I guess*) in an attempt to convey some of the uncertainty about the reasons for the feelings being expressed. It may be, as illustrated here, that some general extender use by a speaker is prompted by the use of a general extender (or two) by another speaker, especially in interpersonal talk that sends a sympathetic message (i.e. "I understand and agree with you"), as illustrated in (11).

In all these examples, from (8) to (11), we've focused on the collaborative, co-constructed nature of the interaction to illustrate positive politeness at work. There are other situations where there isn't necessarily any evidence that a second speaker is collaborating, but we can still observe one of the speakers reaching out with an adjunctive extender to soften a statement about the other speaker's behavior. In (12) and (13), from Aijmer (2002: 216) and Youssef (1993: 298) respectively, one speaker is in the position of telling the other speaker to do something (which may not be what the other speaker wants to hear), so in each case a general extender is attached to the statement to make it seem like they're just taking part in a casual chat among friends. Speaker A's use of *and stuff then* in (12) marks the preceding statement of action (i.e. what to do next) as the obvious one for both of them, because of the information just shared, implementing a strategy of positive politeness.

(12)   A: *does it inhibit exercise of various kinds*
            D: *oh it does absolutely*
                 any large movements
            A: *so you're going to have to – you're going to have to watch your weight* ***and stuff*** *then*

(13)   *But in case you pick up somebody* ***an ting*** *and intend having a sexual relationship you know – you know you try to have safe sexual practices, you know*

In her analysis of (13), Youssef points out that in Trinidad Creole, the general extender *an ting* represents "a discourse feature entailing implicit shared knowledge" (1993: 291). In (13), that solidarity marker is accompanied by another solidarity marker (*you know*), uttered three times, making it sound more like a reminder (of what is known) than an attempt to make the speaker behave in any special way. The counseling is presented as familiar knowledge that they share, a strategy of positive politeness (Brown and Levinson, 1987). We will look at more examples of general extenders in English Creoles in Chapter 8.

3.5   Hedges

While adjunctive forms, as in (12) and (13), are often used in signaling solidarity, disjunctive forms are often used as hedges on the accuracy of what is being said. The term "hedge" was originally introduced into linguistic analysis by G. Lakoff (1972) to describe expressions such as *sort of* and *loosely speaking* which can be used to reduce the speaker's commitment to the accuracy or reliability of what is being said. The motivation behind the use of hedging expressions may be explained in terms of speakers' sensitivity to Grice's (1975: 45) maxim of Quality, which assumes they are not being untruthful to their fellow speakers and not reporting anything for which they "lack adequate evidence." It would seem that *or something* is perfect for this purpose, as it can add an approximating or hedging element to what is stated. The hint of possible imprecision signaled by *or something* can be found with regard to amounts in (14), from Craig and Tracy (1983: 306), a person's age in (15), from Denis and Tagliamonte (2016: 88), an action in (16), from Erman (1995: 141), a location in (17), from Channell (1994: 135), or the use of an appropriate word in (18), from Pichler and Levey, 2010: 21), or the right expression, in (19), from Pichler and Levey, 2011: 451). As Stenström *et al.* (2002: 104) observe with the "somewhat confusing example" in (20), there are occasions when speakers seem to be having genuine difficulty expressing themselves, yet still remember to mark lack of accuracy.

(14)   *for that job he gets – I think it's three weeks or a month **or something** vacation every year*

(15)   S: *How old were you when you were having these dreams?*
       L: *Maybe I was like seven or eight **or something***

(16)   *and he was perhaps sacked for something else, but I don't know, or made redundant **or something***

(17)   *like at work or on a construction site **or something like that***

(18)   *I probably say eh knackered **or something like that***

(19)   *what was the what's the word I'm trying to – em, ulterior motives **or something***

(20)   *yes, he's gon-, told you, yeah the guy's a, he's probably like, like a whatsit **or something***

It is noticeable how often there are contextualization cues in other expressions (*I think, maybe, like, perhaps, I don't know, about, probably, trying, probably, like*) signaling a potential lack of commitment to the accuracy of what is being said in (14)–(20).

Speakers can also signal that information is possibly inaccurate, but add an element that indicates they don't think it's very important, as in the use of *or whatever* in (21), from Overstreet (1999: 116).

(21)   *Because I know when I first moved down here in like what? – nineteen eighty-six **or whatever***

In (21), the speaker signals an approximation (*like*), pauses and questions herself (*what?*) before producing a date that is treated as possibly inaccurate, but also signals with the choice of *or whatever* (rather than *or something*) that the exact year is not really a concern and is of no consequence. We will take a closer look at the ways in which *(or) whatever* is used in Chapter 4.

Example (22), from Aijmer (2002: 244), illustrates the use of *or so* fulfilling a similar hedging function, indicating approximation with regard to a reported amount of time.

(22)   *but I haven't had anyone*
       for the last three – gosh
       *three months **or so***

This particular general extender is rather unusual in the sense that it has strict collocation requirements in contemporary English (cf. Channell, 1994: 59–62).

3.6 Hedging Reported Speech

In fact, the collocation restrictions of *or so* can be problematic for English language learners who may not understand why an utterance such as **He was eating chocolates **or so*** (from Quirk *et al.*, 1972: 930) is considered to be ungrammatical. Clearly *or so* doesn't attach to unmodified plural nouns. We will investigate this challenge to learners of English as a second language in more detail in Chapter 9. We can identify where *or so* may be used instead of *or something* in the earlier examples (14) and (15), but not in any of the others in (16)–(20), where ungrammatical structures would result. According to Huddleston and Pullum, *or so* is an "idiomatic coordinate" that is "combined with expressions of measure or quantification" (2002: 1540), as illustrated in (23)–(24). It is also used with expressions signaling "approximately," for points in time, such as a date in (25), or a day, as in (26), from Mauranen (2004: 185).

(23) Some, including Portland, Oregon, charge $1 **or so** to recycle a tree

(24) A: *How many were in?*
      B: *Four hundred **or so***

(25) *That must have been in 1964 or so*

(26) *I have everything pretty much wrapped up in here by Wednesday **or so***

Three of these examples (23)–(25) are from Biber *et al.* (1999: 112), who comment on the way general extenders "fit in with the communicative purposes of conversation, emphasizing the interpersonal involvement rather than complete explicitness" (1999: 116).

3.6 Hedging Reported Speech

We could cite numerous other examples of this apparent sensitivity to the Quality maxim when mentioning numerical information in data from a wide range of sources. There also seems to be a concern regarding potential inaccuracy when English speakers report the speech of others. Some of the earliest reported examples of this phenomenon date to the seventeenth century, as in (27), from the year 1680, in the *Corpus of English Dialogues 1560–1760* (Kytö and Culpeper, 2006), cited in Tagliamonte and Denis (2010: 365).

(27) *My Lord, my memory hath been exceedingly bruised; but I remember, my Lord, as I was going through the Abby in a rainy afternoon, she said, this Abby was formerly filled with Benedictine Monks, **or something to that purpose**, and saith she, what if it should be so again?*

The speaker in (27) provides a reason, with a figurative appeal to an "exceedingly bruised" memory, for his possible inaccuracy in reporting what was said, while adding an early type of disjunctive extender phrase. By the nineteenth century, the short form *or something* is being used to hedge on the accuracy of reported speech, as in (28), from the novel *Persuasion* by Jane Austen (1818).

(28) *they happened to say, that her brother, Captain Wentworth, is just returned to England, or paid off,* ***or something***

(We will look at more of the historical ancestors of general extenders in Chapter 6.) Both short and long versions of the disjunctive extender continue to fulfill the same function accompanying, and hedging on, the accuracy of reported speech in the contemporary language, as illustrated in (29), from Ball and Ariel (1978: 37), and (30), from Mauranen (2004: 184).

(29) *I was just sitting here with John Dean and he tells me you were going to be sued* ***or something***

(30) *I think it was Mrs said oh good have you come to take them away* ***or something like that***

A similar hedging element can be found when speakers try to relate news reports, as in (31), from Channell (1994: 132), where possible explanations (or speculations) about a tragic disaster involving the space shuttle are doubly marked by disjunctive forms.

(31) *it is possible that the crew, because of some gas in the cockpit **or something** or heart attacks **or what not**, is unable to make the re-entry completely*

The disjunctive phrases *or what not*, as in (31) and *or what*, as in many examples below, are identified by Brinton (2017) as indicators that the speaker is unsure about some aspect(s) of the information being reported. They can be used when expressing uncertainty.

3.7 Expressing Doubts

Speaker uncertainty is manifested in a number of examples from the early nineteenth century that Brinton (2017: 276) cites, as in (32) from 1823, in (33) from 1832, and (34) from Charlotte Brontë's novel *Jane Eyre* (1847).

(32) *I knew not what lulled me – whether it was the broad moonlight; her utter helplessness; her abashed eyes; and pale, speechless lips,* ***or what***

(33) *I don't know whether 'tis misery,* ***or what****, but there are moments when his mind wanders*

(34) *Whether he was incensed or surprised **or what**, it was not easy to tell*

The contextualization cues of *I knew not*, *I don't know* and *not easy to tell* in these examples support Brinton's analysis that *or what* is used "typically in contexts which explicitly express doubt" (2017: 274), and, we might add, frequently in collocation with *whether*. This usage continues to be found in the contemporary language when speakers indicate that they are not sure about the information being reported, as in (35) from Brinton (2017: 274) and (36) from McColm and Trousdale (2019: 84).

(35)   <u>I don't recall</u> what he needed, cows or horses **or what**

(36)   <u>I don't know</u> whether that was a genuine answer **or what**

For McColm and Trousdale, this use of *or what* is "canonically associated with clauses which are complements of mental predicates such as *know*, *recall* and *remember*" (2019: 84). We would simply add that it is the negative of these predicates that characterizes the uses illustrated.

3.8   Interpersonal Entertainment

The use of general extenders to signal that what is being said may not be correct can be extended to the creation of humorous expressions for the entertainment of others. As we noted with examples (19) and (20) earlier, *or something* is frequently used with potentially inaccurate words or phrases. The possibility that the speaker might be producing an inaccurate or approximate expression can also be exploited for humorous effect, as in (37), involving two cartoon characters (*Beavis and Butt-head*), cited in Overstreet (1999: 111).

(37)   B-H: *Why is he, like, walkin' funny?*
       B: *Maybe he has HAMMEROIDS* **or somethin'**

For these young speakers, simply the mention of a word like "hemorrhoids" would be a source of humor, but the mispronunciation to include "hammer" in the word makes it even more hilarious. The addition of *or somethin'* almost seems like "mock" approximation since there is a feeling that the speaker is being intentionally inaccurate in order to make a joke. Also intentionally inaccurate is the "new expression ... coined for humorous effect" (Aijmer, 2002: 247), accompanying *or something* in (38). Here the name of a military regiment can't be fully recalled and is completed with a phrase for a disease that kills cattle ("foot and mouth disease"), creating a nonsense expression.

(38)   *(he) went out in some ghastly regiment of foot*
       Royal Warwickshire foot and mouth **or something**
       And flogged all round Africa

Not intentionally inaccurate, but certainly intentionally humorous is the use of approximate expressions for the noises made by an old truck, incorporating *or something*, that are the cause of laughter for both speakers in (39), adapted from Overstreet (1999: 120).

(39) S: *that truck makes the most amazing snorting noises sometimes*
R: *huh huh huh*
S: *like when you're goin' up a hill*
R: *right=*
S: *=it makes a noise exactly – it sounds exactly like I dunno like a dog or a horse **or something** like like when it's when it's uh discontent heh heh heh it makes the strangest noise – every time it does I just bust out laughing*
R: *huh huh huh haaaah okay*

There is an element of exaggeration in the speaker's analogy in (39) that can be found in other even more outlandish descriptions, where speakers are clearly choosing entertaining scenarios while continuing to feel the need to include a disjunctive extender that indicates not only "not accurate," but purposefully inaccurate in the sense of "impossible." In (40), from Overstreet (1999: 121), the exploits of a well-known handywoman (Martha Stewart) are presented in a list indicating superhuman powers, with the disjunctive extender actually communicating "not really." A similar use of a disjunctive form in (41), from Channell (1994: 135), accompanies the description of an extremely dangerous action that the speaker actually indicates from the start would be unlikely to happen.

(40) *In one of her shows, she took fresh eggs from the hens she raised and made a meal to rival the Last Supper. Ten minutes later she painted a colored diamond on her porch (exhausting just to watch). While the paint was drying, I think she built a house **or something**.*

(41) *I could no more go to a concert of organ music than I could erm I don't know go abseiling down the face of the Woolworth building **or something like that***

(42) *I mean how would we feel if erm I don't know Holland owned the Isle of Wight **or something like that**, I mean, I suppose we'd feel . . .*

Similar to (41), where the extreme idea is bracketed by *I don't know . . . or something like that*, example (42), from Archer et al. (2012: 199), has another irrealis idea within the same brackets in an unreal conditional. We will investigate the use of general extenders as brackets more fully in Chapter 5.

Looking at the inclusion of the general extenders in these descriptions of entertaining scenarios in (37)–(42), all a bit absurd, we can see how speakers can set out to create such scenarios for the amusement of fellow speakers, exemplifying intersubjectivity. However, there is a suspicion that these speakers are also taking the opportunity to express themselves in a particular way for their own entertainment (e.g. *I just bust out laughing*), exemplifying subjectivity, a function of general extender use that we will explore further in Chapter 4.

3.9 Hedging Invitations and Comments

Up to this point we have been focusing on the ways disjunctive forms allow speakers to hedge on the accuracy of the content, or information status, of their contributions, even when being humorous. However, disjunctive forms are frequently found in utterances where accuracy doesn't seem to be a concern, and appropriateness of interpersonal behavior is the focus. As R. Lakoff noted, hedges could be used "for deference (if we are afraid that by making a certain statement we are overstepping our rights)" (1975/2004: 79).

One aspect of interpersonal talk that seems to be treated as "potentially overstepping our rights" is when we make invitations or requests that impinge on the activities of another. In (43), from Overstreet (1999: 105–6), one speaker is trying to invite another to get together in several ways (*hang out, yack, have dinner*) that concludes with *a walk or something*, but only if the other wants to. Giving options is obviously one way to soften any possible sense of imposition that might be involved in this invitation.

(43)   J: *Come over an' hang out*
       D: *'kay*
       J: *We can always y'know – just yack an' have dinner*
       D: *Okay*
       J: *an' we could go*
       D: *But*
       J: *for a walk **or something** if ya wanna go*

The following two examples, (44) from Aijmer (2013: 144) and (45) from Palacios Martínez (2011: 2453), illustrate the further use of *or something* in invitations.

(44)   *We could have dinner that evening **or something***

(45)   *What are you doing tonight, you know, do you wanna go out **or something***

In both these cases, the mention of a possible alternative, to be chosen by the addressee, allows the speaker to soften or mitigate the sense of imposition implicit in an invitation.

Aijmer (2013: 144) draws attention to the modality in *could* in (44) as an additional element that makes the event less than certain. Channell (1994: 130) also notes the use of *could* (twice) along with *sort of* and *or something* in a very tentative-sounding request from a student to a teacher in (46), a social action that might be construed as an imposition. It is worth noting that when the student says *meet or something*, there is no sense of any alternative action being suggested, that is, there is no referential function involved here. As evidenced by the way in which this request is made, the student is very aware of the need for a negative politeness strategy (Brown and Levinson, 1987), that is, "mentioning" the possibility of an alternative, trying to avoid the impression of imposing on the teacher.

(46)   *Could we, when you give us our essays back, and give us titles, could we sort of meet **or something** because, I mean, there might be things we want to ask*

Speakers are often tentative when talking about possibly influencing another person's actions, a predictable scenario for the occurrence of hedging via negative politeness strategies, as in (47), from Tsui (1994: 180).

(47)   *Hey Don, if you have time tomorrow ah at the gymnasium, the English department is playing the ah the students **or something**, you might take a look at it, the gymnasium, right near your place*

Beginning with a conditional clause concerning the other person's *time* (valuable commodity), this speaker pauses or hesitates twice (*ah*), and includes *or something* attached to *the students* (yet there are no others), with a (remote possibility) modal verb in the main clause (*might take*), then repeats the location and notes that the location is *right near your place*, so it won't be difficult to get to. In this situation, the disjunctive extender *or something* is just one hedging element in an utterance saturated with negative politeness.

Lack of certainty about another's past actions can also prompt the hedging use of a general extender, as illustrated in (48) from Channell (1994: 136). Speakers also tend to downplay situations where other speakers appear to be speaking critically about themselves, as in (49) from Ball and Ariel (1978: 36), by making reassuring comments plus a general extender, in this case *or anything*, which helps to create a negative assertion used to deny a possible implication in B's comment.

(48)   *Don't you remember cos didn't you do something – tweak it up there to make it work in a different way or more efficiently **or something***

(49)   B: *All I did was eat all weekend*
       M: *Well, you don't look like you've gained weight **or anything***

The use of *or anything* to hedge on the impact of the speaker's comments can be found in quite different contexts. In (50), the speaker is trying to get a book (with an ISBN), but is unable to provide necessary details, and hence is in a position of apologizing, according to Koester (2007: 49). In (51), from Tsui (1994: 180), the speaker is not apologizing, but being rather assertive about his opinion, yet is in danger of offending the other speaker, so adds the general extender to try to mitigate the impact of the utterance.

(50)   *I don't have the SBN **or anything***

(51)   B: *Teacher training's a good thing to be on*
       C: *Well, I don't want to be a teacher, **or anything***

3.9 Hedging Invitations and Comments

When we investigate the softening, mitigating and downplaying effects in many of the utterances with disjunctive extenders, as in (43)–(51), we realize that we have to study a type of interactive spoken discourse where invitations, requests and comments on others' behavior might be expected to occur. In the survey-interview data collected in many sociolinguistic studies, there is a noticeable absence of examples of disjunctive forms used as hedges with negative politeness where an imposition might occur (because, for example, young interviewees tend not to request or invite adult researchers to do anything). The way we collect the data shapes the data we collect.

4 Personal Function and Subjectivity

In Chapter 3, we focused on the concept of intersubjectivity as a crucial factor in the ability of speakers to make sense of each other by assuming or creating common ground despite individually distinct life experiences. When we investigated the ways in which general extenders could be used to mark an appeal to intersubjectivity (i.e. "you know what I mean"), one clear outcome was that the utterances in focus were addressee-oriented, with attempts to create solidarity with, and avoid imposition on, the other. However, while all interactions will have addressee-oriented features, the focus of some individual utterances may involve another expressive function in terms of a speaker-oriented dimension, known as subjectivity. In one definition, subjectivity involves "the expression of self and the representation of a speaker's perspective or point of view in discourse" (Finegan, 1995: 1). A more detailed description is presented in Scheibman (2002: 1).

> In English conversation, participants are not simply, nor very often really, reporting on events that take place in the world in an unmediated manner. It is the case that what English speakers are consistently conveying in their talk are evaluations, opinions, and attitudes – in short, their points of view – constrained by the exigencies of face-to-face communication.

In their role in this articulation of the self, literally self-expression, general extenders may be analyzed in terms of a speaker's personal meaning. Biber *et al.* approach this aspect of interactive language use by identifying stance markers in their data. From their point of view, stance is a speaker-oriented phenomenon, as spelled out in these two descriptions (Biber *et al.*, 1999: 966, 979).

> In addition to communicating propositional content, speakers and writers commonly express personal feelings, attitudes, value judgments, or assessments, that is, they express a "stance."
>
> Given the high personal involvement of conversation, where it is always topical to talk about oneself, it is not surprising that stance markers are used more frequently in this register.

According to Biber *et al.* (1999: 966–69), stance meanings can be conveyed through lexical choice (*I hate my job*), adverbials (*Unfortunately it's true*), epistemic verbs and modals (*I think you might be wrong*) and adjectives with

4.1 Evaluation

complements (*It's amazing that judges can get away with outrageous statements*), and many other expressions. Among those, we will include certain uses of general extenders as stance markers in the expression of subjectivity.

4.1 Evaluation

Some of the most obvious cases of general extender structures being used as stance markers are those that incorporate lexical material that signals an evaluation of what's being talked about. Overstreet (1999: 5, 135–36) includes a number of examples, shown in (1)–(4), where speakers use general extender structures with terms like *shit*, *crap* and *garbage*.

(1)   now they've got that Kung Fu and Karate **an' shit**

(2)   I still zoom around and do what I do. I'd hate to have to go round thinking about health **and shit like that**

(3)   I was on the phone 12 hours a day making budgets **and all that crap**

(4)   I did not buy the fantasy of Prince Charming **and all that garbage**

There would seem to be little doubt that the speakers in (1)–(4) do not place a positive value on what is being described. Other pejorative terms (*junk*, *mess*, *nonsense*, *rubbish*) have been noted in the position of the proform in the structural template of what are actually specific extenders since they do indicate a very specific evaluation. All of these pejorative forms are low-frequency items in most studies that include numerical data (e.g. Tagliamonte and Denis, 2010: 363) or are completely absent from some reports, particularly the sociolinguistic interview studies (Cheshire, 2007; Levey, 2012; Pichler and Levey, 2011). We suspect that it is the contextually distinct nature of the participation framework in these data-collection situations that creates restrictions on the interviewees' use of "bad language." When teenagers are left in charge of the recordings, as is the case in the *Bergen Corpus of London Teenage Language* (COLT), there is a different effect, as in this observation from Stenström *et al.*, "there is a lot of swearing in the COLT conversations" (2002: 105), and the terms *crap* and *shit* occur more frequently in the extenders the teenagers use. Extract (5) provides a sample of their talk, though the general extender itself in this case is not pejorative. Palacios Martínez (2011: 2453) makes a similar point about teen language, quoting one teenager's contribution as in (6).

(5)   Susie: We come to an agreement and that's our biggest word, fuck. I've got everyone's, oi, Abdullah! What's your favourite swear word?
      Caryl: Bollocks!
      Sharon: I think mine's probably
      Susie: Mine's like, cunt **and things like that**
      Allie: Usually shit and fuck, I think are my vocabulary
      Susie: Yeah, or oh shit, you cunt!

(6)   *I haven't learned my Highway Code **and all that sort of shit***

The speakers in (5) and (6) don't seem to have any difficulty with the vocabulary of negative evaluation in self-expression. However, the study of how speakers express their attitudes and evaluations is not limited to negative lexical material, but includes the use of general extenders such as *and everything, and all (that), or anything* and *or whatever*. Before exploring these indicators of subjective evaluation, we should note an aspect of how speakers can structure their contributions to give voice to the personal expression of their experience(s).

4.2   Subjectivity

One benefit of looking at interactive language use in terms of expressive function is that it may help us understand a feature of spoken discourse that is a bit of a puzzle, especially if we expect speakers to adhere strictly to the Quantity maxim and not to make a contribution "more informative than is required" (Grice, 1975: 45). Why would a speaker not use a common superordinate lexicalized category expression when one is available, such as *housework*, and instead create a list of actions completed with a general extender, as in (7), from Overstreet (1999: 26)? In this transcript, the use of ::: indicates lengthening of the vowel and (.) indicates a short pause or has the length in seconds of other pauses included.

(7)   No::: I've been (.) vacuumin' 'n (1.0) washin': (1.0) clo::thes 'n dustin':
         'n all that stuff

Prior to (7), the speaker's (adult) daughter had asked her (by phone) if she had been taking a nap. In the mother's reply, there are distinct pauses included in the listing of actions, as well as lengthening of some vowels (*No:::, clo::thes*), and the addition of *all that*, with an expanding effect, in the general extender. All these features add up to a much longer turn than if the speaker had just said, "I've been doing housework." If the speaker is being cooperative, there must be a reason why the maxim of Quantity is being flouted. That reason can be found if we focus on the turn as speaker-oriented. All the features of lengthening that we noted result in an utterance that communicates iconically that there was a lot of activity on the part of the speaker and it lasted a long time. The choice of *'n all that stuff* instead of the shorter *'n stuff* expands the basic sense of "there's more" to emphasize that there was "a lot more" involved. The brief interaction we've just reported was based on intersubjectivity, of course, as are all conversations. We have just looked closely at one contribution with a distinct speaker-orientation, or subjectivity, that had a special expressive function for that speaker.

4.3 Maximizing

We can observe the same pattern with a list plus a specific extender, used with expressive function by a speaker in order to signal that there's a lot more, in extract (8), with the original tone unit lineation from Aijmer (2002: 214).

(8)   C: *em we are at the– at the works end*
           of U.C.
      A: *well*
           according to-
      C: *delivery wagons*
           and builders materials
           and joiners
           and pipe layers
           and all sorts of people

In (8), speaker C seems to be flouting Quantity while enumerating the many elements that are present *at the works end of U.C.,* each noun phrase in a separate tone unit, beginning with *and* every time, plus the inclusion of *all* as an intensifier in the specific extender at the end. The contribution of the specific extender here is best seen, not as flouting Quantity, but as magnifying the already long and varied list of "people" in the vicinity. The justification for this message ("there's a lot more") must be based on a negative impact on the personal experience being described and hence how it is expressed. Although there is no overt evaluation included in this extended turn, we are expected to recognize that this speaker has a negative view of all the action being described and is essentially complaining. In Boxer's (1993) analysis, extract (8) would represent an indirect complaint, not aimed at the addressee, but "an expression of dissatisfaction ... about someone/something that is not present" (1993: 24). Although Boxer insists that, in an indirect complaint, the speaker is "sharing" a negative evaluation, "since by definition the indirect complaint is addressed to a third party" (1993: 24), we have to characterize that third party in (8) as more of an audience for the complaint than either a co-participant or a target. In (8), the speaker is using a specific extender to expand on the many reasons for the indirect complaint, attempting to give expression to a subjective experience.

4.3   Maximizing

Another situation in which speakers may seem to be flouting Quantity is when there is something really special or "extraordinary" being described, licensing the expression of "a lot more" through the use of the general extender *and everything*, as illustrated in (9). Prior to this extract, the speaker had expressed the idea that being on holiday is "fantastic because it's so completely different," and goes on to give examples of the ways in which it's really a lot different. The lineation is based on separate tone units, as reported in Aijmer (2002: 238).

(9)   *sort of whole routine*
        and atmosphere
        and climate
        and clothes **and everything**
        you know
        quite extraordinary

The use of *and everything* here is not simply as an adjunctive extender indicating that "there is more," but that there is something special or remarkable in what is being described. The speaker underscores this interpretation with the expression *quite extraordinary* that effectively places the experience described at the high or extreme end of some range of experiences, in the opinion of the speaker.

As already noted in Chapter 1 (section 1.4.3), there is a distinct use of *and everything* in English that provides speakers with a way of indicating that the accompanying information has the feature [+ remarkable], as first noted by Aijmer (1985: 383), or "exemplifies a high value on some inferable scale" (Ward and Birner, 1993: 205). In (10), from Palacios Martínez (2011: 2466), the speaker wants to emphasize the high value of going to Oxford (i.e. the university), presumably on an inferable scale related to level of education, as a way of supporting her initial claim.

(10)   *Her dad's kind of very well brought up. He went to Oxford* **and everything**.

As used in (10), the phrase *and everything* seems to be functioning as a type of intensifier or, more specifically, as a maximizer, "which can denote the upper extreme of a scale" (Quirk *et al.*, 1972: 444). We should be careful not to think of the "upper extreme" as only one-dimensional. What counts as an "extreme" aspect of something necessarily depends on the perspective of the speaker. In his work with preadolescents (10–11-year-olds) in London, Levey (2012: 267, 273) points to the way those young speakers talk about watching horror films where the "extreme" events that are recounted with *and everything*, as in (11) and (12), are on a scale of horribleness.

(11)   *they've ate all their insides* **and everything**

(12)   *and then she comes out and she's got blood all around her* **and everything**

Levey (2012: 273) notes that, in their evaluations of these extreme events (e.g. having their insides eaten), the speakers in (11) and (12) also include *all* as an additional intensifier, helping to maximize the horror in their reports. Supporting this analysis is the inclusion, as in (13), of later information that explains the source of an extremely frightening experience, as Levey (2012: 262) points out.

(13)   *I knew they were going to do it but I never knew what time and I never knew they had <u>all</u> creepy crawly hands **and everything** cos ... spiders come on the TV*

In (13), the young girl is talking about what her friends do to frighten her while she's watching a horror film, using *all* and *and everything* as brackets round the really scary part in *creepy crawly hands*, which plays on her arachnophobia (*spiders come on the TV*).

Although defined in terms of a scale, the maximizing use of *and everything* is clearly not just signaling an upper extreme in a scale of good things, as we have seen in (11)–(13). In fact, the brackets *all ... and everything* can be used to signal very low or negative value, as in (14) from Clancy (2015: 239), recorded while a family is adding decorations to a Christmas tree.

(14)   Son: *Oh look the state of the one mam hate mam hates that because they're+*
       Mother: *It's awful*
       Daughter: *It's rotten*
       Mother: *Don't put it up*
       Daughter: *It's rotten Jimmy*
       Mother: *It's <u>all</u> dirty **and everything***

The final phrase *all dirty and everything* together with the earlier negative adjectives *awful* and *rotten* describing what *mam hates*, leave no doubt about the nature of the mother's evaluation.

Of course, the upper extreme doesn't have to be on a scale of bad things. We can point to many examples such as (15), where the information is presented with high positive value, from Stenström et al. (2002: 149).

(15)   *and he goes to me, it was a Boss h- you know Boss the, make, the clothes and the perfume **and everything***

The young speaker in (15) had earlier expressed a positive opinion of *this amazing Boss hat* that she wanted and interrupts her narrative, using the brackets *you know ... and everything* to allude to the high prestige of this company's range of products.

4.4   Beyond Expectation

A more obvious evaluation of items of high value on a scale is expressed in (16) from Overstreet and Yule (2002: 788). In this example, the speaker (actually, the writer, since this is from an email message) is sending an excited report to a friend who is familiar with New Orleans and the Mardi Gras celebration.

(16)   *Did you do Mardi Gras? Can you believe it's on the internet? King cake, beads **and everything**. It's wild!*

As Overstreet and Yule (2002: 788–89) note with regard to (16), the items *king cake* and *beads* are presented as items on the evoked scale of things connected to Mardi Gras (of which "there are more"), that are marked as being of high value (unlike beer in plastic cups and portable toilets, for example). Notice that in (16), the writer is adding another element (*Can you believe* ... ?) to this use of *and everything*, that the information accompanying it is "hard to believe." The implicit message of "hard to believe" is that the information is unexpected.

It is possible to find *and everything* with an unexpected item in a speaker's description in a written text, as in (17), from Safina (2002: 253), functioning in a way that has been described here for spoken data.

(17) *After college Dave saw the ocean from one of the first really big boats to explore for tuna in the western Pacific. "It was a two-hundred-and-twenty-foot, twelve-hundred ton superseiner – with a helicopter **and everything**."*

What extract (17) and many other written examples illustrate, is that the use of *and everything* doesn't depend on intonation, as has been proposed (Ward and Birner, 1993: 212), in order to be interpreted as indicating an extreme point on a scale. That extreme point in (17), the item to which *and everything* is attached, is certainly worthy of an "unexpected" interpretation. After all, who would expect there to be a helicopter on a boat?

Any type of "hard to believe and unexpected" implication can certainly be reinforced through intonation, as Ward and Birner (1993: 212) demonstrate, and as illustrated even more transparently in (18), from Overstreet (1999: 96). In this extract from a television talk show, the host is expressing a sense of amazement at how sweet and helpful a husband had been to his wife when she was unwell. The vowel in the word *clothes* was pronounced with a lot of lengthening (as indicated by ::::::).

(18) *He washed her CLO::::::thes* **an' E:verything**!

In addition to the emphasis on *clothes*, the articulation of the general extender has heavy stress on the first syllable of *everything*, making it sound like an intensifier and marking the action described as extreme, from the speaker's point of view.

We can also consider some uses of *and all (that)* that can have a similar function to *and everything*. In a BBC news report (November 30, 2019), a puppy that had been frozen for 18,000 years was "amazingly well-preserved," followed by the description in (19), where an "extreme" feature of the discovery is marked by *and all*.

(19) *Its body is nearly intact – fur and all*

It is possible, of course, for an extreme interpretation to be tied to extreme disinterest, especially when a speaker begins with an announcement of

4.5 Contrary to Expectation

personal lack of interest expressed in *I couldn't be bothered* and closes with *and all that*, as in (20), with the lineation from Aijmer (2002: 212).

(20)   *because I I couldn't be bothered with all the palaver*
       <u>*you know*</u> *all the thing of booking up*
       and filling in the forms
       and all that

In (20), the interpretation of *and all that* ("there's a lot more") can be seen as motivated on a literal level by the activities listed between the *you know* bracket and the general extender. This isn't always the case. In (21), from our unpublished American English data, the speaker uses *and all that* twice, as well as in combination with *and everything* one of those times. There are no items listed here. This speaker is reporting what others (*they*) said and using single terms (*gambling, corrupt*) with the general extenders each time to communicate the extreme and problematic nature of the topics. The use of a double general extender has an intensifying effect that, given her later statement, expresses a sense that the extreme element in what *they kept saying* had been unnecessary.

(21)   *they kept saying there'd be y'know gambling y'know and everything an' all that and we were gonna y'know be corrupt an' all that but I haven't been out there so I really don't know*

The clue to this speaker's opinion here is in *we were gonna*, indicating that if the speaker is part of *we*, then it (*becoming corrupt*) didn't happen in her experience. The speaker then adds *but* after the second *an' all that,* plus a couple of self-referencing clauses, not to justify thinking contrary to the earlier expectations of others (because we already know she does), but to retreat from being a knowledgeable informant, as someone lacking adequate evidence, very much in line with Grice's Quality maxim.

4.5   Contrary to Expectation

There is an English formulaic construction, partially instantiated in (21), but more clearly illustrated in (22), involving *and everything/and all (that)*, that speakers use when they are trying to explain behavior that may be contrary to some (implicit) social expectation(s). In (22), from Aijmer (2002: 227), the speaker (A) goes to some lengths to describe a situation where she feels a social expectation concerning an individual exists (*keep him entertained*), with some sorry details about him and his unkempt appearance, and ending with *and everything*, then followed by a *but*-clause in which the speaker explains that the expectation was not fulfilled. The detail of *buttons hanging off his shirt* is presented as an extreme aspect, marked by *and everything* as intensifier, of how

68   4 Personal Function and Subjectivity

pathetic he was, and hence in need of attention, *but* it was a social expectation the speaker could not cope with.

(22)   A: *he was very- he was particularly upset*
            that I couldn't keep him entertained in the evenings rather than the
            mornings
            but I mean
            an evening is a lonely time I guess
        B: *m – right*
        A: *he was obviously*
            just rather pathetic and
            on his own
        B: *yeah*
        A: *buttons hanging off his shirt* **and everything**
            but I wouldn't have been that dedicated

The underlying formulaic construction here is presented in (23), based on Overstreet and Yule (2002: 790), with its assumptions spelled out in detail.

(23)   X *and everything/and all (that), but* Y

        I acknowledge that X is the case and would like to emphasize that certain (implicit social) expectations may arise on the basis of X (*and everything/and all (that)*), yet (*but*) I present Y as explanation for acting/thinking/speaking contrary to those expectations.

Another element that often precedes the use of this formula is an anticipatory *I mean*, indicating that the speaker is attempting to clarify something, typically about the speaker's own behavior. The phrase is used in the third line of (22), and at the beginning of (24), from Overstreet and Yule (2002: 791). In (24), the speaker is referring to a friend who has already been described as irresponsible with respect to a pet dog that died.

(24)   *I mean she is the caretaker of the dog* **and all that**, *but I – I'm real serious about it – if she gets a pet in the next few years I'm gonna slap her*

In (24), the speaker isn't using *and all that* to refer to any other elements, but instead to establish an acknowledgment of the social situation (i.e. the rights of a pet owner), prior to asserting, and being *real serious* about, her intention essentially to behave contrary to an expectation based on that situation, and she won't avoid imposing.

In (25), there is a similar use of the formulaic construction, where a contrast exists, though not marked by *but*, and instead of *I mean*, the speaker begins with *Don't get me wrong*, in an attempt to make sure the message isn't misunderstood.

(25)   *Don't get me wrong, everything is okay with Monica coming, she's nice* **and all**
        It's just that I had just pictured a smaller group in here

4.6 The Minimum Expected

In (25), from Fernandez and Yuldashev (2011: 2633), the speaker acknowledges that the addition of Monica is *okay* and that she is very *nice*, so there would be an expectation that the speaker would have no concerns about her addition to the group, yet he has to explain why he was thinking that, contrary to that expectation, he would rather there weren't any additions. Just another speaker trying to explain his point of view, but including *just* (twice) in the final explanation, with a past perfect (*had pictured*) effectively reducing the current relevance of that earlier opinion, even as it is being articulated.

In all these examples (22)–(25), there is a general sense that the speakers are trying to show that they are aware of social expectations concerning their thinking and acting while needing to explain why they might be thinking or acting contrary to those expectations. Another general extender that has comparable uses is *or anything*, often indicating a minimum expectation.

4.6 The Minimum Expected

The phrase *or anything* is found in questions and, more commonly, in negative statements. In the analysis of Huddleston and Pullum, it would be characterized as a "negatively-oriented polarity-sensitive item" (2002: 823) because it takes part in negative constructions but is not itself a negative form. In its basic uses, it invites an interpretation tied to its function as a disjunctive form with a meaning close to "X (or Y) or any other(s) similar to X (or Y)." This usage is investigated in Adolphs *et al.* (2007: 66–67), based on the frequent occurrence of *or anything* in their healthcare data, particularly in questions that nurses ask of patients, as in (26) and (27).

(26)　*any intense headache or mental confusion **or anything**?*

(27)　*no shortness of breath or gasping for breath **or anything**?*

The open-ended element created by *or anything* in these examples is interpreted by Adolphs *et al.* as a way to "encourage the patient to disclose symptoms" (2007: 67). It could also be a way of making the questions sound more informal, with the same purpose. As a means of eliciting more information, the nurses' questions could be viewed as offering some basic symptoms, or the minimum afflictions the patients might have, as clues for a more general diagnosis. In other uses, this "minimum" element implicated by *or anything (like that)* is much clearer, as in (28), from Macaulay (1985: 118), where a speaker is talking about his father.

(28)　*he wasnae a drinker he wasnae in the pub even once a week **or anything like that***

In (28), the speaker emphasizes, via the information in the structure *not even ... or anything like that*, the minimum one might expect of *a drinker* as a way of creating an emphatic negative assertion. In this usage, *or anything (like that)* loses the sense of "others, or alternatives" and becomes almost formulaic as a way of not only stating a negative, but giving it extra emphasis with an intensifier function.

This emphatic use is not new, having been documented in Jane Austen's novel *Pride and Prejudice* (1813), as in (29), and in Thomas Hardy's novel *Far from the Madding Crowd* (1874), shown in (30), both examples listed in the *OED Online*.

(29)   *I did not once put my foot out of doors ... Not one party, or scheme, **or anything***

(30)   *How soft it is – being winter time too – not chapped or rough **or anything***

As indicated in (30), with the mention of *winter time*, there is often an expectation that is being countered as not being the case with the information between the negative and the general extender. That emphasis is often tied to a minimum expectation not being met, as in (31)–(33), from Overstreet (1999: 86–87). In (31), two nurses are talking about a recently deceased patient and commenting on the absence of something minimally expected (i.e. no family). Similarly, in (32), the speaker is reacting to a friend saying she got married in a small civil ceremony and asking about some minimally expected participants. In (33), the speaker is giving directions to an office, but has to warn the addressee that something minimally expected is missing.

(31)   *I felt so sad for him and no family **or anything***

(32)   *so – but – your parents weren't there **or anything**?*

(33)   *Um hm – it's Kokua Nursing, but it doesn't say that on the door **or anything***

Aijmer (1985: 384) has a similar analysis of a speaker's expectation that there might at least be a phone call, as in (34).

(34)   *so she quite put him off and now he never rings up **or anything***

For this speaker, it seems "hard to believe," in Aijmer's (1985: 384) analysis, that something minimally expected hasn't happened.

4.7   Formulaic Disclaimers

This marking of awareness of a minimum expectation contained in the formula *not ... or anything*, *but*-clause, is analyzed in Overstreet and Yule (2001) as a formulaic disclaimer, as illustrated in (35) from our notebook data.

4.7 Formulaic Disclaimers

(35)   *I know we don't know each other **or anything but** could I ask you something?*

This speaker acknowledges that there is a (perceived) normal precondition on making a request, which is not the case in this situation, so what follows may appear to be a problematic action. The motivation for the *not ... or anything* clause seems to be tied to politeness concerns, in that the speaker has to assert her awareness of the expectation and her concern about imposing, a strategy of negative politeness.

Formulaic disclaimers can be viewed as clear examples of subjectivity in action, as speakers include information that explains or clarifies how they want to be interpreted. The following definition, taking the speaker's point of view, is based on Overstreet and Yule (2001: 51).

(36)   *not X or anything (like that), but Y*

> By using this formulaic disclaimer, I seek to clarify in advance my intention not to violate either a specific social expectation (*not X*) or any other relevant social expectations that we have in common (*or anything*), acknowledging (*but*) that the following clause (Y) may contain something that might constitute problematic action

In many cases, as in (37) from Tsui (1994: 33), speakers actually announce their desire to clarify their intentions by beginning with *I mean* in the left bracket.

(37)   <u>*I mean*</u>*, I'm **not** being insulting **or anything**, **but** I can't see myself being a bank manager*

Given that the other speaker had earlier suggested working in a bank as a career option, the speaker in (37) is clearly in danger of producing a problematic action that is potentially *insulting*, and "tries very hard to clarify his own intentions" (Tsui, 1994: 34). As in (37) and many other cases, the first clause of a formulaic disclaimer contains the expression of a personal concern about inappropriate social action, such as being characterized as "nosey," as in (38), from Overstreet and Yule (2001: 46), or "combative" in (39), from a newspaper report, or "boasting," in (40), from Tsui (1994: 151).

(38)   *I wasn't trying to be nosey **or anything but** I saw the letters on her desk*

(39)   *We're **not** being combative **or anything like that, but** if the prostitutes don't want to go away, maybe our presence out here will keep the johns away*

(40)   *Well I was in the jungles in Zambia y'know and and it's **not** that I'm boasting **or anything but** I have done certain things in my life and they asked about it*

Not being thought of as "boasting" may also be the key to interpreting the speaker's intention in (41), a quotation from the American actor Halle Berry (in *People* magazine, June 3, 2019) where she downplays the level of her ability first before claiming that her ability should not be underestimated.

(41)   *I don't have a black belt **or anything but** I will tell you this: if someone thought they were going to snatch my purse on the street, they better think again*

We should note that examples (37)–(41) all begin with first-person pronouns (*I/we*), more evidence that formulaic disclaimers are ideal structures for expressing subjectivity.

There is some evidence that the structure of a formulaic disclaimer is so familiar to conversational participants that, as one speaker begins to create the first part, another speaker can offer to complete the second part. Towards the end of extract (42), from Cheepen and Monaghan (1990: 119–20), two women co-construct a formulaic disclaimer.

(42)   K: *I was sitting in my living room and without meaning to I was looking out into the garden and I was looking straight into Lawson's house that's the one up in Middle Close on the corner and I saw him get undressed in his living room and there's no reason why you shouldn't get undressed in your living room if you want to*
        C: *yeah*
        K: *and I thought my God*
        C: *yeah*
        K: *if I can see him*
        C: *he can see you*
        K: *and I don't always just get undressed in my living room*
        C: (laugh)
        K: <u>*you know I mean OK I'm sure he's **not***</u>
        C: <u>*peeping*</u>
        K: <u>*peeping **or anything***</u>
        C: <u>***but** he*</u>
        K: <u>*but it just*</u>
        C: <u>*you accidentally saw him*</u>
        K: *that's right*

In line 13 of (42), the speaker (K) begins with the discourse markers *you know* and *I mean* as she attempts to clarify what, on first hearing, seems to be the intention of another individual. However, although apparently referring to this other individual (*him*), the speaker is actually disclaiming a possible interpretation of her own behavior, as described earlier in lines 1–4. The problematic action here, as finally stated by her conversational partner (C), is that speaker K *accidentally saw him* (get undressed). The formulaic disclaimer co-constructed in lines 13–18 is really about speaker K's need to have her reported behavior interpreted appropriately and *not peeping or anything* (i.e. not intentionally trying to secretly watch him). That need is actually satisfied in the co-construction of the formulaic disclaimer (underlined) as speaker C helps K to express her lack of intention in the event because it was accidental. This coordinated performance of a formulaic disclaimer

4.8 On Being Indifferent

In formulaic disclaimers, there is a sense that the speaker is concerned with a form of "impression management" (Goffman, 1959: 208), that is, trying to control a possible negative evaluation and project a positive image of self, even while considering a problematic social action. When we turn to the analysis of another disjunctive general extender, *or whatever*, we find speakers using the form as if the impression they want to give is one of lack of concern or indifference. We should note that, in contemporary English, the word *whatever* has a number of functions, many of them described in Kleiner (1998) and Huddleston and Pullum (2002), with more in-depth studies in Brinton (2017, 2020) and McColm and Trousdale (2019). We will focus on the pragmatic marker uses of *Whatever*, with a capital letter, and *or whatever*, functions virtually unrecorded until the mid twentieth century, but a lot "more salient in the recent history of English" (McColm and Trousdale, 2019: 100). They are typically used with the implication that "it doesn't actually matter whether certain details are exactly correct" (Overstreet, 1999: 123). They are both also used with a dismissive effect on occasion, signaling that the speaker has little interest in the details.

The temptation is to think of the general extender form as the source of the shorter form (i.e. *or whatever* → *Whatever*), but we don't see this kind of change in the uses of other general extenders. There's no contrast in post-position of single word *Something* versus *or something* at the end of a phrase or clause. That is, we find the combination in *like a college or something*, but not *like a college. Something.* There's a similar non-contrast between the single word *Things* versus *and things*. We can use *Something like that* and *Things like that* without conjunctions, but not just the single proforms. Those conjunction-less general extenders will be explored in Chapter 5. For current purposes, we would simply note our suspicion that the two versions of *whatever* might have different functions and different sources.

In Brinton's (2017) investigation of the origins of the single word *Whatever*, used by itself, and the general extender *or whatever*, there is some evidence that their current uses came about through different pathways and one is not the source of the other, a position supported by McColm and Trousdale (2019). However, the similarity in their expression of speaker's evaluation of what has been said can't help but make them reinforce each other as subjective markers.

The single word *Whatever* most likely has its origins in expressions of the type illustrated in (43), from 1854, cited in Brinton (2017: 279). Worth noting is the position of *Whatever* here, at the beginning of an utterance, not a likely position from which the extender phrase might evolve.

(43) So he said in reply, – "***Whatever*** *you please. It is not important to us*"

This nineteenth-century usage has a second-person pronoun subject and any one of a number of specific verbs, as in the structure: *Whatever you please/like/ choose/say* .... According to Brinton (2017: 279), the tone of these uses seems to convey indifference (note the evaluation *not important* in (43)), or even irritation. When the full clause is reduced to a single word (*Whatever*), it is treated as an "interjection," with a quite distinct function, as detailed in McColm and Trousdale (2019: 84), who include the following definition from the *OED Online*.

the function of the interjection is typically to mark a dismissive, ignorant, and/or unengaged stance on the part of the speaker, often in response to a prior comment made by an interlocutor.

This distinctly speaker-oriented function comes into common usage in American English in the mid twentieth century (Brinton, 2017: 272), with an early (and clearly dismissive) example in (44), quoted from a 1965 television program (*Bewitched*). In this situation, a mother (E) doesn't care for her daughter (S)'s husband, frequently getting his name wrong and not being concerned about it.

(44) E: *Good morning, Derwood*
      S: *Darrin*
      E: *Alright.* ***Whatever.***

This usage has become quite widespread and instantly recognizable as a signal from speakers expressing their indifference. In some situations, this indifference can sound like impoliteness, as in (45), from 2005, cited in Brinton (2017: 269).

(45) *Blah, blah, blah. All right.* ***Whatever****. Suit yourself.*

Interestingly, the prior comment of the interlocutor here is represented by *Blah, blah, blah*, another form associated with a dismissive reaction to talk, a function we will explore in section 4.9. Example (45) makes it clear that speakers use *Whatever* with a distinctly dismissive function, not too different from the way in which *or whatever* can be used in the contemporary language.

The alternative path of historical change analyzed by Brinton (2017) tracks the development of the phrase *or whatever*, as used in a general extender role.

4.8 On Being Indifferent

The earliest examples appear to be in parenthetical clauses where the speaker is concerned about the correct expression to use. While the interjection use has its origins in *Whatever you please*, the disjunctive form seems to have originated in expressions similar to *or whatever (else) it may be called*, as illustrated in (46) from the year 1645, and in (47), from 1716, both cited in Brinton (2017: 278).

(46)   We are so ignorant of Truth, or so careless of the profession of it, that any Opinion, or Faction, **or whatever it be called**, should thrust it selfe so farre and so fast into Our Kingdomes without Our Knowledge of it.

(47)   I have stated the true notion of clemency, mercy, compassion, good-nature, humanity, **or whatever else it may be called**, so far as is consistent with wisdom.

When the full clauses of the type shown in (46) and (47), beginning with *or whatever*, are reduced to a two-part short form, it continues to be used where there is uncertainty about the correct expression, as in (48), from the year 1666, and in (49) from a more modern (1905) source, both cited in Brinton (2017: 275–76).

(48)   but commonly the last hath been, who is king, whether called Emperour or Leader **or whatever**, hee is a king

(49)   Poor Professor De Sanctis, the Vice President or Secretary **or whatever**

As in these last four examples, the phrase *or whatever* continues to be found at the end of lists in the contemporary language, always with the implication that there may be "another" or "others" added to the list, but with the added sense that the speaker doesn't care about them or about trying to think of them. Most descriptions of the use of *or whatever* claim that it attaches to lists of nouns, as in the historical examples (46)–(49), and also in the contemporary extracts (50), from Wagner *et al.* (2015: 712), and (51), from Denis (2017: 160).

(50)   and it would be like cousins brothers or sisters and parents **or whatever**

(51)   and of course in the wintertime, I guess, it was getting out, building forts and having a snowball fight or throwing some snowballs at somebody driving by **or whatever**

In (51), we have a list of gerunds describing activities, suggesting that a list consisting of verbs could also be concluded with *or whatever*, as confirmed by extract (52) from the *Church Times*, August 6, 1975, cited in the *OED Online*.

(52)   Now that the Archbishop of Canterbury has "relinquished," "delegated," **or whatever** his metropolitical authority to the local Arab Anglicans

It is noticeable that as the short form *or whatever* has become more common, and conjoined with a wider range of types of antecedents, it is no longer tied to correct naming and has evolved to a basic disjunctive general extender usage (i.e. "there may be others"), yet has retained its sense of (speaker's) indifference to the identification of those "others." In this way, it becomes simply a marker of approximation, with a continued sense that the speaker is downplaying the importance of the information to which it is attached, as in (53) from Wagner *et al.* (2016: 213).

(53) *I had a couple of colds* ***or whatever***, *but I never really got real sick last year at all.*

Having traced the likely development of *or whatever* as a pragmatic marker from *or whatever it may be called*, and similar expressions related to correct naming, we should remain aware of the residual effect of a meta-level function, not only concerned with "naming," but with a more general function that enables speakers to indicate how they would like the message attached to be treated.

4.9   Metapragmatic Awareness

The expression *whatever it may be called* in (46) represents a use of language to reflect on and talk about language, also evident in the use of the short form in *whether called Emperour or Leader or whatever* in (48). This use of language is best analyzed at the meta-level. The prefix *meta-* ("above," "beyond") was introduced by Tarski (1935/1956) in his description of *Metasprache* ("metalanguage") for language used to talk about language. When we use words like "prefix" (as in the preceding sentence) or "noun" or "verb" or any other term for grammatical function, we are using metalanguage. When the author of (49) was trying to identify the correct expression (*the Vice President or Secretary or whatever*), the use of *or whatever* signals potential inaccuracy in the words used, thereby exhibiting "metalinguistic awareness." That is, if I think that what I'm saying might be wrong, I must have the ability to analyze the linguistic forms in what I'm saying. By the same token, when the author of (49) used *or whatever* to signal an adherence to the Quality maxim regarding the accuracy of what is being said, which is a pragmatic function, he exhibited "metapragmatic awareness." That is, if I think that what I'm saying might signal a potentially inappropriate pragmatic message, I must have the ability to analyze what kind of message I might be sending. We can define metapragmatic awareness as the ability of speakers to recognize pragmatic aspects of communication and potential pragmatic interpretations of their utterances (cf. Overstreet, 2010, 2015).

4.9 Metapragmatic Awareness

In our review of the formulaic constructions incorporating *and everything, but* and *not ... or anything, but*, we noted that these formulae, in (23) and (36), allow speakers not only to express a stance, but also to comment on possible evaluations of their behavior. As they offer clarifications of behavior and events that should not be interpreted in terms of normal expectations, speakers are essentially trying to influence the interpretation, not just of the words and phrases used, but also of the pragmatic function of their utterances. This is a good illustration of metapragmatic awareness at work (Verschueren, 1999, 2000) as the speakers demonstrate their ability to comment on and influence the pragmatic impact of what they are saying. In the case of the two formulae described earlier, their use illustrates Caffi's (2009) analysis of metapragmatics as "that area of speakers' competence which reflects the judgments of appropriateness of one's own and other people's communicative behavior" (2009: 625).

When we looked at hedges earlier in Chapter 3 (section 3.5), with examples indicating approximation, as in (54), we noted that the general extender *or whatever* signaled the speaker's sensitivity to an expectation inherent in the Quality maxim regarding accuracy.

(54)   *I know when I first moved down here in like what? – nineteen eighty-six* **or whatever**

While this utterance was mainly about identifying a date, the effect of this speaker's metapragmatic awareness at that point in the interaction results in the addition of a pragmatic marker with two functions. First, *or whatever* indicates awareness that the assumption of dependable accuracy may not be met, and second, it signals that, from the speaker's point of view, the need for strict accuracy is being waived.

We can point to another expression that speakers use that conveys a strong sense of their metapragmatic awareness. Like *or whatever*, the adjunctive form *(and) blah, blah, blah* is a twentieth-century addition to the expressions speakers can use to indicate an awareness that "more" was (or could be) said, yet it is being treated as of no consequence. When we look in the *OED Online* for the source of this expression in *blah*, described as "a derisive interjection, frequently reduplicated," we can find it first used as a way to refer to talk, as in (55) from 1921, then as an interjection, from 1924, in (56).

(55)   *Then a special announcer began a long debate with himself which was mostly* **blah blah**

(56)   *So you heard about it from that femme fatale, did you? Damn that man!* **Bla, bla, bla**

With the spelling *blah* replacing *bla*, the expression continues to be recorded as an interjection, and in the contemporary language is often accompanied by a conjunction when used as a type of adjunctive extender, illustrated in (57) from Overstreet (1999: 138).

(57) *They don't want to give me a paycheck today if I were to take a vacation next week they're like "Wull, we'd hafta like – we'd hafta like mail it to you::: **an' blah blah blah**" An' I'm like "Hhhh! Nevermind."*

We should note that the restricted context for use of this expression is as an addendum to reported speech, which is further illustrated in (58), along with an even more recent type of interjection involving *yada*, performing a very similar function. The earliest entry in the *OED Online* for this alternative expression is from an American newspaper in 1981, shown in (59). It can also be found in the lyrics of current hip-hop music, as in (60), heard on the radio and scribbled down in our notebook, where it combines with another adjunctive form, allowing the rapper to extend the personal expression of how "hot" he is.

(58) *Best actor of his generation, **blah, blah, blah**. Brilliant architect of the method performance, **yada, yada***

(59) *I'm talking country codes, asbestos firewalls, **yada, yada, yada***

(60) *Ain't nobody hottah **and so on and yada yada***

As indicators of the speaker's/writer's point of view, these novel constructions continue to develop new variations, particularly in American English, such as *an' dadada* and *bluh, bluh, bluh*, as documented in Overstreet (1999: 138), and they all signal that the speaker has no interest in providing any further details.

In this chapter we have focused on the way speakers use general extenders and some related interjections to express the "personal feelings, attitudes, value judgments and assessments" (Biber *et al.*, 1999: 966) that we identified in terms of speaker-oriented stance at the beginning of the chapter. In much of that analysis, we have also been incidentally illustrating ways in which speakers indicate metapragmatic awareness. We can conclude this discussion with an observation from Skelton (1988: 381) that was originally used to describe hedges, but applies really well to the speaker-oriented uses of general extenders as expressions with which "a user distinguishes between what s/he says and what s/he thinks about what s/he says."

In the following chapter, we will look at ways in which a "user" indicates awareness of how texts and turns can be constructed with the help of general extenders.

5 Textual Function and Turn Construction

In the previous two chapters we have investigated the role of general extenders in interaction as indicators of expressive function, with a focus on the participants. When we turn to a focus on the actual text of the interaction, that is, the consideration of text as "the verbal record of a communicative act" (Brown and Yule, 1983: 6), we will be attempting to identify features in that record that are indicative of how it is being constructed. We will look at aspects of the internal construction of texts, focusing on some of the uses of general extenders that may be subject to the kind of negative evaluation accorded to vague language from a prescriptive perspective, especially with regard to collocations with placeholders and the use of some forms in what seems to be a punctuating role. We will also present examples of general extender uses that function as parts of brackets and clusters in the internal structure of utterances. When we look at the textual function of general extenders in the larger structure of interaction, we will illustrate their occasional use in terms of foregrounding a topic and also their fairly widespread use as markers of topic shift and turn-completion.

5.1 Performance Fillers and Placeholders

When we look closely at the transcribed verbal record of everyday spoken interaction, we find evidence of speaker uncertainty marked by vague expressions and other features that may be tied to the occasional difficulties participants face as they attempt to construct their turns as they speak. The characterization of general extenders as examples of vague expressions seems to be behind the impression (in these reported opinions) that they are "purely performance fillers" (Channell, 1994) and "vague sloppy language" (Palacios Martínez, 2011: 2455), associated with the "uneducated" (Aijmer, 2013: 145) and hence socially "stigmatized" (Dines, 1980) for some speakers, presumably because "vagueness in reference indicates vagueness in thinking, and hence stupidity" (Overstreet, 1999: 22).[1] Behind these reported negative views there seems to be an assumption that the main, or even sole, reason for speaking is to accomplish successful reference and any indication that this is not being accomplished in what is said leads to a negative reaction.

The important functions served by vague language are well documented (e.g. Channell, 1994; Cutting, 2007; Jucker *et al.*, 2003; Overstreet, 2011), yet it continues to be viewed negatively by some. While it may not be possible to change this type of negative perception of general extenders and other aspects of vague language, we can at least point to the useful function they serve for speakers in terms of text and turn construction. Linguistic (and paralinguistic) features of this aspect of interactive talk are sometimes described as "textual monitors" (Erman, 2001: 1342) that are involved in editing and self-repair while organizing the text. There are many different ways in which these monitors can be realized, with "place-holders" being particularly salient examples, especially when accompanied by general extenders, as in the following two examples from Palacios Martínez and Núñez Pertejo (2015: 441, 444). Here the speakers seem to be experiencing word-finding difficulty as they speak. In both cases, the problem is evident in the use of "vague reference nouns" (Carter and McCarthy, 2006) such as *whatsit* and *thingy*, also described as "placeholders" (Channell, 1994: 157–64).

(1) *Jason took a box in today cos they've got ta do er – whatsit, a Christmas decoration **or something***

(2) *cos you wanna thingy like maybe raise a family **or anything***

We can see a definite pattern here in the way the placeholders are accompanied by a filled pause (*er*) plus a distinct pause (–) in (1) or markers of uncertainty (*like maybe*) in (2) before the chosen expression is selected, yet accompanied by disjunctive extenders to indicate that the expression is still just an approximation to what the speaker is trying to say.

Similar features occur when speakers try to explain an earlier misconception, as in (3), from Channell (1994: 161), where confusion over the appropriate name for a drink is represented in the text, introduced by *I thought* twice. The word-finding problem in this case involves non-English terms for the drinks, indicated first by the placeholder *whatsit* before the terms and then two uses of disjunctive forms after them.

(3) *Oh the whole glass is blue I thought it was the liquid that was blue (laughter). I thought it was erm that whatsit piña colada **or whatever it is** – it's bright blue – curaçao **or something***

The word-finding problem can become so acute on occasion for a speaker that the general extender attaches to the placeholder and, within that utterance, allows the speaker to finish the utterance fluently, but remain "somewhat confusing," according to Stenström *et al.* (2002: 105), the source of example (4). This speaker maintains fluency, but not comprehensibility.

(4)   *Yes, he's gon-, told you, yeah the guy's a, he's probably like, like a <u>whatsit</u> **or something***

The speaker of (4) may not find the words for successful reference here, but the attempt is structured in a regular way, with *like* before and *or something* after the placeholder. We will describe this structure in terms of "brackets," a feature of text organization we will explore further in section 5.3. The use of general extenders with placeholders is not the only text-structuring feature that might result in their receiving a negative evaluation as vague language. In some utterances, the general extenders might appear to be adding nothing at all.

5.2   Punctors

Among the many insights from his in-depth analysis of the speech of one individual, a Scottish coal miner (A.S.), Macaulay (1985: 114) makes the following observation about the occurrence of the general extender *and that*, described at the time as a "terminal tag."

about one-fifth of the terminal tags are open to rather subtle set-marking interpretations of this kind, but a more likely interpretation is that A.S. is not using them as set-marking.

Macaulay (1985: 113) presents a number of examples, with his interpretation, where no set-marking function seems likely, as in (5) and (6).

(5)   *but I remember him when he worked in the pits **and that*** (i.e. when he worked in the pits and nowhere else)

(6)   *he was flying from Prestwick to Ireland **and that*** (i.e. to Ireland and nowhere else)

Macaulay (1985: 112) notes that when the speaker includes *and that* as a tag, it is weakly stressed and often difficult to decode at first because it is uttered so quickly. He goes on to suggest that many general extenders used by this speaker operate like oral punctuation marks.

these expressions seem to function less with respect to the semantic interpretation of the words than as a kind of punctuation feature, almost the oral equivalent of a comma or full stop, depending on the intonation.

It is clear from this analysis that Macaulay (1985) doesn't think the general extenders have an exclusively semantic interpretation in terms of sets, and he proposes that they are often used instead with other roles in conversational interaction. In a later study, Macaulay (2002: 762–63) notes that a large number of pragmatic markers such as *you know, I mean, you see*, as well as *and that* (and we would add *and stuff* and *and things*) have a similar iambic structure that may contribute more to the rhythmic structure of the discourse than to any aspect of propositional structure.

The specific role played by the general extenders in examples (5) and (6) is very similar to that described in terms of "ponctuants" in Montreal French by Vincent (1983) and later as "punctors" by Vincent and Sankoff (1992). These are tokens that are not part of the semantics of an utterance, but "have lost all or most of their original meaning or function" (1992: 206), are phonologically assimilated to the preceding phrase, have no independent intonational pattern and are absent from the written language. They are punctuation marks and have a structural role similar to those used in the written language and should not be considered irrelevant either in writing or in speaking.

Aijmer (2013: 142) notes that some general extenders in her data have this punctuating function, even suggesting that they can be used like (filled) pauses as the speaker plans what to say. In (7), *and things* is used at the end of each segment describing the individuals.

(7) *and um so she's (.) has a lot of problems getting around **and things** and the next one had a (.) major problems with drugs and she spent a lot of time in psychiatric wards **and things***

In Pichler and Levey's taxonomy of the functions of general extenders they present the fragment in (8), as transcribed in the original, as illustration of a general extender that is, in their estimation, "devoid of referential and pragmatic meaning" (2011: 452).

(8) S1: *Although it's actually in your opinion more Geordie you would [still] prefer the Scots. Why?*
S2: *[yeah]*
*Just cos eh some of my family's Scottish **and that**, and I don't really like getting called a Geordie*

Because speaker 2 had already mentioned that all his family were from Scotland, there is no hint of any further reference signaled by the adjunctive extender *and that*, which the researchers say only "serves to punctuate the discourse" (Pichler and Levey, 2011: 452). This phenomenon is not restricted to English, as Winter and Norrby (2000: 4–5) demonstrate with the following extended example from Swedish. The English translation is presented first in (9), with the Swedish version in (10).

(9) S1: *one thing that differs also different hardcore styles from one another that's the texts you know (.) straight edge hardcore or they sing quite a lot about that you should n- become a vegetarian and you shouldn't kill the animals and you should like (.) **and all those things** [then that they stand*
S2: *[m*

5.2 Punctors

S1: *for (.) like (.) those who play (.) aand eh- bootcore **and so** they sing quite a lot about I suppose (.) "how awful it is with war **and such**" quite a lot that like (.) y- you shouldn't- or that this here with Vietnam **and so** [(.) like this that it's so terrible that they killed people and (.)*

S2: *[mm*

S1: *in that way **and so** (.) and eh- against Nazis (.) a lot (.) **and (.) so** (.) against fascism on the whole against the police [against- against like against (.) the system **and so***

S2:   *[mm*

S1: *a bit more anarchistic (.) okay*

(10) Original of (9)

S1: *en sak som skilyer också olika hardcorestilar från varann de e ju texterna (.) straight edge-hardcore eller dom sjunger ju ganska mycke o matt man sla i bli vegetarian å man ska inte dööda djuren å man ska liksome (.) å **alla dom där grejerna** [då som dom står för (.) å eh-*

S2: *[m*

S1: *(.) typ (.) såna som spelar känghardcore : **å så** : dom sjunger väl ganska mycke om (.) "hur jävligt de e me krig **å sånt**" ganska mycke att liksom (.) ma ska inte- eller att de här mr Vietnam **å så** [(.) liksom de här me att de e så jävligt att man dödade folk åå*

S2:   *[mm*

S1: *(.) på dee sättet **å så** (.) och eh- mot nazister (.) mycke (.) **åå (.) så** (.) mot fascism äverhuvudtaget mot polisen [mot= mot liksom mot (.) systemet **å så** (.) mer*

S2:   *[mm*

S1: *lite mer anarkistiskt (.) okej*

In her extended turn, speaker 1 begins with a general description of a type of musical style and a full general extender with *grejerna* ("things"), but as she continues, she frequently ends her descriptions of additional features of one version of the musical style with a short adjunctive extender. Regularly ending each point with essentially the same form of extender has the effect of creating a punctuated list of things the music is protesting against.

The translated English forms *and so, and such* in (9) are literal versions of the Swedish forms, but are not typical forms of adjunctive extenders found in conversational English. Given that this is the speech of a young person, describing something from the lives of young people, we would guess that *and stuff* or *and that* might be more typical translation equivalents here.

For some American English speakers, *and stuff* has become an almost automatic reflex in the process of self-expression, often in conjunction with *you know*, especially in situations where an explanation seems to cause some difficulty for the speaker, as in (11), where a young student is talking about learning how to fix horseshoes. We can imagine the difficulty in describing what (for many) might be a rather gruesome scenario. This example is cited in Aijmer (2013: 142), with lineation as in the original.

(11)   *we start out,*
        ... with,
        .. dead horse hooves.
        I mean,
        the eh the canneries,
        *<u>you know</u> **and stuff** <u>you know</u>?*
        ... The people that
        ... that
        *.. kill the horses for meat **and stuff**?*
        *.. <u>You know</u> they have all these legs **and stuff**?*

Overstreet (1999: 103–4) also recorded an example of another American English speaker (one nurse talking to another) who used *you know* and *and stuff* in combination, as in (12), almost compulsively, in structuring her turn, again addressing what might be a difficult topic.

(12)   S1: *Yeah, I was real concerned, **you know**, it'd affect him*
        S2: *what about the organs?*
        S1: *Yeah, right, see I was real concerned we're gonna have a problem*
        S2: *grow, yeah*
        S1: *But **y'know 'n stuff**, as he got a little bit older **'n stuff**, **y'know** doctor told me ... and Justin was fine and has no problem. But as he's gotten older you can see he's (.) flattening out (.) **y'know, an' stuff**, an' he's uh, his muscles are developing **'n stuff**, and I even run my hand across his chest **y'know** and I can tell it's flatter. **Y'know**, so he's, yeah*

The pattern illustrated in (12), with a repeated combination of *y'know* and *'n stuff* (in either order), suggests that these forms have a similar function in terms of inviting the listener to have the same point of view as the speaker, but their most salient contribution to the discourse is to create a rhythmic pattern, similar to the use of short general extenders presented earlier as punctors.

In Macaulay's (1991) later discussion of the use of *and that* by a single speaker, as described earlier, he noted that the speaker "uses approximately fourteen tags per thousand words compared with just one per thousand in the rest of the lower-class interviews" (1991: 70) which, in his calculations, accounted for 85 percent of the general extenders in his interview data. He identifies a large number of those forms as serving as spoken punctuation marks, or punctors.

In her study of regional and social-class variation in the use of general extenders, Cheshire also pointed out that "individual speakers vary greatly in the extent to which they use general extenders" and "some individuals used as many as 24 in a one-hour interview while others used only one or two" (2007: 163). As illustration of what she considered a punctor, Cheshire presented the

5.2 Punctors

example in (13) "where *and everything* seems to simply break up the flow of discourse" (2007: 186).

(13) A: *and is there anyone you really admire? I mean you must have lots of sort of sporting heroes do you?*
W: *er I admire my best friend*
A: *Oh right*
W: *cos erm he's had a lot of problems **and everything** with his family **and everything** so and he's still coping **and everything***

The use of pragmatic markers as punctors is not restricted to general extenders and may be a feature of "optional" constituents in speech. Romaine and Lange (1991) report on a speaker who used *like* as a pragmatic marker "at a rate of 20 times per minute" (1991: 250). Similar accounts of other markers being used with very high frequency can be found in the discourse-pragmatic literature, as exemplified in the following short extract in (14) from Holmes (1990: 195), where the young speaker (talking to friends) uses *sort of* as a rhythmic element punctuating the series of predicates.

(14) *and literally <u>sort of</u> quite out of phase*
and <u>sort of</u> doing things
and eventually <u>sort of</u> ends up circling two <u>sort of</u> skips down the page

Another form used frequently as a punctor is *you know* (*y'know*), as pointed out by Stenström (2011: 543). This common feature of spoken discourse was recognized by Watts (1989) as a form that some speakers used so much that others would comment on it. In the revealing anecdote in (15), from Watts (1989: 231), one "bloke" is identified solely by his frequent use of *you know* as essentially a punctor.

(15) *we ran a shop up to nineteen fifty four and before the war when I was that high there was a bloke who lived on the other side of the road . . . and at that time he was a pensioner and he used to come over the shop and buy his tobacco . . . and he- this is before the war used the phrase "you know" so much . . . and my mother ca- never knew his name called him "Mr. you know" and we all adopted it "Mr. you know."*

This anecdote is valuable not only as evidence of speakers' awareness of how other speakers use pragmatic markers, but also as a caveat against simply counting all occurrences of a particular pragmatic marker in a corpus and making claims about usage based on that aggregate data. Individuals who are extremely high-frequency users of a form will inevitably influence the results in a particular direction. As Brezina and Meyerhoff have pointed out, "using aggregate data is unreliable as it can be skewed if one individual speaker is a heavy user of a particular language feature" (2014: 45).

Other researchers have commented on this phenomenon. In a note on the frequency of general extender use in his data, Denis identified one speaker (aged 62) as "having an exceptionally high rate of *stuff* type general extenders for her age" (2011: 67), something considered in more detail in Chapter 7. Other researchers have tried to minimize the effect of high-frequency general extender use by individuals in their token counts. Wagner *et al.* were clearly sensitive to this issue in their study of general extenders in American English when they identified one speaker who "appeared to be using general extenders at an anomalously high rate compared to other speakers" and, based on a measure for identifying statistical outliers, "was found to be significantly deviant from the rest of the sample and excluded accordingly" (2015: 728).

The possibility that some general extenders can come to be used as punctors will be explored further when we investigate grammaticalization in Chapter 6, but for the moment we should remain aware that simply counting and aggregating tokens of general extenders in a corpus collected from a speech community has the potential to misrepresent their prevalence (or not) in that community.

5.3 Brackets and Clusters

The combination of the two pragmatic markers *you know* and *and stuff* (or *y'know, 'n stuff*), as illustrated in (12), seems to be an extreme version of a pattern of textual organization in which other pragmatic markers such as *sort of* or *like* and stance adverbials, such as *probably* or *maybe*, co-occur with general extenders in spoken interaction. Overstreet noted that, in her data, *you know*, a marker often taken "to indicate assumed similarity of participants' experience" (1999: 74), was regularly used in conjunction with general extenders. In her analysis of discourse markers, Schiffrin notes that "*y'know* is likely to occur with another device through which speakers appeal to general understanding, i.e. set expanders such as *and stuff like that*" (1987: 340). The analytic term "set expanders" (for general extenders) has not been generally adopted, but Schiffrin's (1987: 36–37) proposal that discourse and pragmatic markers can be used as "brackets" round units of talk has proved to be useful in the analysis of utterance structure. Aijmer offers some examples of *you know* and general extenders in combination and also notes the prevalence of what she describes as collocations of general extenders with a range of other pragmatic markers that, in her analysis, "serve the function of coordinating the speaker's and hearer's point of view" (2002: 228). Her examples seem to function in their contexts as summaries of what has been said, typically involving long forms of the general extenders, and, as shown in (16) and (17), marking the end of the speaker's turn (2002: 229).

(16)   *he does sound changes*
         and all that sort of thing
         you know

(17)   *this is to run their coordinating machinery*
         you know
         to establish the standards
         and all that kind of thing

The same structural arrangement can be employed as a way of using *you know* and *and so on* like parentheses around "what the speaker assumes to be shared (or old) information for the listener," as in the analysis of (18) by O'Keeffe et al. (2011: 159).

(18)   *They had Robert Fisk one year.* *You know* *the famous middle-east correspondent* ***and so on***

There can be a lengthy segment of discourse between *you know* and the turn-final general extender, as in (19), from Erman (2001: 1343), where *you know* serves to introduce details in an elaboration of the topic (*a completely slapstick farce way*) that concludes with *and things*. A very similar pattern is shown in (20), from Denis (2017: 176), where *general agriculture* is further elaborated between *you know* and *and things*.

(19)   *they did it in a completely slapstick farce way, you know, the- the men who were dressed up supposed to be women had great big balloons and had rosy cheeks and wigs **and things***

(20)   *it was all uh just general agriculture gen- you know grain farming and varieties of animals **and things***

From a structural point of view, Erman and Kotsinas point to a distinction between the two different positions of *you know* in examples (16)–(20). When *you know* occurs finally in a turn, as in (16), it has "a confirmation-seeking function" (1993: 88). When it occurs before information (that concludes with a general extender here), as in (17)–(20), *you know* has a function tied to introducing an elaboration or "a justification for a previous claim" (1993: 87).

Though much rarer, a construction with *you know* inside the general extender has been documented, as in example (21), from Margerie (2010: 327), where a request is being made and confirmation of what the speaker is *hoping* for is being sought (very tentatively).

(21)   *I was just kinda hoping you'd read over and say this has to be changed **or** *you know* **whatever***

The combination in *just kinda hoping* marks this utterance as an attempt to downplay the sense of imposition implicated in this request (from an undergraduate to a more senior graduate student), reinforced by the unusual cluster *or you know whatever* that indicates that any suggestion would be welcome. In this case we have a rather clear indication that the general extender, together with the other pragmatic markers, is being used as part of a strategy of negative politeness ("avoid imposing"), as discussed in more detail in Chapter 3.

Cheshire (2007: 185) and Pichler and Levey (2010: 17) document some typical patterns of co-occurrence, quantifying the frequency of general extenders being used with a range of other expressions in their data. In fact, Pichler and Levey report that "almost half of the 783 general extender tokens in the corpus co-occur with one or more discourse features" (2010: 22). That rich data source provides many of the examples presented in this section, unless otherwise indicated. To describe the structural configuration involved in these patterns, the term "bracket" is used in a way similar to the description of the positioning of discourse markers by Schiffrin as "sequentially dependent elements which bracket units of talk" (1987: 31). There is a left-hand bracket position for a marker prior to a structure or phrase and a right-hand bracket position after it (Schiffrin, 1987: 36; Watts, 1989: 208). In this type of analysis, general extenders are consistently used as right-hand brackets. However, other markers are more flexible in their possible positions. In (22), *you know* is in a left-bracket position, and in (23), in a right-bracket position, a distinction already illustrated in (16) and (17).

(22)   and all the wives were *you know* doing the nets **and stuff like that**

(23)   she skinned rabbits **and that** *you know*

The pragmatic marker *like* can also be used in both positions in structures with general extenders, as in (24) and (25), though it is more common as a left bracket, as in (26) and (27), from Levey (2012: 263–64). As shown in (27) and (28), some markers, such as *just*, are much more likely to occur as left brackets.

(24)   *It's not very like fashionable and artistic **or anything***

(25)   *it's old boy patter **and that** like*

(26)   *I watched the ... things all about like the Germans **and things***

(27)   *cos sometimes you just forget by an accident and like sometimes you just think that you gonna get it wrong **and that***

(28)   *usually hear about Berwick Rangers just on the sport **and that***

Pichler and Levey analyze "the syntagmatic arrangement" in examples (24)–(28) as "a double bracketed configuration" (2010: 21), a description that will actually apply to all the examples in this section, including those with multiple pragmatic markers.

One of the most common left brackets is *sort of*, as illustrated in (29), from our notebook, jotted down during a BBC radio interview (October 2019) with

5.3 Brackets and Clusters

author and naturalist, Sir David Attenborough, where he is describing his early career advocating for environmental awareness and using a double bracket to mark off a negative characterization by others.

(29)   *At the time I dare say people thought we were <u>sort of</u> cranks **or something***

Here the speaker is subjectively presenting an image of self that is based on the perspective of others (*people thought*), but is downplaying the accuracy of the negative characterization (*cranks*) by surrounding it with approximating expressions, implicating an inaccurate characterization. In other words, while the perspective of others is being presented, it is not being validated from the subjective perspective of the speaker. Other examples of *sort of* as in (30), and *and kind of* in (31)–(32), from Kärkkäinen (2003: 75) and Farr and Riordan (2015: 188) respectively, are quite commonly found as left brackets.

(30)   *at one time there was a resident <u>sort of</u> surgeon there **and everything***

(31)   *<u>you know</u> she's <u>kind of</u> all sophisticated **and everything***

(32)   *<u>You know</u> <u>like</u> have <u>kinda</u> exercises **or something** to fall back on*

As illustrated in (31) and (32), there may be multiple forms used in double brackets, also in evidence in (33) from Stenström *et al.* (2002: 99). Epistemic stance markers (e.g. *I think*) can also occur as part of a bracket, as in (34) from Kärkkäinen (2003: 60) and (35) from Cotterill (2007: 97).

(33)   *they <u>like</u> wanna see <u>like</u> how we talk **and all that** <u>you know</u>*

(34)   *He got on the train on <u>like</u> <u>I think</u> Twelfth Street **or something***

(35)   *<u>I think</u> he was <u>kind of</u> shouting **or something***

Just as in (34) and (35), when the general extenders are used to express approximation or tentativeness, they may be reinforced by expressions of uncertainty in both brackets, as in (36), or (37) from Aijmer (2002: 244).

(36)   *they were <u>probably</u> gypsies **or something** <u>I dunno</u>*

(37)   *he must have been born in <u>about</u> eighteen fifty-eight **or something like that** <u>I suppose</u>*

When two or more brackets occur together, they are described as a "cluster" (Aijmer, 2002: 30–31). In their analysis of clusters, Pichler and Levey (2010: 18) include filled pauses (*em*) as relevant discourse features, as in (38), and also draw attention to the occurrence of other pragmatic markers that may be in an utterance in addition to the clusters, as in (39), where the initial *I dunno* establishes the tentativeness that will be further expressed by the clusters in both the left and right brackets. A similar clustering of what she calls "discourse-pragmatic features," including the general extender *and that*, is present in (40), from Tagliamonte (2016: 120).

(38)   *you know, you're on about like sort of em Tweedmouth and Spittal **and that***

(39)   *I dunno, people kind of associate Newcastle wi like sort of rougher people **sort of thing** you know*

(40)   *I think she wants to work with people like you know like sort of these trouble shooters people **and that** you know*

All of these examples illustrate the common cluster *like sort of* which signals to the listener that there is some uncertainty about the information being expressed, as in (38), or the appropriateness of a description, as in (39), or the accuracy of a label in (40).

In accounts of the larger structural organization of discourse as social action, a distinction is drawn between initiating and terminating brackets (Goffman, 1974: 255), but in our narrower focus on the textual function of utterance structure, we will restrict the analysis to those phrasal sequences containing general extenders as brackets. It is worth noting that the basic information (*people associate Newcastle wi rougher people*) in (39) is suffused with six pragmatic markers, beginning with a left bracket that expresses some lack of confidence in the validity of what is to follow (*I dunno*) and ends with a bracket (*you know*) appealing to the listener not only to understand the speaker's meaning but also to recognize the speaker's caution in expressing the opinion, as indicated by the other four pragmatic markers, all signaling "approximation" in different ways. We can tell that the speaker in (39) is almost reluctant to use the description in *rougher people* here because of the clusters before (*like, sort of*) and after (*sort of thing, you know*), which function to mitigate the force of the potentially negative opinion. The density of pragmatic marker combinations, as illustrated in (39), may also signal a sense of the difficulty the speaker is experiencing in formulating and expressing that opinion. A similar sense of difficulty, this time in terms of the correct label (*trouble shooters people*), is signaled by the six pragmatic markers in (40). It may be that clusters more typically occur when speakers are being tentative or when they are not sure how to express something, as in (38)–(40), as well as in the three-item cluster that initiates the utterance in (41).

(41)   *I mean, just like the words we combine **and that**, you can tell it's Berwick*

If we remove the pragmatic markers from (41), it becomes clear that the speaker has topicalized *the words we combine* within brackets marking approximation before completing the utterance. It may be, of course, that some of the "difficulty" we are witnessing in some of these speakers' uses of mitigating brackets and clusters, as in (38), (39) and (41), may have been

5.3 Brackets and Clusters

caused by their lack of experience, as "a group of working class speakers," when it came to discussing aspects of language in terms of their "use of local dialect words, as well as their attitudes towards their locality and dialect" (Pichler and Levey, 2010: 19).

It is unfortunate that the interactive context is rarely cited in the debate over whether the co-presence of discourse-pragmatic features indicates that a particular general extender variant is being used with newer pragmatic functions or not. Cheshire (2007: 185) proposed that, based on the analysis of her data, as general extenders develop new pragmatic functions, they are more likely to be shorter and to co-occur with fewer of the other features. Tagliamonte (2016) argues that the trend in her data is in the opposite direction, with "more co-occurring discourse-pragmatic features with short general extenders" (2016: 132). Apart from the fact that the two data sets involve quite different locations, participants and topics, the source of the discrepancy may lie in the fact that the interpersonal role of variables of social interaction, usually tied to the circumstances of the data collection, is generally ignored and the researchers tend to rely solely on token counts. The advantages and disadvantages of relying on a quantitative approach to the study of general extenders will be explored in Chapter 7.

It may be that the particular circumstances and topics involved in data collection are more responsible for differences in token counts and token combinations than other factors. Although Cheshire (2007) and Pichler and Levey (2010) are both reports on general extender use in contemporary British English, and both have *and that* as a high-frequency token, it apparently doesn't seem to co-occur much with *you know* in Cheshire's data (2007: 186), whereas the two forms occur quite frequently in double brackets in Pichler and Levey's account (2010: 24). This may be a reflection of a general change that Pichler and Levey propose in terms of age-grading whereby the youngest group (aged 17–23) record much higher uses of *like* and lower uses of *you know* than the two groups of older speakers in their population. The participants in Cheshire's study (2007: 160) were even younger (14–15-year-old adolescents) and, following Pichler and Levey's argument, may simply be part of a young cohort favoring one of these pragmatic markers (*like*) over the other (*you know*) in general, and with general extenders in particular. Some of Cheshire's (2007: 167–68) examples seem to support this, with *like* occurring where *you know* could just as easily occur in the double brackets in (42) and (43). Younger speakers may be in the process of making a subtle shift in their choice of pragmatic markers, yet they are continuing to use those markers in the same structures, such as double brackets with general extenders.

(42)   *you can just get like a bus and get straight into Hull **and that sort of thing***

(43)   *they're probably more into like Indie music **and stuff like that***

We will return to the investigation of how younger speakers differ from older speakers among other aspects of social variation in more depth in Chapter 7. Whatever the reason for the discrepancies between token counts in different data sets, there is ample evidence that general extenders can be used within a range of mitigating constructions in a way that reinforces, and is reinforced by, the other pragmatic markers in the brackets and clusters.[2,3]

5.4 Foregrounding

In terms of their textual function, general extenders not only take part in the internal structuring of utterances, as we have been illustrating, they have other distinct functions in terms of marking a new topic by foregrounding and also marking the end of a topic and/or a turn within interaction. A rarely documented textual function identified by Pichler and Levey is the use of a general extender "to foreground a new discourse entity and to introduce a new topic" (2011: 452), as illustrated in (44), with the transcription and lineation of the original.

(44) S1: *But don't you think the Scots get a better deal?*
      S2: *Well, th- their rates **and that**, everything's cheaper*
          [the water rates] and everything. When my niece
      S1: *[mhm mhm]*
      S2: *told me what she paid for her water, you know.*
          What we pay here. I think it's terrible like.

Pichler and Levey (2011: 452) are quite specific in their analysis that *and that* is not being used to implicate a larger set (e.g. "things that are cheaper in Scotland than in Northumberland"), but instead signals a focus on a specific feature (*rates*), as evidenced by the extended discussion of that specific feature in the rest of the speaker's turn.

In example (45), from Stenström *et al.* (2002: 100), two adolescent boys are sharing their experiences of encounters with a woman (*she*) who has been checking on them because of their truancy from school. The new topic is not only introduced, but is immediately given a negative value by the speaker in the phrase with the general extender (*Shit like that*).

(45) S1 *Did she go to you I'm on your side?* **Shit like that.**
      S2: *Well she she tried to act like really friendly like*
      S1: *Yeah I know*
      S2: *She really cares about me. Is that er*
      S1: *And she said er, did she go to your mum, oh you've done a good job and,*
          [laugh] ***and shit and stuff****. I hated it.*

In (45), the topic seems to be "things the woman said," which is immediately downgraded (from the speaker's perspective) at the same time as it is being foregrounded. The negative attitude becomes part of what is being foregrounded: something like "things (I hated that) the woman said." The ensuing discourse confirms this analysis with more indications of downgrading (*and shit and stuff*) and negative attitude (*I hated it*).

5.5 Turn Construction

In (46), from Levey (2012: 267), the speaker has already expressed a lack of certainty (*I think*) about the time stated (*9 o'clock*) before a pause (.), then added the general extender (*something like that*). Note that the general extender is not attached to the immediately preceding constituent (*I think*), but to the whole utterance. This general extender not only reinforces the sense of possible inaccuracy, it also marks the end of the speaker's turn.

(46)   *it's on at 9 o'clock I think (.)* ***something like that***

The turn-yielding use of general extenders is characterized by longer forms, often beginning with a pause rather than a conjunction, as in (46), and also in (47) from Cheepen and Monaghan (1990: 21).

(47)   *so it's not it's not to do with building, its to do with who owns (.) the bit of ground (.) under the building it was very much property law (.)* ***that kind of thing***

In the analysis of general extenders being used in turn construction, we can occasionally find some tokens that reveal a distinction between the functions of short and long forms. Norrby and Winter (2002: 4), in their description of Australian English, provide a clear illustration of the difference between a short form of a general extender (*and stuff*) being used with a phrase only, and a long form (*things like that*) being used to close the speaker's turn in (48).

(48)   *Well, when I've finished school I go home ... Walk home ... Um ... Get changed ... usually do my homework first ... play some computer games* ***and stuff ... things like that***

In (48), the speaker produces the short form, attached to and in the same tone unit as the preceding element, then after a pause (instead of a conjunction) produces the long form in a separate tone unit, clearly separating that form from the rest of the utterance before it, and marking the end of that utterance and the speaker's turn as well.

A very similar pattern, with both short and long disjunctive forms, is illustrated in (49), from Aijmer (2002: 246–47). In B's first turn, the short form *or something* is used inside a tone unit, then at the end of B's second turn, in a separate tone unit, the form *something like that* (without a conjunction) marks the end of the turn.

(49)   A: *OK*
                 right
           B: *we can have lunch **or something***
           A: *yeah*
                 what time do you usually have lunch
           B: *well*
                 I usually go about
                 quarter past twelve
                 half past twelve
                 something like that

A similar turn-yielding effect can occur at the end of a list, as in (50) from the Canadian data of Tagliamonte and Denis (2010: 355), where the speaker signals an expectation that the listener will recognize the types of activities being listed (*you know*), followed by the conjunction-less general extender (*stuff like that*), completing the turn. In this case, the combination of the final two pragmatic markers creates a cluster that completes the turn, a structural feature involving general extenders that we examined earlier.

(50)   *Yeah, we used to play hide-and-seek a lot and hopscotch, ah baseball and we would swim all the time, you know, **stuff like that***

In (51), from Aijmer (2002: 225), the topic of American (English) is mentioned and illustrated by speaker B, then picked up and further illustrated by speaker A before *that sort of thing*, marking the end of a turn, and potentially the topic.

(51)   B: *I mean American you know really has different tenses and different prepositions it's getting to that point if you look at it at all close*
           A: *m*
           B: *things like in back of matching in front of*
           A: *yes*
                 that's right
                 and eh and do you have
                 instead of have you got
                 that sort of thing

In all these examples (46)–(51), the final tone unit features a pause plus a long general extender form that seems to function as a turn-yielding signal. There is no requirement that there should be a pause and that the conjunction be omitted in order to complete a turn. In an example from their northern British English data, Pichler and Levey note that the speaker in (52) concludes her utterance with *And stuff like that* (as transcribed in the original), using it "as a turn-yielding signal, an effect which is achieved by the production of the general

5.5 Turn Construction

extender in a separate tone unit and with a falling intonation contour" (2011: 451).

(52)   But I quite like my accent. It's got touches of different sort of maybe a bit of American when I speak, and a bit of Scottish. **And stuff like that**.

One general extender form, *(or) whatever*, has been studied specifically in terms of its use to mark "topic shift" or as "a means of bringing a topic to a close" (Brinton, 2017: 277). In (53), from written examples in Brinton (2017: 276), the writer uses *or whatever* with a term summarizing the topic and marking the end of that topic. In (54), from the same source, there is a clear shift from general concepts, ending with *or whatever*, to a concern with different, quite specific and more personal events. In (55) from Kleiner (1998: 610), the speaker not only marks a shift with *Whatever*, but actually goes on to say that a *New topic* will be announced.

(53)   But a girl has to live. And it isn't as easy as it looks. And so a girl can make a mistake, marry the wrong guy and the wrong family, looking for something that isn't there. Security, **or whatever**.

(54)   One may not like England or France because of imperialism, past wars, war debts, **or whatever**. But suppose burglars were breaking into houses of friends.

(55)   T: *Well – again. I mean I think that you're – that you're generalizing again.*
A: **Whatever**. *New topic. How do you feel about interracial dating on campus*

The development of the "stand-alone" form *Whatever* has already been charted in Chapter 4 as it became an interjection with subjective function, but its use as a topic closer or turn-yielding signal was not explored in detail. One outcome of changes in usage during the early to mid twentieth century has been described by McColm and Trousdale (2019: 103).

whatever can function as a stand-alone turn that signals not only the speaker's view on what has been said before, but also the view that discourse should come to an end.

McColm and Trousdale (2019: 100) illustrate this point with examples such as (56), from a written source. Brinton (2017: 269) provides an array of other examples that support the analysis of *whatever* as having developed a "stand-alone" feature that can be used to signal an attempt to close the topic, as well as yielding the turn, shown in (57) and (58).

(56)   Mama frowned at her mother-in-law. "**Whatever**." Grandma sighed.

(57)   It doesn't matter. I don't care. **Whatever**.

(58)   Fine, fine, be that way. **Whatever**.

In most of these examples, we have been focusing on turn yielding as part of "turn management," but without any indication in the reported data about what kind of response was received from any other(s) taking part in the interaction. In a corpus-based study of British and Irish English, focusing specifically on the use of general extenders (or "vague category markers" in their analysis) as a "turn management resource" and "an important factor in the smooth coordination of turns in conversational interaction," Vaughan et al. (2017: 209) report on their use as "noticeably frequent just prior to speaker change" (2017: 210). As turn-final items in conversation, general extenders are described as "triggers" that prompt "a listener response within the framework of turn architecture" (2017: 211). Vaughan et al. were able to document listener responses to turn-final general extenders, such as *yeah*, *yes*, *right*, and backchannels such as *mm*, *uhuh* as part of a process of "collective affirmation" (2017: 217) within the turn-taking system. This process can be as simple as a turn-final general extender followed by a next-turn *yeah*, as in (59), from Vaughan et al. (2017: 216), or the series *Oh, okay, right* in (60), from Overstreet (1999: 76), followed by the very explicit expression of understanding in *Yeah, I- I know what you mean. Yeah.*

(59)   S1: *Fifty to sixty is an honour too*
       S2: *Yeah*
       S1: *Or fifty-five to sixty-five **or something like that***
       S2: *Yeah*

(60)   S1: *Wull, that's the way- that's who I was until*
       S2: *Uh huh*
       S1: *I got a PhD **or something***
       S2: *Oh, okay. Right.*
       S1: *So it was umm-*
       S2: *Yeah, I- I know what you mean. Yeah.*

A more complex connection can be illustrated when multiple speakers co-construct a collective affirmation of what they're all talking about. In (61), from Vaughan et al. (2017: 217), speaker S1 uses turn-final *or something*, with *yeah* as the response from speaker S2, and the general extender is echoed by a third speaker (*a film or something*) before speaker S1 completes speaker S2's turn and effectively concludes the segment on that topic.

(61)   S2: *I think that is so I always think that gate. It's just so sad.*
       S1: *It's freaky isn't it it's like a cemetery **or something**.*
       S2: *Yeah it looks like a scene from like the-*
       S3: *A film **or something**.*
       S1: *the Adams family.*

Vaughan et al. (2017: 217) also illustrate, in (62), how the turn-final use of a general extender by one speaker can elicit a repetition of that form by another

5.5 Turn Construction

speaker, who then produces the *yeah* response (repeated), resulting in a collective affirmation that they're all on the same page.

(62) S1: *Er what was the American equivalent to er ENSA? What's its United States-*
      S4: *Erm*
      S1: *-en entertainment forces **or something like that**.*
      S5: ***Something like that. Something like that.*** *Yeah.*
      S1: *It's the same idea.*
      S5: *Yeah. Yeah.*

It is noticeable that the examples used by Vaughan *et al.* (2017) to illustrate the turn-constructional role of general extenders are all disjunctive forms that seem to be used to signal a lack of certainty. The responses in those examples are all in the form of assurances that the speaker is not mistaken and the participants are all in agreement. The advantage of Vaughan *et al.*'s (2017) data presentation is that responses to turns ending in general extenders can be tracked, analyzed and illustrated. In many other studies, including our own in the past, examples of utterances ending in general extenders are offered as illustration without providing the responses of next speakers.

Having described the different functions of general extenders in present-day English, we occasionally had to appeal to earlier uses in order to work out how current uses might be interpreted. In the next chapter, we will take an in-depth look at those forms in earlier uses that may be the source(s) of contemporary forms.

6 Historical Development and Change

In this chapter, we will look into the origins of expressions used as general extenders in modern English. This turns out to be a fairly speculative undertaking because of the limited resources available for the study of spoken interaction throughout the historical period. Even when we think we can identify general extender types of constructions in the written record, we can't be sure that they are representative of the speech of the day or that they are perhaps limited to a particular group or even an individual. Indeed, there are many reasons for being cautious when making claims about the generalizability of any findings based on the rather fragmented record of earlier stages of the language, especially spoken language. Nevertheless, there do appear to be patterns of development and change in general extender-type structures and we will tentatively explore some of them in this chapter.[1]

We suspect that there must be examples of constructions similar to general extenders in the historical record from the Old English period, but so far there have been no dedicated studies in this area. The example in (1) is from Ælfric's grammar from the year 1020, where an early version of *and so forth* is used, apparently on the assumption that the reader knows what would come next in this declension of the Latin word *primus* ("first"). The marking of a continuation of a text is a frequent use of this fixed expression, which can be found with little change throughout the historical record. We will include, in square brackets, an indication of the year in which the examples were recorded in the various historical corpora that we, and others, have used in the reported research, such as the *Oxford English Dictionary Online* (OED). We will not include bracketed citations where we cite examples from recent studies, the general source of which we will identify as "Present Day English" (PDE).

(1)   *primus se forma, prima, primum,* **and swa forð**

[1020 ÆLFRIC *Gram.* (Z) xxv. 144 OED]

We have much more success documenting the occurrence of expressions from the early Middle English period. Some of the expressions we discover appear to function in a way similar to general extenders in today's English, though they are no longer in common use. In other expressions we will identify what look like precursors of the forms used currently as general extenders and trace their development through the historical record since the fifteenth century. In that review, we will try to make sense of an apparent conundrum: if there's an established principle that forms become reduced through frequent usage, why doesn't the principle apply in the relationship between long forms such as *and things like that* and short forms like *and things*?

6.1 From *ant so vorth* to *and so on and so forth*

As we noted in Chapter 1, there are fixed expressions functioning as general extenders in some of the oldest records of the language that have survived virtually unchanged from early Middle English into the contemporary language. We are indebted to the work of Ruth Carroll (2008), whose groundbreaking research is the source of a number of the following examples, including her translations. The older forms of *ant so vorth*, as in (2) and *&c* (*et cetera*), as in (6), are clearly the source of very similar forms in use throughout the history of English, as in the samples shown in (3)–(5) and (7)–(9).

(2)   *Tac a lutel radel ant grynt to thin asise . . .* ***ant so vorth****, as I seyde er*
        ("Take a little red ochre and grind into thin sizing . . . and so forth, as I said earlier")

        [c1325 *Recipe Painting* (1) s. v. *sō* (adv.) 5(c) MED]

(3)   *othere colours, as is whit and blew or whit and blak or blak and reed* ***and so forth***
        ("other colors, as is white and blue or white and black or black and red and so forth")

        [c1390 CHAUCER *CT. Pars.* S. v. *rēd* (n(2)) (a) MED]

(4)   *saienge to ham: 'Dredeth nouȝt! ȝe secheth Jesu!'* ***and so forthe***
        ("saying to them, 'Fear not! You seek Jesus!' and so forth")

        [c1430 (a1410) *Love mirror* s. v. *and* (conj.) 1c (b) MED]

(5)   *the accidentes of brede or wyne, that is to seie, the colour, the sauour,* ***and so forth*** *. . . mowe not be, but in the substaunce of breed or wyne*
        ("the accidents [outward characteristics] of bread or wine, that is to say, the color, the taste, and so forth . . . may not be, but in the substance [essential nature] of bread and wine")

        [c1430 (a1410) *Love mirror* s. v. *accident* (n.) 2(a) MED]

(6)   *and bedding, hangings* ***&c****; to the Parson of Tasley*

        [1418, Fifty Earliest English Wills MEC]

(7)   *A charme for to stawnchyn blood ... 'In nomine patris **et cetera** ... '*
        ("A charm for stanching blood ... 'In the name of the father' et cetera")

        [c1450 Stockh. *Recipes* s. v. *charme* (n.) (a) MED]

(8)   *The words of saynt Paule, It is impossible that they whiche haue once been illumed, **&c.***

        [1532 T. More *Confut. Tyndale* in Wks. 612/1 OED]

(9)   *from Hamborg, and Dansk, Lubeck, **&c***

        [1586 LYCESTE 200, CEECS]

These uses signal continuation, either of lists or (known) texts, while typically marking the end of a segment of spoken or written text, functions investigated in detail in Chapter 5. These functions continue into PDE, as exemplified in (10) and (11). Example (10) is from our notebook (noted during a discussion on public television, January 24, 2020), while (11) and (15) are from Biber *et al.* (1999: 117).

(10)   *What about decorum in terms of paying attention? Are they sitting in their seats, are they staying in the chamber, **and so forth**?*

(11)   *The Libertas catalogue menu offered a choice of six search modes (author and title, title, subject, **etc.**).*

The use of these fixed expressions, to which we might add *or thereabouts* as an antique disjunctive form,[2] is currently associated with formal spoken registers of language use, especially in academic discourse, as described in Chapter 7. It may be when an expression used as a general extender has existed virtually unchanged for such a long time in the language that it becomes the traditional form, associated with written language norms, and established as indicative of educated speech. Although not attested in the historical record as early as *and so forth*, the phrase *and so on* has the same association with formal spoken language (cf. Aijmer, 2002; Biber *et al.*, 1999), especially in the academic register, as described in Chapter 7. Two examples in the corpus of *Early English Books Online* (EEBO; www.english-corpora.org/eebo/) from the late sixteenth century (12) and early seventeenth century (13) reveal a function of marking the continuation of a pattern, especially involving numbers.[3]

(12)   *you may augment your rancks, from three to five, and so to seauen, then to nine and eleuen, **and so on***

        [1591 Gyles Clayton *A briefe discourse, of martial discipline* EEBO]

(13)   *so nothing can be second, which hath not a first before it; no third, which hath not a second,* ***and so on****, in all the rest*

[1622 Martin Fotherby *Atheomastix clearing foure truthes, against atheists and infidels* EEBO]

The frequency of the phrase *and so on* has increased since that time, and not only in phrases attached to numbers, as exemplified in (14), and (15) from Biber *et al.* (1999: 117). It is now more common than *and so forth* in PDE, though they can be found together, as in the functional reduplication in (16), from Walsh *et al.* (2008: 9), signaling that much more could be said. Both (15) and (16) illustrate the common position of *and so on* at the end of lists in PDE.

(14)   *Till, in time, the English we now speak is become as obsolete and unintelligible as that of Chaucer **and so on***

[1724 L. Welsted *Epist.* 123 OED]

(15)   *It includes information about the file such as its size, history,* ***and so on***

(16)   *... post-colonialism, multi-culturalism, structuralism, feminism, postmodernism,* ***and so on and so forth***

When we turn to the investigation of expressions currently found in informal uses, we find varied paths of development, but they all seem to undergo a shift over time from functioning as specific extenders to become general extenders.

6.2   From Specific to General

Some of the difficulty involved in our attempts to discover the origins of today's general extenders in earlier periods of the language is the simple fact that many of the expressions used in the past were quite different from those found in the contemporary language. Carroll (2008) reported on the occurrence in the *Middle English Dictionary* (MED; see Kurath *et al.*, 1952–2001) of early equivalents of the word *such* in phrases that appear to be used in extender-type constructions, as in (17)–(19), in each case preceded by versions of the word *other*.

(17)   *seinte Sare **& monie opre swucche***
         ("Saint Sarah and many other such")

[c1230 (a1200) *Ancr.*, s. v. *swich* (adj.) 5d MED]

(18)   *Iob, Iosep,* ***and mony opere suche*** *weren riche of pite*
         ("Job, Joseph, and many other such were rich in pity")

[c1400 *Bk. Mother* s. v. *riche* (adj.) I (c) MED]

(19) *oþere membris þat mouen hem bi hemsilf as þe lippis **and oþere siche*** ("other members that move by themselves, as the lips and other such")

[c1475 *Mandeville* (Wel 564) s. v. *swich* (adj.) 5d (b) MED]]

(20) *that is to say glotonye lecchorye rapyn **and such other***

[1485 ANONYMOUS *Here begynnys a schort and breue tabull on thes cronicles* EEBO]

(21) *all these Treators **and such other wicked people***

[1586 WiFLEETWOOD 308 CEECS]

Toward the end of the fifteenth century, the reverse pattern is recorded, as in (20) and (21), shifting from versions of *and other such* to *and such other*, which eventually establishes the introductory sequence of constituents in *and such* as the basis of a range of other adjunctive forms. Carroll (2008: 29) points to the frequency with which these *such other* and *such like* expressions collocate with negative words and concepts, as in (21) and (22). In the *Corpus of Early English Correspondence Sampler* (CEECS; see Hofland et al., 1999), we not only find forms with specific extenders as in (21) and (22), but shorter forms, as in (23) and (24), also following negatively evaluated references. When used non-specifically, as in (23) and (24), the expression has shortened and seems to function as an adjunctive extender.

(22) *common receivers of seminaries **and such like bad persons***

[1597 WCECIL 115 CEECS]

(23) *certen horstealers, cutpurses **and such lyke***

[1585 WiFLEETWOOD 297 CEECS]

(24) *treacherous weapons, as knifes **and such like***

[1639 BHARLEY 51 CEECS]

It is not hard to imagine that these sixteenth- and seventeenth-century uses are the likely source of a form (*and such*) that can still be found in PDE, as in (25).

(25) *He was doing the lambing **and such***

This example is from Tagliamonte (2016: 120), who counted fourteen tokens of the phrase in what is described as the "Roots Archive" (Tagliamonte, 2013). This is a data collection from the early 2000s, containing recordings of the speech of "the oldest living generation in each of the peripheral communities" (2016: 119), one in northern England, one in southern Scotland and two in Northern Ireland. These communities were intentionally selected as representing "relic areas" which "because of their peripheral geographic location and/or isolated socio-political circumstances tend to preserve older features of a language" (2016: 118). Since no other researchers report any examples of *and such* (in any relevant numbers) among general extenders in collections of contemporary spoken discourse, we can identify this phrase as having an archaic sense. It is still found in formal registers, in broadcast media, for example, and among older, perhaps rural speakers in Britain. The one example we encountered earlier was in the translation of a Swedish speaker's use of *å sånt*, as in (26), from Winter and Norrby (2000: 4).

(26)   *hur jävligt de e me krig **å sånt***
       ("how awful it is with war **and such**")

We have already noted, in Chapter 5, the oddness of this English translation of what is reported to be contemporary teenage speech. More appropriate here might be *and stuff* or *and that* in the translated version. The use of a formal-sounding or uncommon phrase (in informal situations) is an interesting aspect of general extender use noted among some speakers of English as a second language that we will investigate further in Chapter 9.

Still used in some registers, but not reported to be common in recent studies of everyday spoken data in PDE, the phrase *and such* does allow us to trace a distinct pattern in its history, from a specific version, as exemplified by *and such like bad persons* to a form *and such*, with more general usage. We can also note that there is a pattern of change from a longer form to a shorter form, retaining only the first two constituents of the longer expression. As we discovered, this is a typical direction of change throughout the history of general extenders.

The pattern is reflected in the change Carroll (2008) traces in the use of the word *other*, in its different instantiations, from examples such as (17)–(21) earlier, through specific examples (without *such*), as in (27) and (28), to a short form, reduced to only the first two elements, as in (29). These latter three examples reveal a structural change in fifteenth-century English that led to the creation of an adjunctive extender type of phrase (*and oþer*) that begins to be written in a more familiar form, as in (30), around 1500. The phrase *and other* in (30) seems to have come into use and fallen out of use in late Middle English and is no longer found in recent data collections.

(27)   *wilde boores, wolues **and oþer byteng beestis***
       ("wild boars, wolves and other biting beasts")

       [c1410 York *M Game* s. v. *bēst(e)* (n.) 3(c) MED]

(28)   *ympes and herbes **and oþer feele thinges That growed in þat gardyn***
       ("shoots and herbs and other excellent things that grew in that garden")

       [c1450 (c1405) *Mum & S. (2)*, s. v. impe (n.) I(d) MED]

(29) *hostiary, reader, benette, accolette **and oþer***
("ostiary, reader, benet, acolyte and other")

[?a1475 (?a1425) *Higd* (2) s. v. *rēder(e)* (n. (I) MED]

(30) *and as mocke as we need to have of 00 thynge **and other***

[1502 Ranulf Higden *Tabula* EEBO]

In contrast, the grammatically plural version *and others* can be found throughout the history of English, beginning in the early records, as in (31) and (32), where it is attached to groups of proper nouns, especially the names of people. By the fifteenth century, the phrase is found with ordinary (non-human) nouns, especially at the end of a list, as in (33). It continues to be used very much like a fixed-expression type of general extender into the current century, as in (35). It also retains a strong preference for attachment to human referents, unlike its near translation equivalent *et cetera*, exemplified earlier in (6)–(9), which is more often attached to non-human referents. The phrase *and others*, unlike *et cetera*, is also commonly used as part of a specific extender, as in (34), where *the Ale-draperie* refers to the business of selling ale. Both of these expressions can be used to signal the continuation of a list, as in (31)–(34), but only *et cetera*, not *and others*, is used to indicate the continuation of a (known) text, as illustrated in examples (7) and (8) earlier, and discussed in more detail in Chapter 2.

(31) *Witnesses: John Bokeointe, Daniel de Stebehee, Geoffrey Waterlader, Robert Badding **and others** (named)*

[?a1221 *Descriptive Catal. Deeds Public Rec. Office* (1890) OED]

(32) *In that grete mouthe and baye, beth ilondes Calchos, Patmos, **and others***

[1385 J. TREVISA tr. R. Higden *Polychron* (1865) I. 57 OED]

(33) *to be well learned in the making of confections, plates, gandequinces **and others***

[c1475 *Coll. Ordinances Royal Househ.* (Harl. 642) (1790) 81] OED]

(34) *hvmbly sueth to your current Excellency, your vncustom'd drooping Suppliants, the Vinters, and Innekeepers, **and others** of the Ale-draperie*

[1609 T. DEKKER *Worke for Armorours* sig. G OED]

(35) *The attitude of the self-exiled leader had forced him **and others** to quit the armed struggle*

[2016 *Dawn* (Pakistan) (Nexis) 23 Oct. OED]

6.3 From *or sum oþer þing* to *or something like that*

Having traced the genesis of earlier forms of (potential) general extenders in the phrases *and such* and *and other(s)*, we may be able to identify other expressions including the words *such* and *other* as possible sources of phrases that develop into the general extender forms in use today. One of the earliest recorded phrases is *or sum oþer* from Middle English, as shown in (36).

(36)   þan preyed þe ryche man Abraham, þat he wide sende Lazare, **or sum oþer wham**, to hys breþryn

[1303 R. MANNYNG *Handlyng Synne* 6694 OED]

The form *wham*, an earlier version of *whom*, is best translated here as "person," giving us a specific extender *or some other person*. During the fifteenth and sixteenth centuries, a large number of phrases with a similar structure can be identified, typically used as specific extenders, as illustrated in (38)–(41), although a very early form, as in (37), cited in Carroll (2008: 13), is clearly not a specific extender. It is also, unusually, a short form, appearing before longer forms with similar basic structure. This represents an exception to the more widespread trend of longer forms appearing before shorter forms. Those specific extenders have some unfamiliar lexis, as in (38), where *disgisee* conveys "new fashioned," (39), where *avail* means "benefit," (40), where ʒeven is "given," and (41), involving "a strong weapon." By the mid sixteenth century, as shown in (42), and (43), from the *Michigan Early Modern English Materials* (MEMEM; see Bailey *et al.* (1975/1994), http://quod.lib.umich.edu /m/memem/), quoted in Carroll (2008: 8), the phrases are being used as disjunctive extenders.

(37)   *he may passe to Ieen or Venice **or sum oþer***

[1425 Hamelius, P. (ed.) 1919 *Mandeville's Travels* 214/27–28 OED]

(38)   *To roste a small hastelet or make a steike **or sum oother disgisee thing***

[c1430 *Pilgr. Luf Manhode (*1869) I. cxliv 74 OED]

(39)   *a riʒt forto ... haue certeyn fruytis **or sum othir avail***

[c1449 R. PECOCK *Repressor* (1860) 392 OED]

(40)   *If money **or sum oþer þing** be ʒeven to hem*

[1475 (a1400) Apol. Lollard Doctr. (1842) 11 OED]

(41)   *The father takkis ane batton **or sum vthir sterk vappin** to puneise his sonne*

[c1550 Complaynt Sctl. (1979) iii. 22 OED]

(42) and blotte the same againe with a spunge **or some suche other thynge**

[1550 R. EDEN tr. Peter Martyr of Angleria Decades of Newe Worlde III. xi f 161 OED]

(43) Crownets of Bayes, of Gold, of Myrtill, **or some other thing**

[1590 s. v. *be* MEMEM]

It is quite noticeable that phrases beginning with a version of *or some other* ... are by far the most common disjunctive forms during this period, with versions of *or some other thing* occurring quite frequently. During the late sixteenth century and into the seventeenth century, there is evidence that the *other* element is disappearing and the combination *or something* is found more often in the record. One of the earliest occurrences of the basic expression may be the version shown in (44), clearly a general extender usage, but others can be found, as in (45), where it isn't clear if *or something* is an independent phrase (i.e. a general extender) or a phrase combined with a restrictive relative clause, making it more of a specific extender.

(44) pray ye give me some of my goods againe, a ring **or something**

[1590 Robert Wilson *The pleasant and stately morall, of the three lords and three ladies of London* EEBO]

(45) they hold it also an unbeseeming thing, for a man to make himself ready, without putting on a girdle; **or something**, that may divide the lower part of the body, from the upper

[1650 Modena, *The history of the rites* EEBO]

More typically during this period, the *or something* element is the beginning of a longer phrase, often qualifying the accuracy of a spoken report, as in (46) from 1680, and (47) from 1692, cited by Tagliamonte and Denis (2010: 365), based on data from Kytö and Culpeper (2006).

(46) My Lord, my memory hath been exceedingly bruised; but I remember, my Lord, as I was going through the Abby in a rainy afternoon, she said, this Abby was formerly filled with Benedictine Monks, **or something to that purpose**, and saith she, what if it should be so again?

(47) he said he would not give it to me, but if I brought any of our Masters, he would slit their noses **or something to that effect**

As we noted in Chapter 1, an early version of a shorter form of the phrase can be found in the following line (48) from a theatrical comedy in the mid eighteenth century, once again signaling uncertainty as to the accuracy of a report.

(48) a sort of Queen or Wife **or something or other** to somebody

[1752 S. FOOTE *Taste* II 25 OED]

6.3 From *or sum oþer þing* to *or something*

Marking a concern with the accuracy of a report continues to be a salient function of *or something* when it appears more often as a short general extender in the early nineteenth century, as evidenced in two examples from the novels of Jane Austen: (49) from *Mansfield Park* and (50) from *Persuasion*, first noted in Overstreet (1999: 117).

(49) *There were generally delays, a bad passage **or something***

[1814 J. AUSTEN *Mansfield Park* I. xi. 223 OED]

(50) *they happened to say, that her brother Captain Wentworth, is just returned to England, or paid off, **or something**, and is coming to see them almost directly*

[1818 J. AUSTEN *Persuasion* (1961: 52)]

During the nineteenth century, the approximating element involved in hedging the accuracy of a report spreads to other uses, especially involving terminology, as illustrated in (51) and (52).

(51) *May I be a prompter, or call-boy **or something**?*

[1874 F.C. BURNAND *My Time* XV. 130 OED]

(52) *The Galleries shut at the absurd hour of 3 ... in order that the officials may have some absurd meal, a mittagsessen **or something***

[1899 R. FRY *Let.* Oct. (1972) I. 174 OED]

By the end of the nineteenth century, a very general approximating function has become the typical use of the short form *or something*. It is about this time that we start to find examples of the modern long version *or something like that* in the historical record, as shown in (53) and (54).

(53) *she's a sewer, I think – a manty-maker **or something like that**, I would suppose, from the needle-marks on her fingers*

[1891 H. JOHNSTON *Kilmallie* I. xviii OED)

(54) *The man who has it now works nights – he's some kind of a head waiter at Rector's **or something like that**, and he's out till three or four*

[1914 S. LEWIS *Our Mr. Wrenn* xiv. 188 OED]

In both these examples, the sense of uncertainty about the accuracy of the information is marked through expressions such *as I would suppose* and *he's some kind of* as well as the long general extenders.

What all these examples involving *or something* and longer versions serve to demonstrate is a fairly regular process of change over a long period of time whereby a variety of longer, more specific forms coalesce into one shorter, less

108   6 Historical Development and Change

specific form, which then later develops a longer, non-specific form incorporating *like that*. Speculating on a reason for this later change, we might say that the longer form, with the backward reference in *that*, allows the speaker to make the approximation less vague by connecting it more closely to the preceding expression. Why these longer forms with *like that* became suddenly more common in the late nineteenth century and early twentieth century remains to be explained.

6.4   From *or any other thing rounde* to *or anything like that*

We can trace a very similar pattern of change in the development of the negative polarity disjunctive extender *or anything (like that)*. As in the evolution of *or something (like that)*, the word *other* was a regular component in early versions, as illustrated in the following examples from the sixteenth century.

(55)   *I enrolle, I rolle up a writing,* **or any other thing rounde**

[1530 J. PALSGRAVE *Lesclarcissement* 537/1 OED]

(56)   *Whether yt were poldavis* ("linen cloth") *for saylis,* **or any other thing**

[1552 T. BARNABE in J. Strype *Eccl. Mem.* (1721) II ii App. E. 152 OED]

(57)   *Glasse or Tinne* **or any other thing glassed***, it doth penetrate*

[1577 J. FRAMPTON tr. N. Monardes *Three Bookes* 1.f.8 OED]

(58)   *La garniture d'vn lict, d'vne espée, ou quelque chose*
         ("*the garniture or furniture of a bed, a sword,* **or any other thing**")

[1580 C. HOLLYBAND *Treasurie French Tong* (at cited word) OED]

(59)   *Anie part ... of foule linen cloth ... as shirt, handkercher, napkin* **or any other thing**

[1590 in R. Pitcairn *Criminal Trials Scotl.* (1833) I.II 218 OED]

Once again, some of the earliest forms are specific extenders, with the attributes of *rounde* in (55) and *glassed* in (57), limiting the referential range of *or any other thing* in these cases, while the examples in (56), (58) and (59) seem to include general extenders.

In other attestations, the word *such* is also used where our examples (55)–(59) had favored the word *other*. Examples (60) and (61), from the mid sixteenth century, show that *or any such thing* was being used as a disjunctive extender at about the same time as *or any other thing* and continued to be used into the nineteenth century, as in (62) and (63).

6.4 From *or any other thing rounde* to *or anything* 109

(60) *Wherfore yf for honour, beauty, cōnyng, **or any such thing**, we be moued vnto pryde, the best is to humble oure selues before god*

[1545 Desiderius Erasmus *A shorte recapitulacion or abridgement of Erasmus Enchiridion* EEBO]

(61) *that trust in their owne learning, wysedom, riches, power, frendes, **or any such thing**, they do not truly beleue in God*

[1548 Thomas Cranmer *Catechismus, that is to say, a shorte instruction into Christian religion* EEBO]

(62) *I value a Pistol, or a Blunderbuss, **or any such thing**, no more than a Pop-gun*

[1749, H. FIELDING *Tom Jones* IV. x. vi. 47 OED]

(63) *If a feather, a straw **or any such thing**, be observed hanging at a dog's nose or beard*

[1807 J. HOGG Mountain Bard vi, in *Poet. Wks.* (1838) II. 331 OED]

At the beginning of the seventeenth century, we can find examples, as in (64) and (65), of the basic disjunctive form (*or anything*) already being cited. Interestingly, from the earliest citations, as in (64), the phrase can have human referents as antecedents, evidence that the "thing" element was being used without its original (i.e. non-human) referential function.

(64) *take him, what euer he be, papist, atheist, swaggerer, theese, drunkard, **or anything**, care not*

[1603 John Dod The bright star which leadeth wise men to our Lord Jesus Christ EEBO]

(65) *with her nimble fingers stroake my haire, play with my fingers endes, **or anything***

[1607 Francis Beaumont and John Fletcher *The woman hater* EEBO]

By the nineteenth century, examples without either *other* or *such* become more common, as we noted in Chapter 4 with examples repeated in (66) from Jane Austen's *Pride and Prejudice* and (67) from Thomas Hardy's *Far from the Madding Crowd*.

(66) *I did not once put my foot out of doors ... Not one party, or scheme, **or anything***

[1813 J. AUSTEN *Pride & Prejudice* III. ix. 166 OED]

(67) *How soft it is – being winter time, too – not chapped or rough **or anything***

[1874 T. HARDY *Far from Madding Crowd* I. iii. 36 OED]

This usage continues into the twentieth century, as in (68), which illustrates one of the earliest constructions used as a type of formulaic disclaimer involving *or anything*, a construction analyzed in detail in Chapter 4.

(68)   *Don't imagine I'm huffed **or anything**, little heart, I'm only weary*

[1906 J. M. SYNGE *Lett. To Molly* (1971) 50 OED]

It is during this period in the early 1900s that we find examples of the longer and more explicitly cohesive form *or anything like that*, as in (69) and (70), where *icky-boo* means "ill."

(69)   *Are you engaged to be married to a little-footed China doll, **or anything like that**?*

[1911 K. D. WIGGIN *Mother Carey's Chickens* xxxv. 346 OED]

(70)   *The jolly old tum-tum is not icky-boo **or anything like that***

[1930 "SAPPER" *Finger of Fate* 188 OED]

As we observed with the development of *or something*, the modern use of the short form *or anything* may have derived from longer expressions, but not from the longer form *or anything like that* which, as in the case of *or something like that*, comes into existence after use of the short form is already established in the language.

6.5   From *and moche other stuffe* to *and stuff like that*

The development of the common modern adjunctive forms seems to begin with lexical items (*stuff, things*) that were originally used with specific reference before evolving the non-specific vague meaning that is found in their general extender uses. Carroll (2008: 30) points out that *stuff* should not be interpreted as a "vague noun or general noun" in examples from the Middle English period, but is used to refer to different types of "materials." It was possible early on to make the word plural, as in (71), where the reference is to "property" in a will. As we saw in early versions of the disjunctive forms, the word *other* often accompanies *stuff* in early extender constructions, as in (72) and (73), from Carroll (2008). In (72), the reference is to "embroidery materials" and in (73) to "materials for war," a fairly frequent use of the expression at that time, as we noted in Chapter 1.

(71)   *All his other godes **and stuffes** meveable that he leveth vnto hem*

[1439 in F. J. Furnival *Fifty Earliest Eng. Wills* (1882) 126 OED]

6.5 From *and moche other stuffe* to *and stuff*

(72)   *gold silke **and other stuff***

[1448 *Pet. Hen. VI* s.v. *stuf(f)e* (n.) 3(b) MED]

(73)   *men of Armes & Archers, **And moche other stuffe** þat longeth to were*

[a1500 *Brut -1419* s.v. *stuf(f)e* (n.) I(a) MED]

During the sixteenth century, the short form without *other* comes into use, as in (74), where there may still be a referential meaning involving "valuable materials." By the next century, it is possible to find examples, as in (75), where the short form has become non-specific and no reference seems to be intended. Similarly, in (76), we also have evidence of a grammatical change in which the typically non-count *stuff* is attached to two plural forms. The grammatical change is obviously complete by the nineteenth century, as illustrated in (77), from a novel by Thackeray, with the same type of connection.

(74)   *They encountered the sayde people yt caryed the sayde Treasoure **and stuffe** & parforce toke it from the knyghtes*

[1513 R. FABYAN *New Cronycles Eng. & Fraunce* (1516) I. cxxiii. F. lix OED]

(75)   *She turned to me and said, 'Lewis, I find you pretend to give the Duke notions of the mathematics **and stuff***'

[1697 J. LEWIS Mem. *Duke of Glocester* (1789) 66 OED]

(76)   *When they talk'd of their Raphaels, Corregios **and stuff***

[1774 O. GOLDSMITH *Retaliation* 16 OED]

(77)   *And as for you, you want a woman ... to sit at your feet, and cry 'O caro! O bravo!' whilst you read your Shakspeares, and Miltons, **and stuff***

[1852 W. M. THACKERAY *Henry Esmond* III. iv. 110 OED]

During the nineteenth century, there is some evidence that the longer version *and stuff like that* is being used in American English, as in example (78) from the *Corpus of Historical American English* (COHA; see Davies (2012), www.english-corpora.org/coha/), but we could find no other examples before 1920, as shown in (79).

(78)   *natives are deadly afraid of magic, the evil eye, witch doctors **and stuff like that***

[1868 T. S. Arthur *After a Shadow and Other Stories* COHA]

(79)   *I'm pretty practical about foundations and radiation **and stuff like that***

[1920 Sinclair Lewis *Main Street* COHA]

112   6 Historical Development and Change

The distribution of the longer form never matches the widespread use of the short form *and stuff* as it eventually spreads from American English into the everyday talk of younger speakers throughout the English-speaking world, as documented in Aijmer (2013). It is noticeable that, while these two citations, in (78) and (79), are from written stories, they are actually part of characters' speech in the stories.

6.6   From *and other Thynges* to *and things like that*

The origin of the general extender *and things* may be found in constructions where specific reference is involved, as in (80), from Caxton, in a context where there really were those marvelous "thynges."

(80)   *The poetes ... sayen and rehercen many fables **and thynges meruayllous***

[1483 W. CAXTON tr. Caton G vj b OED]

As we enter the early modern period, we find those two common collocates, *other* and *such*, that we have noted already, present in versions of extender constructions with *things*. There is a definite sense in these early examples that there were actual referential objects meant by *thynges* in these lists.

(81)   *Mylke, chese, pulleyn, **and other thynges***

[1523 L. D. BERNERS tr. J. Froissart *Cronycles* I. cccciii. 701 OED]

(82)   *The kyng sent William Blacknall esquyer, Clerck of hys Spycery with siluer vessell, plate **and other thynges***

[1548 *Hall's Vnion: Henry VIII* f. lviii OED]

(83)   *The Carauan presented his rude like maiesty with water, bread, hearbs, figs, garlike, **and such things** as he had*

[1614 W. Lithgow *Most Delectable Disc. Peregrination* sig. N3 OED]

The phrase *and other things* is commonly used to complete lists with clearly referential function throughout the sixteenth century, but beginning in the late sixteenth and early seventeenth century, the short form *and things* comes into use, even appearing in the plays of Ben Jonson, as in (74), and Shakespeare, as in (75).

(84)   *And with-all calles me at his pleasure; I knowe not how many Cocatrices, **and things***

[1601 B. JONSON *Fountaine of Selfe-love* IV. lv. Sig. I2 OED]

(85)   *With Ruffes and Cuffes, and Fardingales, **and things***

[a1616 W. SHAKESPEARE *Taming of Shrew* (1623) IV. Iii. 56 OED]

6.6 From *and other Thynges* to *and things*   113

From that time until very recently, *and things* served as a very common adjunctive extender, as in (86), and is still being used by some young speakers, as in (87) from Levey (2012: 258). However, as documented by Cheshire (2007) and Tagliamonte and Denis (2010), the phrase has been declining in frequency more recently as *and stuff* advances. According to Tagliamonte and Denis (2010), the process is best described as "lexical replacement" as one form supplants the other. According to Denis (2017), analyzing Toronto English, adjunctive extenders with *thing* are "rapidly moving toward obsolescence" (2017: 169).

(86) *The Japanese supper with the Japanese room and mats **and things***

[1894 *To-day* 13 Jan. 14 OED]

(87) *they teamed up on to him and started hitting him with weapons **and things***

The long form with the modifier, *and things like that*, first appears in the late nineteenth century in American English examples, as in (88) and (89), and early twentieth century in British English citations, as in (90). Although all three sources in (88)–(90) are novels, these examples are not from the narrative, but from dialogue. The association with speech continues into PDE, as in (91).

(88) *I should so like a ring, and a pin, **and things like that***

[1879 Augustin Daly *Little Miss Million* COHA]

(89) *we do a great deal of work together, for the parish; widows and orphans **and things like that**, you know*

[1886 Bronson Howard *Kate* COHA]

(90) *I shall take odd jobs. Something always comes along, cholera duty in India **and things like that***

[1915 W. S. Maugham *Of Human Bondage* lxiv. 329 OED]

(91) *There've been relentless personal attacks calling her a 'prom queen', 'an airhead', **and things like that***

[1985 *Washington Post* (Nexis) 9 June F1 OED]

In support of the analysis of longer general extenders with *like that* as late nineteenth- and early twentieth-century innovations, we find examples of the short version of *and everything* in Shakespeare's *Twelfth Night* from early in the seventeenth century, as in (92), but it isn't until the early twentieth century that we find the long version in use, as in this example from American English (93). The short version is very frequent in PDE, but not the long form.

(92)   *By maid-hood, honor, truth, **and euery thing**, I loue thee so=*

           [a1616 W. SHAKESPEARE *Twelfth Night* (1623) III i. 148 OED]

(93)   *my aunt lets me go to a matinee, and to the moving picture shows, **and everything like that***

           [1914 Jane L. Stewart *The Camp Fire Girls on the Farm. Or, Bessie King's New Chum* COHA]

By now it must have become clear that the direction of development is from shorter forms (*or something, and things*) earlier to longer forms (*or something like that, and things like that*) later.

6.7   From *and that* to *and that sort of thing*

The most common adjunctive form in many areas of Britain is *and (all) that*. We suspect that the basic form *and that* may have been widely used in casual speech before it is found in the written record. In his *Grammar of Late Modern English*, Poutsma (1904–1926) cites several examples of *and that, and all that* and *and that sort of thing* from the mid-nineteenth-century novels of William Thackeray, but provides no indication of how they developed.

Cheshire (2007: 165) notes that older speakers in her study used the following adjunctive forms most frequently: *and that, and all that, and (all) that sort of thing*. For those speakers, the three forms might be on a cline from a basic adjunctive form, simply signaling "there is more" (*and that*), through a more emphatic, hence louder version incorporating the intensifier (*and all that*), to an even longer and more elaborate construction identifying the "more" in terms of a *sort* or *kind* or *type*, as a form of classification (*and all that sort of thing*). We would suggest that this was the sequence of development and, although we don't know when the earliest versions of *and that* were in use, we can say that the other two forms appear in the record at least a century apart. There is evidence that *and all that* was in use in the seventeenth century, as in (94), and the early eighteenth century, as in (95) and (96), the latter example from an edition of *The Spectator* (1711).

(94)   *His spirits exhale with the heat of his passion, **and all that**, and swop falls asleep*

           [1672 DUKE OF BUCKINGHAM *Rehearsal* II. 16 OED]

(95)   *They did it to Purpose, carried all before them, subdued Monarchy, cut their King's Head, **and all that***

           [1702 D. DEFOE New Test. In *Coll. Scarce & Valuable Tracts* (1751) III. 14 OED]

(96)   *And what a poor Figure would Mr. Bayes have made without his Egad **and all That***?

[1711 *The Spectator* No. 80, Friday, June 1. P. 345]

The long form (*and that sort/kind of thing*) appears about a century later, as in (97), and is found in fictional writing during the mid nineteenth century, as in (98). To complete the set of SKT constructions from the historical record, the long form with *type* isn't much in use before the mid twentieth century, as in (99), and remains fairly infrequent. This sequence of occurrence follows the historical path of the elements *kind of* (used in Old English), *sort of* (in the 1400s) and *type of* (in the 1900s), as detailed in Keizer (2007).

(97)   *Ben used to say that Latin, **and all that kind of thing**, was of no more use to a sailor than a fourth mast to a ship.*

[1806 R. SEMPLE Charles Ellis I. ii. 19 OED]

(98)   *I suppose you would go properly dressed, – white tie, kids, **and that sort of thing**, eh?*

[1853 C. BEDE Adventures Mr. Verdant Green vii 65 OED]

(99)   *Lots of people they plan and put this away for when they get old **and that type of thing**.*

[1965 N. DUNN *Talking to Women* 40 OED]

From this evidence, we might hypothesize that the long form came into use after the short form, possibly in order to emphasize a stronger cohesive tie, a development we have observed with other examples of long forms. However, at the moment, our proposed connection between *and (all) that sort of thing* and *and (all) that* is really only a hypothesis which may be tested through a more thorough investigation of the historical origins of *and that* in British English, a project for future research requiring a more fine-grained analysis of older texts.

Having surveyed the historical record for examples of older forms and their more recent instantiations, we now turn to some of the mechanisms of change that resulted in the current forms. These mechanisms have been described in terms of grammaticalization.

6.8   Grammaticalization

The grammaticalization of general extenders, as described in Cheshire's (2007) original and detailed account, "consists of a collection of interrelated language changes within a construction" (2007: 166). It is important to recognize the "interrelated" nature of those changes because, as we describe them, we tend to identify the individual changes and analyze them separately, yet they must be assumed to be connected, although they "may not unfold concurrently," as emphasized by Pichler and Levey (2011: 462). The study of grammaticalization is considered to begin, in the modern era, with Meillet's (1912/1958) investigation of how new grammatical categories evolve. It becomes a greater focus of contemporary research after Traugott (1982) in the work of Lehmann (1985), Heine *et al.* (1991), Hopper (1991) and Traugott and Heine (1991). It is from Hopper and Traugott (2003: 18), basing their analysis on Kurylowicz (1965), that we get the most frequently quoted definition:

the change whereby lexical items and constructions come in certain linguistic contexts to serve grammatical functions, and once grammaticalized, continue to develop new grammatical functions.

The focus on the historical development of grammatical markers in earlier studies has been expanded to include structural changes in other expressions, including pragmatic markers. As we emphasized in Chapter 1, expressions such as general extenders are treated in this type of analysis as constructions that are part of the grammar and serve grammatical functions. Although we think of them as pragmatic markers rather than as grammatical markers, this distinction seems to have no consequences for the study of their grammaticalization, as explicitly stated by Traugott, "in my view 'grammar' is communicative and covers the full range of expressions in a language" (2012: 20), and repeated, with general extenders included, in Traugott (2016). The justification for this perspective is that the mechanisms of change that result in pragmatic markers are essentially no different from those that have been discovered for grammatical markers.

Most studies are concerned with specific mechanisms of change that account for the consistently observed reduction in formal structure of words and phrases over time. That process of reduction follows a very general pattern whereby expressions that are used frequently become less fully articulated in both syntactic and phonological terms (Bybee, 2003). We will investigate the ways in which general extenders follow that pattern. One well-documented mechanism of change is described as decategorialization (or "decategorisation" in Cheshire, 2007), through which linguistic expressions lose some aspect of their earlier grammatical structure and function.

6.9 Decategorialization

Heine and Kuteva (2005) describe decategorialization as a "loss of morphosyntactic properties characteristic of the source form" (2005: 579). In the case of general extenders, we have evidence of multiple source forms undergoing this change. In grammatical terms, short general extenders consist of

6.9 Decategorialization

a coordinating conjunction (*and, or*) and a proform that is syntactically a noun phrase (*things, stuff, something, anything*). In an early observation about the underlying structure of general extenders, Ball and Ariel pointed out that "built into the phrase structure rules for coordination, only constituents of the same category can be coordinated" (1978: 37). This would lead to an expectation that each one will be coordinated with another noun phrase (i.e. NP *and/or* NP). This expectation may be fulfilled in the case of examples such as (100), from Levey (2012: 263), where two plural, non-animate noun phrases, the "host" NP, underlined, and the extender NP, are coordinated. We include a simple grammatical analysis beside each of the following examples, mainly to draw attention to the unexpected combinations. In the case of (100), an alternative interpretation might see *and things* as coordinating with the whole verb phrase *playing with skipping ropes*. This is a notorious problem in the interpretation of the scope of short general extenders, but not a delimiting one. We have chosen a viable interpretation of the utterance, and present it as an illustration of what two "constituents of the same category" look like.

(100)   *we've been playing with the skipping ropes* ***and things***
        [NP plural, non-animate and NP plural, non-animate]

However, as most of the linguistic research has emphasized (e.g. Erman, 1995), this type of expected coordination is not always what we find. When we encounter a mismatch between the coordinated elements, in terms of their grammatical categories, we uncover evidence of decategorialization at work, resulting in the erosion of the original morphosyntactic characteristics of the extender noun phrase (cf. Heine, 2003: 579).

Among the many mismatches that have been cited, we can illustrate some that would occur if the source form *things* is assumed to be a "plural noun with non-human reference," as it is in most uses other than in an adjunctive extender. In (101), from Cheshire (2007: 182), *things* is coordinated with a noun phrase with human reference, in (102), from Aijmer (2002: 240), with a verb phrase, and in (103), also from Cheshire (2007: 180), with a whole sentence, reporting an idea. We have witnessed, in example (89) earlier, a combination involving human referents in the phrase *widows and orphans and things like that*, suggesting that decategorialization of this type is not a new phenomenon.

(101)   *it's American about these American singers **and things***

        [NP human and NP non-human]

(102)   *I've been bumbling around through the West and talking to old friends **and things***

        [VP and NP]

118   6 Historical Development and Change

(103)   *I look at nursing and then I think "that'd be a nice thing to do to help people"* **and things**

         [S and NP]

We can find a similar range of mismatches involving the lexical item *stuff* if "non-count, non-animate noun" are assumed features. In (104), from Pichler and Levey (2011: 445), it coordinates with a plural noun phrase, in (105), from Evison *et al.* (2007: 138), with a verb phrase, and in (106), from Winter and Norrby (2000: 6), with a sentence.

(104)   *it's usually all on history programmes* **and stuff**

         [NP plural and NP non-count]

(105)   *I'm going to do everything. Fry chips and wait tables* **and stuff**

         [VP and NP]

(106)   *I go out with my friends* **and stuff**

         [S and NP]

We might expect the disjunctive form *or something* to coordinate with other "singular, non-animate nouns," but mismatches can be found, as in (107), from Mauranen (2004: 184), with a plural noun, in (108), from Cheshire (2007: 181), with two singular human proper nouns ("footballers"), in (109), from Erman (1995: 143), with two plural, human nouns, in (110), from Ball and Ariel (1978: 37), with an adjective, in (111), from Channell (1994: 137) with a verb phrase, and in (112), from Cheshire (2007: 180), with a sentence reporting speech.

(107)   *they'll have sandwiches* **or something** *for tea*

         [NP plural or NP singular]

(108)   *Gianno Franco Zola or Ruud Gullit* **or something**

         [NP human or NP non-human]

(109)   *it wants almost boys or schoolgirls* **or something** *singing it*

         [NP plural, human or NP singular, non-human]

(110)   *Are you crazy* **or something**?

         [Adj or NP]

(111)   *what about things like when you read sentences* **or something**

         [VP or NP]

(112) *people say "watch out" you know "you might get mugged" **or something***

[S or NP]

We could continue to illustrate this widespread decategorialization of other short general extenders, but examples (101)–(112) provide enough evidence of the process at work. From the examples in (107)–(112), we can be fairly sure that the phrase *or something* is no longer restricted to category-based coordination. We might also say that, in its general extender use here, the conjunction *or* has lost some of its formal (logical) coordination function and become part of the extender phrase, which attaches to a preceding phrase or clause, with a modifying function (i.e. "there may be others"), rather than coordinating grammatically equivalent expressions.

In adjunctive forms, as illustrated in (101)–(106), the conjunction *and* no longer seems to be the equivalent of a logical operator between two equivalent predicates, but is part of a phrase that attaches (optionally) to a preceding item, typically with the function of signaling "there may be more."

In order to illustrate the process of decategorialization of the proforms in short general extenders, we began with the simplifying assumption that, for example, the morpheme *thing*, as part of *or something*, could be analyzed in terms of its grammatical features, such as syntactic (NP singular) and semantic (non-human reference), and concluded that the absence of coordination constraints associated with those features undermined their relevance for the analysis of the general extender. Examples (101)–(106) for *and stuff* and *and things* also illustrate the same type of decategorialization process that disconnects general extenders from grammatical constraints. Our finding is that short general extenders are attached to phrases and clauses, but they are not necessarily coordinated with them.

6.10 Morphosyntactic Reanalysis

Accompanying the changes in terms of an external relationship with preceding items are two related internal changes that are involved in the transformation of short general extenders. These other processes cause erosion of the independence of the morphosyntactic status, along with the phonological attrition, of the separate elements within the whole phrase.

The process of morphosyntactic reanalysis has been well documented in the evolution of the modern element *gonna* in the expression *I'm not gonna go* as deriving from a fully explicit form (*go* + *ing* + *to*) with lexical status (motion verb plus preposition). These three morphemes are combined, through the effect of frequent usage, to become a single reduced form with a more grammatical role marking future temporal reference. The original lexical verb (*go*) continues to be used with its "motion" meaning, as in *I'm* *not going to town*, while disappearing into an expression with a "future" meaning, as in *I'm not gonna go*, and grammatically distinct from the earlier use. That is, it loses the "motion" sense, as in the ungrammatical **I'm not gonna town*. This phenomenon is described as "layering" (Hopper, 1991) for a situation "where a full form and a reduced form co-exist" (Hopper and Traugott, 2003: 124).

As Erman (1995) pointed out, a very similar process can be seen at work with the original components (*or* + *some* + *thing*) undergoing reduction to become a fixed phrase (*or something*). The three separate components combine into a single form, morphosyntactically speaking, in a development known as "fusion" (Hopper and Traugott, 2003: 44), or "automatization" (Bybee, 2003: 603), which results in a single processing unit. The result, as Cheshire has noted, is that forms "that were formerly separate become stored and processed as a prefabricated phrase" (2007: 166). The layering phenomenon is also discernible in this case, with the noun *thing* continuing to have a use as a morpheme with referential potential (*Where's my blue thing?*), yet disappearing into a general extender (*I think it was blue or something*) where it is no longer a separate morpheme and no referential function remains. As a result, the phrase can be attached to syntactic units other than noun phrases, as we illustrated in the previous section.

A comparable layering effect can be identified in the use of the noun *stuff* with a referential function, as in talking about personal possessions (*Have you seen my school stuff?*), that loses its separate status and referential function when used as part of the adjunctive extender (*I see my friends at school and stuff*). As forms that were separate morphemes become part of a fixed expression, there is a concomitant process of phonological change as the formerly distinct elements are no longer pronounced separately.

6.11 Phonological Attrition

A really consistent finding from studies of diachronic change is that linguistic expressions tend to lose phonological substance as they undergo decategorialization and reanalysis, based on the simple fact that "expressions that undergo phonological reduction do so because they are frequent" (Boye and Harder, 2012: 29). When we look at this effect in the case of general extenders, we find two aspects of phonological development, one at the suprasegmental level and the other involving the loss of phonetic segments, more generally known as phonological attrition.

One of the major differences between long forms and short forms of general extenders is in terms of their pronunciation. Long forms are more likely to occur as separate constituents in a distinct tone unit, while the short forms are more

6.11 Phonological Attrition

often found inside a tone unit with other constituents. In the Hong Kong English corpus examined by Warren, the short form *or something* "was almost always spoken in the same tone unit as the item that it is tagged with" (2007: 187), while long forms typically occurred in a separate tone unit. In Aijmer's (1985: 370–71) analysis of British English data, the short forms *and things* and *or something* were overwhelmingly used inside a tone unit, whereas their longer counterparts with the modifier *like that* were typically in a separate tone unit by themselves. In addition, short forms were used much more frequently. Channell (1994: 137) reported a similar pattern for *or something*. As the short forms become minimal elements in the pronunciation of utterances, they simply become part of the rhythm, with very little phonological presence.

The pronunciation of short general extenders has also been subject to a process involving the reduction or loss of phonetic segments. In Cheshire's (2007) study of general extender use in three English towns, two of the most frequent forms are listed as *and that* and *or something*. However, as Cheshire notes, "the unstressed *and* is reduced to /n/ in every case and *or* in *or something* is almost always pronounced as a schwa" (2007: 168). In both these forms, it is the conjunction that undergoes most phonetic reduction, potentially reducing its role as a marker signaling any kind of cohesive link and contributing to the impression that these short general extenders have undergone reanalysis as single forms (while continuing to be transcribed with two constituents). In her analysis of the grammaticalization of *or something*, Erman (1995) argues that the form should be treated as a single unit, using phonetic reduction as evidence: "it should be pointed out that a more adequate representation of *or something* in these examples would have been *o'someth'n*" (1995: 144), as illustrated in (113) from British English. Other researchers occasionally provide evidence that the use of *or something* was heard in a reduced form, as in (114) from Drew (2014: 232), also from British English, and (115) from American English (Guthrie, 1994: 85).

(113) you get it out of the computer every six months **o'someth'n**

(114) I'll give you a call then tomorrow when I get in **'rsumn**

(115) there was like eight ta ten of 'em **er somethin'**

When we look at the pronunciation of other extenders, we find more examples of reduced forms reported in some of the data. Both Brinton (2017) and McColm and Trousdale (2019) report on examples of reduced forms of *or whatever* (e.g. *or whatev*, *or wev*) as becoming increasingly common in contemporary usage, particularly in web-based communication.

In Levey's (2012) study, the most frequent form used by the young (London) speakers was *and everything*, which was typically pronounced as /ənɛvθɪn/. Compared to the careful articulation of the constituents in *and everything*, there is a loss of a consonant /d/ and a middle syllable /rɪ/, plus the very common change from the velar nasal /ŋ/ to the alveolar /n/. In Jefferson's (1990) detailed transcriptions, the representation of the *and* element is almost non-existent, as in (116), supporting our earlier observation that it is probably no longer being treated as a conjunction. A similar absence of *and* is found in other transcribed examples, such as the representation of *and that* in (117) from Overstreet (2014) and *and stuff* in (118) from Guthrie (1994).

(116)   *Did she do the cooking en take over'n everything*

(117)   *we were having a party 'nat before leaving*

(118)   *there was a sugar shortage an' a-like he sold pot 'nstuff*

Example (118) is from American English where, according to Overstreet (1999) and Aijmer (2013), the use of *and stuff* has not only become reduced in form (*'nstu*), it no longer has to attach to an antecedent phrase. As we noted in Chapter 5, some speakers use a version of *and stuff*, as in (119) from Overstreet (1999: 103), that is so reduced in phonetic substance that it seems to have no other function than to be part of the rhythm of speech as a punctuation element, or punctor (Vincent and Sankoff, 1992).

(119)   *But y'know 'nstuff as he got a little bit older 'nstuff y'know*

We might interpret this use of the reduced form of the general extender as almost the equivalent of a filled pause, with a role in the prosodic structure of the utterance, but with no role in terms of information content, a function consistent with its phonologically reduced form. This is the phenomenon that Pichler and Levey (2011: 452) identify as the final stage in their taxonomy of semantic–pragmatic change in general extenders.

To summarize, we can propose that in contemporary English, the spoken versions of *and that* (*'nat*), *and stuff* (*'nstu*), *and everything* (*'nevthin*), and *or something* (*'rsumpn*) offer evidence that these forms have grammaticalized and, in some situations, have become the equivalent of oral punctuation marks. In addition, the effect of lexical replacement has reduced the frequency of *and things*, illustrating a similar process of language change that resulted in the loss of earlier phrases used as general extenders, including *and such like*, *and other*, *or some other* and *or any such thing*.

6.12   Pragmatic Shift

In the preceding discussion, we have mostly been concerned with the formal changes associated with grammaticalization. There are also accompanying changes in the meaning potential of the words and phrases undergoing those changes. While carefully investigating the historical record to identify changes

6.12 Pragmatic Shift

in form and structure, it is important not to lose sight of the fact that these changes "result not from purely language-internal factors, but from verbal interactions among speakers" (Hopper, 2010: 181). When we look at what speakers are doing, we are inevitably going to be talking about the pragmatics of language in use.

What Meillet (1912/1958) described as "affaiblissement" ("weakening") is an effect more commonly known now as "semantic bleaching," which results in lexical items losing some of their original meaning as they grammaticalize in particular uses. This is what happened to the "physical motion" meaning of *go* when it grammaticalized as part of a future marker in *gonna*: the source meaning disappeared in the new usage (cf. Sweetser, 1988: 392). We have already noted this effect in the case of the lexical items *stuff* and *thing* as they lost their "physical" or "concrete" semantic features when they were co-opted into pragmatic markers in the form of general extenders. This change coincides with a shift from referential function to interpersonal function, the primary change identified by Pichler and Levey (2012: 452) in their description of the stages in a historical sequence of functional changes, an analysis adopted by Traugott (2016). We investigated the interpersonal function in detail in Chapter 3, but a couple of examples here may serve to illustrate the effect of pragmatic shift on two of the most common general extenders, in (120), from Overstreet (1999: 101), and (121), from Channell (1994: 135), already noted in Chapter 3.

(120)   *I talked to the grad division yesterday an' it's so weird, y'know, I call – I call the school **an' stuff** an' everybody's so nice*

(121)   *Could we, when you give us our essays back, and give us titles, could we sort of meet **or something** because, I mean, there might be things we want to ask?*

In the case of *and stuff* in (120), there is a signal that more could be said, but following the conversational maxim of Quantity (i.e. avoid being over-informative), it would be deemed unnecessary for the current purposes of the interaction since the speaker can assume that the addressee (her friend) has experience of what's involved in calling the school. There is no semantic content, or referential target, in this use of *stuff*, but in addition to signaling an assumption of shared experience, there is another pragmatic effect based on that assumption, that the speakers are socially close, an interpersonal function commonly fulfilled by *and stuff*, which has been described as creating a sense of "rapport" (Aijmer, 1985: 386) or "solidarity" (Overstreet and Yule, 1997b: 250).

A related pragmatic shift takes place as disjunctive forms come to be used with interpersonal function. Inherent in the use of *or something* is the sense that there is an alternative to what is named, with the effect of downplaying how accurate the accompanying information may be, a motivation tied to the conversational maxim of Quality (i.e. avoid being inaccurate). When *or something* is part of an invitation or request, the possibility of an alternative removes some of the imposition associated with those speech acts and adds a sense of negative politeness (i.e. avoid imposing) to the utterance. There is no alternative to *meet* implied in (121), there is only a sense of making the request sound less demanding, a distinctly pragmatic function.

We could also include the formulaic structures involving *and everything* and *or anything*, described in Chapter 4, where other potential expectations are clearly involved, exemplifying even further dimensions of pragmatic shift in the use of general extenders. As we hope to have demonstrated, the grammaticalization framework provides a perfect instrument for the analysis of the development of general extenders in English. The use of that framework among sociolinguists was just part of their analysis of variation in the ways in which general extenders have also become social markers, the topic of Chapter 7.[4]

7 Social Marking and Variation

In contrast to the relatively few studies of general extenders in terms of diachronic variation, there are many more studies of synchronic variation. Indeed, in the first serious study of general extenders, described here as "terminal tags" by Dines (1980: 20), their social relevance in terms of variation is made clear.

> Below the level of consciousness, terminal tags are salient across the speech community, although speakers may vary in their conscious awareness and consequently in their control of the feature. This is the pattern of salience which we have come to expect with phonological and syntactic variables. It supports the case for regarding the terminal tag as a socially diagnostic discourse variable.

In her approach, a major concern for Dines (1980), and subsequently for most of the sociolinguists who have undertaken variationist studies, is whether discourse-pragmatic variation, as recorded in general extender use, can be analyzed in the same way as phonetic variation was in the original studies by Labov (2006) on social variation. The problem is essentially a matter of being able to count tokens of variants, not such a problem when it is the pronunciation of post-vocalic /r/, for example. Tagliamonte (2012: 270) presents the issue in the following way.

> If variationists adhere to the most rudimentary notion of the linguistic variable, namely that variants must mean exactly the same thing, discourse-pragmatic features cannot be studied quantitatively.

This strict, though "rudimentary" notion would require us to treat *and stuff* and *and things*, for example, as having the same meaning, an idea that seems hard to justify from a strictly linguistic point of view. Instead, we have to find a method of categorization that is appropriate for the type of constituent under investigation. Rather than investigate differences tied to variation in the phonetic realization of a phonological category, we can look at the various phrasal realizations of a discourse category. As Cheshire (2005: 481) expresses it, "the conditions of strict semantic equivalence can be relaxed if variants can be shown to be equivalent in their discourse function." This echoes Dines'

125

(1980: 15) earlier decision to "propose that variables may be postulated on the basis of *a common function in discourse*" (emphasis in the original). If everyone agrees that "general extender" represents a discrete category at the discourse level, with a set of recognized instantiations (including *and stuff* and *and things*), then, by analogy, we can try to connect variation in the linguistic forms and uses of general extenders with the social categories of speakers in different communities. This is exactly what sociolinguists have tried to do and the approach has rewarded us with a wealth of information and a fairly definitive picture of who uses which general extenders, and how many, in which social circumstances.

In this chapter we will report on a number of studies that have looked at general extenders as linguistic variables that may align with social variables, becoming social markers in different communities. This research is mostly quantitative, using electronic corpora to find patterns in the use of particular expressions according to a number of social criteria, with results presented in aggregated token counts. Social variables involved include age, with a particular interest in younger (teenage) speech (versus adult) and a concern with whether the results support a "real-time" (age-grading) process versus an "apparent-time" process as an explanation of differences documented. Other variables involve the gender and social class of speakers, and any interactions of these variables with age, in order that the researchers can identify clear differences in the speech of, for example, young working-class males versus middle-class females, within a range of comparisons. We will also note some differences in general extender use according to location, particularly among local varieties in British towns, among speakers of Montreal French, and among speakers of international varieties of English. A different sense of "location" is relevant for other studies of variation, notably those involving register differences, which we will illustrate from studies of the academic register and the business register.

7.1 The Age Factor

In terms of overall general extender use, most studies find higher tokens among younger speakers, leading to the generalization that "general extenders are typically associated with youth speech" (Tagliamonte, 2012: 260). In their New Zealand data, Stubbe and Holmes (1995: 72) reported that a younger group recorded almost double the number of general extenders than an older group. Those higher token counts are achieved through a limited set of forms, mostly shorter versions, whereas older speakers use fewer tokens overall, but include a wider variety of forms, particularly longer versions. As Palacios Martínez concludes, from a survey of British studies, "adolescents concentrate their use of extenders, especially in the case of adjunctives, on a small number of items,

7.1 The Age Factor

with the opposite being true with the adults, who seem to use a wider repertoire" (2011: 2460). As exemplification, Secova's (2017) report on London English (recorded 2010–2014) had high token counts of *and stuff* among teenagers (16–19-year-olds), but older speakers (60+ years old) didn't use that phrase at all. Unlike the teenagers, older speakers recorded longer expressions such as *and all that lark* and *and all the rest of it*, indicative of their wider variety of forms.

In the most comprehensive review of age-related variation, Tagliamonte and Denis (2010) compared the results of a number of studies to arrive at some generalizations that seem to capture the older–younger divide in terms of token counts. In their Toronto population, Tagliamonte and Denis (2010: 349) report that the highest-frequency use of general extenders was in the age range 20–29 (44 tokens). This is close to the same ratio (39 tokens) found in a similar age range (18–34) in the Wellington (New Zealand) study by Stubbe and Holmes (1995). (The number of tokens displayed in each case is per ten thousand words.) In both these studies, frequency of general extender use was similarly lower among older speakers in the age range (30–39), and the decline continues among speakers over 40, with about the same number (19) of tokens in both studies, a number that remains stable for speakers in their fifties and sixties. These are remarkably similar token counts for two populations in really different geographical locations and at least a decade apart. In both cases, it is adult speakers of the language who are using the most general extenders.

However, when we look at some of the results from recent quantitative studies of British English, we find a distinct difference between token counts for Canadian and British speakers in the younger age groups. In the younger teenage populations (14–15-year-olds) that were the focus of Cheshire's (2007) study in three different English towns, general extender use was, in some cases, substantially greater than in the Canadian data. Among groups of 13–16-year-olds, the Toronto count was about 35 tokens, while the counts for different English towns were about 41 tokens in Milton Keynes, about 56 in Reading and about 59 in Hull. Some of those younger teenagers in England are using a lot more general extenders than their Canadian counterparts. Very similar to the British English counts are those from an earlier Australian study by Winter and Norrby (2000), who report a token count of 51 among 15–16-year-olds in Melbourne. All these data sets were collected at about the same time, late 1990s for the English and Australian studies and during 2002–2006 for the Canadian study. The basic data suggests that in Toronto and Wellington the greatest use of general extenders is not actually in "youth speech," but among adult speakers in their twenties, while in Melbourne and the English towns, it really is in youth speech that we find the largest numbers. Other than potential differences in the circumstances of data collection, and the fact that they are clearly in different locations, we have no explanation for the widely diverging frequencies of use among these younger speakers in Toronto versus Melbourne versus Hull.

Rather puzzling is a relatively low count for young teenagers in London, reported by Stenström *et al.* (2002), and a similar low token count (about 28) among young speakers reported by Levey (2012: 272) for his younger preadolescent group (7–8-year-olds) in London. Surely we are not to deduce from these reports that young people in the London area just don't use general extenders very much. This seems unlikely. Levey (2012: 271) points out that, in another group (10–11-year-olds), boys continued to produce approximately the same number of tokens as their younger counterparts through adolescence, but girls more than doubled their token count (69). For Levey (2012: 272), this divergence is not simply gender-based, but signals a difference in the pragmatic function of general extenders used, with girls possibly showing "a more marked concern with the affective component of talk" (2012: 273). This observation reminds us that age is not the only factor that may be responsible for the variation we find in these token counts, as we will see in the following sections.

Despite some puzzles, the generalizations we reported earlier in terms of frequency and type of general extenders in use by younger versus older speakers seem to hold true in British English. Some local observations reveal very specific differences, as pointed out by Pichler and Levey, based on their data from Berwick-upon-Tweed: "In the oldest group, infrequent variants are highly favored in non-nominal contexts" (2011: 46). It may be that in order to investigate the age factor more thoroughly, we will have to fine-tune our analytic constructs beyond simply the number of years lived and look more closely at the discourse context and the potentially different functions of forms in the speech of individuals inside those sociolinguistically defined populations at different points in their lives. Not all individuals "act their age." For example, we might speculate that a 62-year-old woman, possibly spending lots of in-group time with her grandchildren, might sometimes sound like them. Denis (2011) identifies such a person whom he recognizes as a genuine outlier whose high-frequency use of *and stuff* he attributes to "high gregariousness" (2011: 67).

Meanwhile, taking the information we have so far, we can offer a brief review, in Table 7.1, of forms to be found in the speech of younger and older speakers. Although most forms can be found in the speech of most groups, we can nevertheless identify some forms as strongly represented in the recorded talk of younger versus older speakers. The division of forms in Table 7.1 is based on numerical data reported for British (London) English in Aijmer (2002: 233), Stenström *et al.* (2002: 89), Palacios Martínez (2011: 2460) and Secova (2017: 9). We can also add Murphy (2010: 107) to that group, based on her study of Irish English, where the phrase *and stuff* was

Table 7.1 *English general extenders associated with younger and older speakers*

Younger	Older
and all	*and so on*
and stuff	*and things*
and stuff like that	*and things like that*
and everything	*and all the rest of it*
or anything	*or so*

used by both male and female speakers in the youngest cohort (in their twenties), but was not used at all by speakers in two older cohorts (in their forties and seventies). The ratio of token counts (per 10,000 words) for younger versus older speakers can be provided for *and all* (71/5), *and stuff* (39/6), *and stuff like that* (56/1), *and everything* (74/22), *or anything* (34/5), *and so on* (3/110), *and things* (6/46), *and things like that* (10/23), *and all the rest of it* (0/30), *or so* (0/29).

7.1.1 Age-Grading

In two studies of general extender use in French (discussed more fully in Chapter 8), one in Montreal (Dubois, 1992), and the other in Paris (Secova, 2011), younger speakers in both varieties were much more prolific users of the forms than older speakers. Both researchers interpret this difference in terms of age-grading, which reflects "change in individual use as the speaker progresses through life, unrelated to community language change" (Secova, 2017: 3). Dubois (1992) reported a very regular rate of decline, noting that "extension particle use was strongly conditioned by age, with younger speakers using the most and the rate of use per 1000 lines dropping off by 4.4 particles per 10 years of age" (1992: 185). This steady decline in the use of what Dubois (1992) described as "extension particles" (our general extenders) is a dramatic representation of the kind of change through time that the term "age-grading" is intended to capture. More specific evidence for age-grading is presented by Secova (2017: 8) in a discussion of her London teenage data.

younger speakers also use derogatory terms (e.g. *and shit*), which is consistent with the theory of age-grading whereby the use of non-prestigious forms (e.g. slang) peaks at adolescence and decreases as speakers reach middle age.

Stenström *et al.* (2002), also reporting on the speech of London teenagers, noted that younger speakers, more often males, used pejorative terms while older speakers did not, an example of which was presented earlier in example (45) in Chapter 5.

In an example of our current understanding of what may be taking place in English, we can start with the observation that the adjunctive extender *and stuff* is used with high frequency among younger (teenage) speakers. If it is an age-graded phenomenon, as those young speakers become adults, they will use *and stuff* less frequently, changing aspects of their speech patterns as they go through life. It is important to emphasize that age-grading is a way of explaining what happens in individuals as their linguistic repertoire changes during their lifetime, sometimes called age-specific variation. An alternative explanation would be that the whole language is changing during a particular period, a process described as change in "apparent time" (Labov, 1972, 1994), so that we would be able to document ongoing change in the "community language," as Secova (2017) describes it. This is change that washes through a community, sweeping most individuals with it. In this scenario, those younger speakers will continue to use *and stuff* into their adult years, resulting in a large-scale change in the language and not just in individual speakers (Eckert, 1997; Sankoff, 2018).

Our earlier attempt to track the history and grammaticalization of general extenders through the historical record (Chapter 6) was based on an analysis in real time, from which we can postulate changes in apparent time. Cheshire (2007), looking at synchronic data, interpreted the observed variation in general extender forms in her data as evidence of ongoing change in terms of grammaticalization, which has to be treated as an apparent-time change. However, when other researchers have since investigated the use of general extenders in English using different sets of synchronic data, they have not been able to support Cheshire's (2007) conclusion. It now seems that the processes involved in grammaticalization are more likely to have been at work through a longer period of time than can be revealed in synchronic data. When researchers looked closely at other data, inspired by Cheshire's (2007) foundational study, they decided that grammaticalization was not a good analysis (Tagliamonte and Denis, 2010; Pichler and Levey, 2011). As Pichler and Levey (2011) argue, grammaticalization changes "may have unfolded centuries ago" and "the temporal span included in conventional apparent-time analyses will be inadequate to identify and chart the full progression of such changes which are typically slow and protracted" (2011: 463). These researchers note (2011: 464) that while younger speakers in their corpus tend not to use *or whatever*, the form continues to be used by older speakers and there is no sense that it is about to disappear from the language. The concomitant increase in the use of *and stuff* by those younger speakers is interpreted in terms of change over time and not just age-grading, an interpretation that is echoed by Tagliamonte and Denis (2010) and Denis (2011), looking at data from Toronto and York (England) respectively. The conclusion, at least currently, is that the phrase *and stuff*, having risen in popularity in American English, has been enjoying a very "fashionable" period among some young speakers in different English-speaking communities. In Cheshire's (2007) study, the phrase was strongly favored by middle-class speakers, but not among working-class speakers. The continuing dominance of *and that* among young working-class males in Pichler and Levey's (2011) study is more evidence that not everything is changing. Among working-class speakers of British English, *and that* has been a stable linguistic feature for generations (Cheshire, 2007: 165).

However, we should remember that there is no competing form *and that* in North American varieties, where *and things* is treated as the nearest alternative to *and stuff*. As both Tagliamonte and Denis (2010) and Denis (2017) point out, a process of "lexical replacement" has led to reduced counts of *and things* and very high counts of *and stuff* in their Canadian data. As Denis reports, "the rise of *stuff* general extenders resulted in a massive reduction of variation" (2017: 165), which leads to fewer instances of *and things*. Looking at the time frames reported by Denis (2017) in his attempt to track changes in general extender use in Ontario, Canada, using archival data, there had already been an increase in the use of *stuff* general extenders among those born in the 1940s, before a sudden large increase during the 1960s and a continued high-frequency use thereafter. For the next thirty years, as documented, the high level of *stuff* general extender use did not decline. From our own experience of North American English, use of the highest-frequency form *and stuff* has not declined in thirty years since. This would seem to represent a clear form of linguistic change, with a new form becoming established in American English and continuing into the present as the dominant adjunctive form, in a process that might be better analyzed as change in apparent time.

We should treat this suggested analysis as tentative, and certainly only limited to one adjunctive extender, and look for opportunities to test it against data with sufficient time-depth to identify the types of incremental changes that might reconcile an apparent-time and/or an age-grading explanation. Studies using age as a factor have, as yet, not really tried to replicate the type of close analysis of small, narrowly focused research projects, starting with younger speakers who are monitored over extended periods, that characterize the typical study of language change (usually involving pronunciation) in segments of lifespan, as detailed in Sankoff (2018). We believe that the future study of general extenders in lifespan data will eventually provide better answers to questions about the age factor than we have settled on for now.

7.2 The Gender Factor

When we turn to the analysis of general extender use by speakers identified by their gender, we should remember that we are focusing on the social gender of those counted as male and female. We have already noted a difference in frequency of general extender use according to gender in Levey's (2012) London study, in which adolescent females (10–11-year-olds) used the forms twice as often as males. This is in contrast to Cheshire's (2007) comprehensive report on the speech of teenagers (14–15-year-olds) in three English towns, in which she notes individual variation in the use of general extenders, but finds "no consistent patterns of gender variation in our data" (2007: 162). Both of these reports are in contrast to the results of Pichler and Levey's (2011) analysis of data from another northern English town, where they found that "males in every age cohort, particularly the youngest, use general extenders more than females" (2011: 454). Pichler and Levey's (2011) youngest group were closer to an adult age range (17–23-year-olds), making them a lot older than Levey's (2012) adolescents. The populations in these two studies were working class, while Cheshire (2007) included both middle-class and working-class participants. Are we to conclude from these British studies that males and females have similar levels of general extender use in their preadolescent years (7–8-year-olds), that females use more during the adolescent period (10–11-year-olds), that there is no difference in frequency of use during the mid teens (14–15-year-olds), after which in their later teens and early twenties (17–23-year-olds), males use more than females? That is actually an empirical question that might best be answered through a study of those different age cohorts within a single stable population, or following individuals through time, rather than trying to make comparisons across very different corpora, as Macaulay (2002) and Pichler (2010) have argued.

Alternatively, we can try to look more closely at the different results from the two populations identified as working class to check if they really are comparable. They turn out to have such different high-frequency forms that we can probably attribute the differences to different types of data-collection events, undermining the idea of a sequential relationship between them as presented in the speculative question above. Whereas Pichler and Levey (2011) report the highest frequency for *and that* (31%) compared to *and everything* (4%), that relationship is reversed in Levey's (2012) report, where *and everything* is most frequent (20%) and *and that* is less (15%). Additionally, in Levey's distribution, another form *and all that* is listed as frequent (18%). From a gender perspective, Levey's results reveal some very interesting tendencies. Females use *and everything* more than twice as often as males, a relationship that is reversed with *and all that*. Both these phrases can have an intensifying effect as the young speakers produce their personal narratives, but there is a distinct gender preference. For males, the dominant form *and all that* in Levey (2012), an intensified version of the dominant male form *and that* in Pichler and Levey (2011), is in line with a male/female dichotomy among the young London population in Stenström *et al.*'s (2002) study. In that study, the ratio of male/

7.2 The Gender Factor

female tokens for *and all* (55/20) is reversed for *and everything* (21/56). For younger speakers of British English, we can propose that, based on earlier reports, males exhibit a preference for *and (all) that* while females choose *and everything* more often for a similar function. This conclusion is supported by token counts from Murphy's (2010: 107) study of gender in a corpus of Irish English, recorded in Limerick and Cork, where *and all (that)* was the most frequent adjunctive form for males in their twenties (the youngest group) yet was completely missing from the speech of a matched group of females, who recorded higher token counts of *and everything*. In the Australian English data reported by Norrby and Winter (2002), a similar preference for *and that* variants is found among males compared to females (64%/36%), which is reversed in favor of the alternative adjunctive form *and stuff* among females (35%/65%).

The existence of a possible male/female distinction in choice of adjunctive forms can sometimes be proposed for the use of the most common disjunctive form. In informally recorded interaction, females are reported to use *or something* more than males (Stenström *et al.*, 2002: 103). However, when interviewed, males use *or something* more than twice as frequently as females, often with a distinct function. As Levey (2012) reports, males exhibit a "greater preoccupation with the referential accuracy of the information they are supplying" (2012: 273), as evidenced by high use of *or something* with an epistemic interpretation, accompanied by other markers of epistemic stance. This observation is very similar to a conclusion reached by Cheshire (2005) that the males in her study were much more concerned with the accuracy of details than females. Cheshire (2005) reports that males were much more precise in answering questions. When asked about where they lived, for example, they gave their full street address, yet females rarely did so, and the males often used clarification requests to check precisely what the focus of a question was. In Holmes' (1990) report from a New Zealand study, male speakers used "imprecision signals" such as *I think* and *you know* to indicate uncertainty twice as often as females (1990: 199–200). This distinction mirrors a reported tendency of males to be more information-oriented and females to be more interaction-oriented, possibly accounting for different patterns of uses of pragmatic markers in general (Erman, 1992; Stubbe and Holmes, 1995). Apparently, this is not only true in English, for the same phenomenon is proposed for French discourse particles by Beeching, who observes that "women use particles to structure discourse while men use them to add referential detail or to signal repair work" (2002: 209). This shift in focus from linguistic form (token counts) to discourse function (marking imprecision) leads to the realization that we may have to use a more fine-grained analytic approach to the investigation of what males and females are doing with general extenders under different circumstances. As things stand, we do not have a clear picture of

Table 7.2 *English general extenders associated with male and female speakers*

Male	Female
and that	*and things*
and all (that)	*and everything*

gendered variation in general extender use overall, largely because different researchers, using different groups and methodologies, have reported conflicting results. When we narrow our focus to individual general extenders, we still find conflicting results for the common phrase *or something*, largely attributable to different data-elicitation events. The one robust finding, supported by several studies of British English, even with different populations and methodologies, is that females have a clear preference for *and everything* versus *and all that* (preferred by males), with a similar gendered difference for *and things* versus *and that*, as detailed in Table 7.2, based on data from Cheshire (2007), Pichler and Levey (2011), Denis (2011), and Levey (2012). There is still clearly a need for a more definitive, gender-focused study of general extender usage.

7.3 The Social-Class Factor

We have already had to refer to social class as a factor in the analysis of variation in general extender use, based on a dichotomy between working class and middle class known to exist in British English. The most detailed investigation in this area that we are familiar with is reported in Cheshire's (2007) detailed study of the frequency of general extender use in two groups of young speakers (working class and middle class) in three English towns. In terms of overall frequency, middle-class speakers used more general extenders, especially the most common forms (2007: 164). The disjunctive form *or something* occurred with consistently higher frequency in the middle-class groups, even when a non-standard form such as *or summat* was included in the working-class token count for one of the towns. There were also some clear differences in the choice of particular adjunctive forms according to social class. We can illustrate this (British) dichotomy with two examples from Cheshire's (2007: 167, 173) study, where (1) is from an interview with a middle-class speaker and (2) is from one with a working-class speaker. We will try to include any known background details with the utterances, as shown after (1): [British English, Male, Teenager, Middle Class].

7.3 The Social-Class Factor

(1) T: *I quite like the English food actually I love roasts **and things like that***
    A: *Do you cook?*
    T: *uh I cook occasionally (.) on weekends **and things***

[BrE, M, Teen, MC]

(2) *I wear his socks (.) his jumpers **and all that lot** (.) when I ain't got no new socks **and that** I borrow his*

[BrE, F, Teen, WC]

Example (1) is from data collected in Milton Keynes where a lot of *things*-variants are recorded among middle-class speakers, but no examples of *and things* are used by working-class speakers. In contrast, looking at (2) from the town of Reading, Cheshire reports that "*and (all) that lot* was almost entirely confined to working class interviewees" (2007: 164), as is the very common phrase *and that*. As Cheshire (2007: 164), notes, "there was a robust social-class distinction" in the choice of certain phrases, with *and that* established among working-class speakers, while middle-class speakers used *and things* and *and stuff* more frequently. Although not focused on the analysis of social-class differences, both Pichler and Levey (2011) and Tagliamonte (2016), investigating working-class speech in smaller towns in northern England, northern Ireland and southern Scotland, reported on the dominance of *and that* among those speakers. Given the limited amount of research on this topic, we can tentatively suggest that the expressions included in Table 7.3 are good indicators that those who use them in British English are likely to be identified as belonging to one social class or the other.

There have been relatively few studies of general extenders in terms of social-class differences outside of the British Isles, but some of those studies have resulted in observations worth recording. Based on their New Zealand study, Stubbe and Holmes (1995) noted that, in their younger population, "working class male speakers and middle class female speakers produced the highest frequencies" of general extenders (1995: 76). Few details are given of the different forms used, though one phenomenon seemed worthy of report.

Table 7.3 *English general extenders associated with different social classes*

Working class	Middle class
and that	and stuff
and all that (lot)	and things
or summat	or something

In the interview sessions (not conversation), middle-class speakers produced a lot of what Stubbe and Holmes (1995: 79) called "prestige variants" *and so on* and *or so*, indicating that those middle-class participants seem to have treated the interviews as formal events. In an earlier study of New Zealand English, Britain (1992), cited in Stubbe and Holmes (1995: 65), reported higher frequencies among working-class speakers, especially females, matching the findings of Brotherton (1976) and Dines (1980) in their studies of Australian English. At some point in the future we trust that some of these discrepancies in token counts of general extenders across varieties will be reconciled and a clearer picture of social-class differentiation in spoken language use will emerge.

Before leaving this topic, we should note that studies of general extenders in North American English have not investigated social class as a variable at all. However, an early study of North American French pointed to some major differences. Dubois (1992) found a clear difference in the general extender-type expressions used most frequently by working-class speakers compared to speakers identified as "professional/managerial" class. Dubois (1992: 190) described two ways to represent the English phrase *(and) things like that* in Montreal French with the distinct components *choses, affaires* ("things") and *comme ça, de même* ("like that"). Middle-class speakers preferred the noun *chose*, while working-class speakers used *affaire*. Choice of modifier also differed by class, with *comme ça* associated with middle class and *de même* with working class (1992: 189). While the middle class said *choses comme ça* most often, working-class speakers used both the expressions *affaires de même* and *choses de même* over five times more frequently than the professional-class speakers. Clearly *de même* is a social marker in this variety when it functions as the modifier element inside the long general extender construction. In English, as we have illustrated, social marking is more likely to arise from the choice of the proform (noun or pronoun), not from the choice of the modifier. This aspect of general extender structure is not only a distinguishing feature between the two languages French and English, but also between the two varieties of Montreal French and Parisian French, as described in more detail in Chapter 8. Other common phrases in this variety are *toute l'affaire* and *tout le kit* (both translated as "and everything"), *ainsi de suite* ("and so on") and *patati patata* (similar to "blah, blah, blah"). For Montreal French, based on Dubois (1992), we list some of the relevant forms in Table 7.4 and would encourage further studies of these novel differences.

We will return to the investigation of general extenders in French, among other languages, in Chapter 8. Within each society, there is an additional source of variation in language use that is typically associated with different educational and employment environments, generally described in terms of variation in register.

Table 7.4 *Montreal French general extenders associated with social class*

Working class	Middle class
(des) affaires de même	*choses comme ça*
(puis) toute l'affaire	*(et puis) ces choses-là*
(puis) tout le kit	*et cetera*
patati patata	*ainsi de suite*

7.4 Register

Although we are familiar with the idea that different professions have their specialized uses of language, there has been relatively little research into the choice and distribution of general extenders in those domains. The work that has been done in this area has mostly been undertaken by British researchers in the study of register, defined by Matthews (2007: 321) as follows:

a set of features of speech or writing characteristic of a particular type of linguistic activity or a particular group when engaging in it.

There are potentially dozens of different activities and groups that can be characterized through specialized linguistic usage, notably in terms of specific lexical items, the professional jargon. General extenders have not been previously analyzed as examples of jargon, though there are some forms that are strongly associated with certain domains of language use. There is also the occasional expression that can be identified as a special feature in the talk of a relatively small and localized community of practice.

One of the broadest distinctions is between written (mainly printed) discourse and spoken (mainly face-to-face) discourse, as noted by Biber *et al.* (1999: 116), who list the most frequent forms in the written mode as *et cetera, and so on* and *or so*, and in the spoken mode as *or something, and everything* and *and things (like that)*. Modeled mostly on the written language, and often partially scripted in it, formal spoken language also tends to feature *et cetera* and *and so on* as the most frequent general extenders (Overstreet, 1999: 7). These are the only two phrases consistently used to indicate that more could be said, typically at the end of lists, in data from debates in the parliament of the European Union, a situation fostering use of a formal spoken register (Cucchi, 2007). Having focused on aspects of informal spoken language variation in the earlier parts of this chapter, we will pay more attention in this section to features of formal spoken language in two registers that have been studied most: in the academic world and the business world. We should note that the frequency of general extender occurrence in data from the study of business discourse is reported to be half of what is found in social conversation and even less in academic discourse than in business (McCarthy, 2020: 207).[1]

7.4.1 The Academic Register

Although the high-frequency forms in Biber *et al.* (1999) were derived from written academic discourse, they are essentially the same as those reported for spoken academic discourse. O'Keeffe (2006) also noted that expressions most common in political interviews were very similar to those in academic discourse. Walsh *et al.* (2008) reported that, in the LIBEL corpus (*Limerick-Belfast Corpus of Academic Spoken English*), 60 percent of general extender use featured *and so on* (48%) and *et cetera* (12%). They also noted very frequent reduplications, as in *et cetera et cetera* or *and so on and so forth*, making those doublets a very distinctive feature of the academic register. Taking the Walsh *et al.* (2008) study as their starting point, Kozman and Swales (2008) looked at general extenders in LIBEL and MICASE (*Michigan Corpus of Academic Spoken English*). Although not as frequent as in the Irish data, *and so on (and so forth)* was the most frequent adjunctive form, though closely followed by *and stuff (like that)*, which initially seems out of place until the data is examined more closely. The MICASE corpus contains spoken data from both professors and students, which Kozman and Swales (2008) later analyzed separately. The difference between the general extenders used by each group was very marked. The ratio of tokens of *and so on (and so forth)* for faculty/students was 249/8, a huge difference, and the ratio of tokens of *and stuff (like that)* was 30/276, another huge difference, in the opposite direction, helping to explain how these two very different forms came to be most frequent in the data overall. This finding matches what Simpson had reported from an earlier study of MICASE data: "the most frequent differentiating expression for professors is the phrase *and so on*" (2004: 47), rarely used by the students. Those students may have been participating in the academic world, but they weren't using the academic register, at least as far as adjunctive extenders were concerned. This type of difference may also emerge from the study of intra-register variation, where situational factors can have a stronger effect than individual social characteristics (cf. Poos and Simpson, 2002; Schleef, 2008; Barbieri, 2012). McCarthy (2020: 211) provides a typical example of the most frequent expression being used in the academic register, as in (3). Examples of the two other frequent forms are in (4), from Bamford (2004: 117), and (5), from Mauranen (2004: 185), both reports of studies of academic lectures.

(3) *Before we go on to the third lecture where we talk about the liver and the pancreas **and so on** . . .*

[BrE, M, Adult, MC]

7.4 Register

(4) *We're not really interested in these but we have to put them in into the regression just to take out the fact of education capital **et cetera***

[BrE, M, Adult, MC]

(5) *V-perpendicular T is on the order of ten to the minus two **or so***

[BrE, M, Adult, MC]

What Biber *et al.* (2004) call "lexical bundles" (multiword phrases) are particularly prominent in the academic register. Long general extenders are among the most frequent four- to six-word lexical bundles recorded. Even when attempting to introduce exemplification from everyday, non-technical situations, lecturers may still end them with formal adjunctive expressions, as in (6), from CANCAD (*Cambridge and Nottingham Corpus of Academic Discourse*), cited in Evison *et al.* (2007: 151).

(6) *the fact that er a woman is assumed to have a smaller car than a man **and so on and so forth***

[BrE, Adult, MC]

The implication in this long (six-word) expression is iconically that there is much more that could be said on the topic or, as Kozman and Swales put it, such forms "are more confident sounding, in the sense that they give the impression that the speaker could easily further exemplify if needed" (2008: 4). Not all long forms signal continuation, as in (6), but can signal reference to a category, especially if incorporating the classifying terms *kind/sort/type of*, as in (7), from McCarthy (2020: 210), where a supervisor is advising a research student. Note once again that a five-word bundle (*and that sort of thing*) is being used, not the kind of casual two-word adjunctive extender more typical of informal language use.

(7) *Have you done anything on the intentional fallacy and the affective fallacy **and that sort of thing**?*

[BrE, Adult, MC]

One interesting feature of the academic register is the extent to which it can infiltrate the everyday conversational speech of some professional academics, as illustrated in (8), from the speech of a professor talking about her husband, from Nikolaou and Sclafani (2018: 247).

(8) *One was the war itself that <u>you know</u> he couldn't return right away (.) um to see his parents **and so forth** because of his um <u>you know</u> because of his party affiliations **and so forth***

[BrE, F, Adult, MC]

The formal-sounding *and so forth* is used twice here in double brackets with the very informal *you know*, which would seem to fit the conversational context more appropriately, suggesting that the speaker is indeed taking part in the informal interaction, but unable to let go of the favored adjunctive extender expression. Example (8) provides another small piece of evidence that register variation is not strictly defined by the physical situation (i.e. the academic world), but is in the discourse of members of a community of practice (i.e. professional academics), even when they are not speaking in their professional role.

One of the outcomes of these studies of speakers using the academic register is the opportunity to identify clear markers of that register and, when faced with the results from another corpus study, to check if it is characterized by those markers. We feel that, with the benefit of hindsight, the much-cited *London-Lund Corpus* (LLC; Svartvik and Quirk, 1980) now looks as if it involved some of those speakers. As listed in Aijmer (2002: 221), there is a very high token count in that corpus for *and so on* and a surprisingly high count for *and all the rest of it*. These two adjunctive forms represent one established formal expression and one long six-word bundle of a type that has low frequency otherwise. There are also a number of the reduplicated forms identified earlier, cementing the impression that the participants in this corpus included a number of individuals who were used to speaking in the academic register.

7.4.2 The Business Register

The business register provides some notable contrasts with the academic register. According to token counts provided by Malyuga and McCarthy (2018: 44), the expression *and so on* is not frequent at all (in tenth place in the frequency list) and *or so* is even less frequent in business meetings. However, that other frequent form in academic discourse, *et cetera*, is among the most frequent in the business data. We should be clear that we are talking about frequency in a British corpus known as CANBEC (*Cambridge and Nottingham Business English Corpus*), which is the source of most of the examples in this section and described in detail in Handford (2010). In this corpus, the two most frequent forms are *or something (like that)* and *or whatever*, both disjunctive. Malyuga and McCarthy (2018) focus on the high frequency of *or whatever*, which seems to be used without the "I don't care" element we identified in conversational uses earlier in Chapter 4. Referring to example (9), from a sales negotiation event, Malyuga and McCarthy propose that the disjunctive form "opens a wider door to conceptualization, speculation and different courses of action" (2018: 46). In a similar vein, Handford notes that (10) is uttered by a sales person in his first visit to a company, trying to signal shared understanding (*you know*) of what normally happens.

7.4 Register

(9) *and obviously you can tell us then how many you can produce a day **or whatever** to give us an idea*

[BrE, M, Adult, MC]

(10) *if somebody doesn't want props **or whatever** you know you're not gonna get anything back from it*

[BrE, M, Adult, MC]

Based on examples like (9) and (10), we can say that the general function of *or whatever* in sales negotiations is not dismissive of other options, but rather seems to be involved in the positive creation of options.

We might say the same for another unusually frequent expression, *and everything else*, in the business data, illustrated in (11), from Malyuga and McCarthy (2018: 45). (We will review the use of *and everything else* and related expressions in more detail in Chapter 10.)

(11) *all I'm saying is that you need to be away from here in reasonable time allowing for – allowing for traffic **and everything else***

[BrE, M, Adult, MC]

In order to account for some of these uses, where speakers seem to be acting as if they have things in common (though not necessarily the case), Handford (2010) provides an insightful explanation of the difference between "external" meetings, involving discussions with others outside a company, and "internal" meetings, involving peers/colleagues of similar status within a company. It is during external meetings that *and everything else* is more common, along with *et cetera*, and "can be used tactically by company representatives to create a positive, convergent impression" (2010: 179). In sales negotiations with representatives in other companies, Handford sees the use of certain general extenders as an attempt to send a signal along the lines of: "I know your business, we are very familiar, you can trust me" (2010: 164).

While some general extenders are more frequent in the external meetings and used to try to create a closer relationship, other expressions are used within the internal meetings as a reflection of the existence of assumed shared knowledge and experience. One example is *and (all) that sort of thing*, as shown in (12), from McCarthy (2020: 207), which is more likely to occur in meetings involving peers inside the company, and used in a way similar to its function in (7) earlier to connect supervisor and student in their academic meeting.

(12) *Any teams which have ongoing product lines like toothpaste **and all that that sort of thing**, they will work on the new way*

[BrE, M, Adult, MC]

McCarthy (2020: 207–8) points out that this speaker is signaling that there is no need to elaborate the list of product lines already known by others in the "in-group" taking part in the internal meeting.

One expression that is unusually prominent in the internal meetings is one of the longest general extenders in English: *and this, that and the other*. Given its unusual length as a single phrase, this multiword string would be expected to signal iconically that there is not only "more," but "a lot more" that could be said. This is confirmed by an earlier example from the *OED Online*, as in (13) from 1863, as well as (14), from some time in the 1990s, cited in McCarthy and Carter (2002).

(13)   *Odds and ends, and omnium gatherums,* **and this, that and the other**, *enough to fill nine museums*

[BrE, Adult]

(14)   *She said, "We've come out to furnish it and buy the furniture* **and this, that and the other***."*

[BrE, Adult]

Example (13) makes it clear that there is a very large number of additional items being referenced (*to fill nine museums*!). In the context of example (14), the speaker has just bought an apartment and is signaling that a lot of items will be needed to furnish it. One of the implications of this general extender seems to be that there will be miscellaneous additional exemplars, which are occasionally added after the general extender, as in (15), from Malyuga and McCarthy (2018: 45).

(15)   *They're forever having dinners and dances* **and this, that and the other** *and Halloween parties and you know get to meet your favorite footballers*

[BrE, M, Adult, MC]

As Evison *et al*. (2007) observe, this adjunctive extender is completely absent from their corpus of academic discourse, is occasionally found in their conversational data, but is recorded as three times more frequent in the corpus of business English, as described in Handford, who notes that "this cluster appears to be more frequent in business English than in everyday conversation" (2010: 165–66). However, it is not found in all business meetings and seems to be used in a very restricted set of contexts within the business world. Its frequency is greatest in very specific types of meetings. In Handford's analysis, the expression "is used solely by men from Great Britain" and he concludes that "*and this, that and the other* tends to be used by a small number of clearly defined communities of practice ... usually in internal meetings between British males, and mainly from the sales and marketing departments of certain manufacturing companies" (2010: 166). This is a remarkably limited context, yet one that fits in with Handford's (2010: 165) explanation that the expression reflects detailed in-group shared knowledge among the participants. Clearly it is also a social marker for its users.

Up to now we have looked at variation in general extender use in terms of different micro-sociolinguistic constructs, focusing on the linguistic output of individuals as representative of their age, gender, social class and, to a lesser extent, professional life. In the following sections, we will adopt more of a macro-sociolinguistic perspective and focus on the linguistic similarities and differences in varieties of a language such as English in different countries.

7.5 International Variation

The study of general extenders in different varieties of a language has been described as part of "variational pragmatics" (Aijmer, 2013: 131), which seeks to account for linguistic features used with pragmatic functions that may be "variety specific" (Barron and Schneider, 2009: 429). Most of this research in English has been undertaken in the major varieties, which we describe in the following sections. Some studies of other varieties have also provided insights into special preferences in the use of general extenders. Aijmer (2013) notes that, among speakers of Singaporean English, long forms of general extenders dominate, though the most frequent phrase is *and all that*, an "ethnic marker which is closely associated with Singaporean identity" (2013: 143). This is exemplified in (16) from Aijmer (2013: 141), who notes that local varieties will inevitably have local references establishing common ground that may be opaque to non-speakers of that variety, as exemplified in (16) and (17).

(16) *Ge Lan was uhm a star you know during the time when there was Ling Chui **and all that***

[SingE]

(17) *[a] phrase from Cantonese opera **or something** I don't remember really*

[HKE]

In a study using the *Hong Kong Corpus of Spoken English* (Cheng et al., 2005), the effect of educational background was cited as a possible reason for different general extender choices. While Warren (2007: 187) focused on the analysis of aspects of the intonation of *or something* in the corpus, exemplified in (17), Cheng (2007: 176) actually reported finding fewer examples of the disjunctive form *or something* in Hong Kong English than in descriptions of other varieties, attributing the difference to the fact that the speakers who were recorded "are more formal in their language use" and the role of "formal school teaching

Table 7.5 *General extenders in international varieties of English*

USA	UK	Canada	Australia	New Zealand
or something	*and that*	*and stuff*	*or something*	*and stuff*
and stuff	*and stuff*	*or something*	*and stuff*	*or something*
and everything	*or something*	*or whatever*	*and that*	*or whatever*

which does not cover patterns such as these" (2007: 176–77), referring to general extenders. Bearing this type of cautionary note in mind, we will investigate variation in general extender use among different Englishes, benefiting from Aijmer's (2013) earlier comprehensive survey of a group of international varieties.

Although there is substantial variation in the expressions used as general extenders within every corpus analyzed, there is a general uniformity in the phrases used most frequently (cf. Aijmer, 2013, Ch. 4). The top two expressions are *or something* and *and stuff* in data from the USA, Canada, Australia and New Zealand. In Britain, *and that* is the most frequent, followed by the two other popular phrases just mentioned. The three most frequent forms for each country are displayed in Table 7.5.[2]

7.6 America, Britain and Canada

Our results for the USA are based on Overstreet and Yule (1997b) and the *Santa Barbara Corpus of Spoken American English* (Du Bois et al., 2000–2005), referenced in Aijmer (2013) as representative of American English. Both data sets were collected during the 1990s. Similar results can be found in the *Fisher Corpus* (Cieri et al., 2004–2005), compiled from phone conversations in the early 2000s, and referenced in Wagner et al. (2015). However, a different corpus collected in Philadelphia in 2005 and reported in Wagner et al. (2016: 213, 222) has different phrases as most frequent: *and everything*, as in (18), followed by *and things like that*.

(18)   *but like with my grandmom **and everything** I would speak all Chinese*

[AmE, F, Teen, MC]

It is very unusual in informal spoken interaction to find a long-form general extender (*and things like that*) among the most frequent phrases used, which leads to a suspicion that there was something special in the way this data was collected. The very high frequency of *and everything* suggests that the speakers (teenage females) may have been talking about special or extreme events and ideas. Another corpus with *and everything* as the most frequent form is

7.6 America, Britain and Canada

described in Levey (2012), involving adolescent speakers (7–11-year-olds) in London. One clue to the high frequencies of the top two phrases (*and everything, and all that*) is possibly to be found in the elicitation procedure in which "the children were encouraged to share narratives of personal experience centered on topics of high emotional involvement such as arguments, fights, accidents and personal mishaps" (Levey, 2012: 266). It may simply be that topics of high emotional involvement give rise to high numbers of tokens of *and everything*, regardless of whether the young speakers are in London or Philadelphia.

Levey's (2012) London data has *and that* as the third most frequent form. As shown in Table 7.5, based on data (from British teenagers) reported in Cheshire (2007) and Secova (2017), *and that* is the most frequent form overall, followed by *and stuff* and *or something*. The two studies, looking at data from different places in England, are published ten years apart, yet they report similar forms as high-frequency general extenders. The frequencies in Secova's (2017) London data are influenced by the impact of substantially more general extenders overall in the speech of young people.

(19)   *there's a wide range of what you can actually do in terms of like we're studying with- group of foundation like (.) students **and stuff like that** and whereas we're on a-level standards like we're just wanna work **and stuff** and actually do something with our lives they're just about playing games and (.) fighting each other **and stuff like that***

[BrE, F, Teen, MC]

As illustrated in (19), from Secova (2017: 3), those young people can have well-articulated opinions and they use *and stuff (like that)* a lot, whereas older speakers (60+ years old) produced none. Older speakers used *or anything, and things* and *and all the rest of it* a lot more often than younger speakers. It is difficult to make generalizations about frequency in a variety without taking account of differences in social influences among speakers of that variety, as we have illustrated earlier. A similar point can be made about Cheshire's study. Cheshire (2007) reports a strong preference for *and that* in the north of England (Hull), similar to the results from another northern town (Berwick-upon-Tweed) reported by Pichler and Levey (2011), where *and that* was over three times more frequent than the next phrase used as a general extender. Among other small northern British towns in Tagliamonte's (2016) study of archival data (older speakers), the most frequent form was also *and that*, exemplified in (20) from Tagliamonte (2016: 123).

(20)   *Pickering chemist, he was a big friend of Josh **and that***

[BrE, M, Adult, WC]

As Cheshire observes, "*and that* has been firmly entrenched in working class speech for at least three generations" (2007: 165).

In contrast, in towns in the south of England (especially Reading) in Cheshire's (2007) study, the most frequent form by far was *or something*, used over three times more often than in the northern data. Which general extender should we treat as most typical of British English? The answer is both, one adjunctive and one disjunctive. Perhaps it will be neither of those in the near future as *and stuff* continues to increase in frequency in both the south and north, mainly at the expense of *and things*, which has become one of the least frequent adjunctive forms. As we noted already, this change is interpreted in terms of "lexical replacement" by Tagliamonte and Denis (2010) in their study of the Canadian English of Toronto where *and stuff* is recorded as the most frequent form (over *or something* and *or whatever*) and *and stuff like that* is by far the most common long form. The phrase *and things* is being replaced and is way down the list in terms of frequency. In an interesting verification of those earlier findings, Wagner et al. (2015) looked at a small subset of the Toronto data (nine younger female speakers out of an original total of eighty-seven speakers), and found them using the same three most frequent forms in the same order as Tagliamonte and Denis (2010) reported.

7.7 Australia and New Zealand

When we look at the Australian English data from Winter and Norrby (2000) and Norrby and Winter (2002), involving 15–16-year-olds, collected in the mid 1990s, we find the same first two phrases ordered as in the USA data from the same time period, but the more distinctly British *and that* in use as well. However, there is a noticeable difference in forms used by males and females. There is a marked preference for *and stuff* among females and for *and that* among males, by about two-thirds in each case. In examples (21) and (22), from Norrby and Winter (2002: 1, 6), the two young females may have different opinions about what they like, but they signal their appeal to shared understanding with the same adjunctive extender, repeated in both.

(21) *I go out with my friends **and stuff** ... just I'm not into ... big club things **and stuff***

[AusE, F, Teen, MC]

(22) *I like t- I like dancing **and stuff** ... I like partying ... dance parties **and stuff***

[AusE, F, Teen, MC]

The high frequency of *and stuff* in Australian examples from the 1990s is in marked contrast to the minimal use (only two examples) recorded in Dines'

(1980) study of Australian data from about twenty years earlier. The preference for *and that*, especially among young male speakers, matches Dines' (1980) earlier data and maintains its association with what Norrby and Winter describe as "Australia masculine reticent heroes" (2002: 7).

In Dines (1980: 20), *and things like that* is the most frequent form recorded. This long form is used six times more often than the short form *and things*, suggesting that the talk that was recorded may have occurred in a more formal context than the later data. Dines' (1980) second most frequent form is *or something*, a phrase that rises to most frequent overall in Winter and Norrby's (2000) token count.

In New Zealand English, as reported in Terraschke (2007a), the three most frequent forms and their ordering matched the Canadian data overall, with *and stuff* and *or something* being used with almost equal frequency and substantially more often than any other forms. When Aijmer (2013) reports on the New Zealand data in the *International Corpus of English* (ICE) (Greenbaum, 1996), she includes *and that* as the second most frequent form between *and stuff* and *or something*, yet it has very low frequency (only three tokens) in Terraschke's (2007a) report. Based on earlier observations, we know that *and that* is generally a feature of working-class speech, especially among males, in places with historical connections to British English. This group may have been among those recorded in the ICE data but not in Terraschke's (2007a) study involving (likely middle-class) university students. As we have already noted, it can be quite difficult to generalize about frequency in different varieties while remaining aware that there are likely to be differences within that variety based on social factors.

7.8 Ireland and Scotland

Among the many recent studies of pragmatic aspects of Irish English (e.g. Amador-Moreno *et al.*, 2015), there have been several investigating general extenders (usually identified as "vague category markers" by these researchers). O'Keeffe's (2004) study of vague expressions recorded from *Liveline*, an Irish radio phone-in show, revealed a general preference for longer forms (*X like that, all that kind of thing*). This would be consistent with the perception by the participants of a more formal context (public broadcasting) than casual face-to-face interaction. Other aspects of the data that support this analysis are the lower frequencies of *or something*, *and stuff* (only 3 tokens) and *and everything* (1 token), all of which occur less often than *and so on*. A similar pattern is reported in Evison *et al.* (2007) in their discussion of the *Liveline* data. In a comparison of British and Irish data, Vaughan *et al.* (2017) note that every type of general extender is more frequent in the British data. They make the very interesting point that "due to the higher use of other, more traditional, pragmatic markers such as *like* and *now* in Irish English, Irish intimates tend to perform indirectness and imprecision in a different way" (2017: 220). They also propose that "the Irish pragmatic system may not use vague category markers interpersonally to the same extent as in British English" (2017: 214). Investigating this large claim is beyond the scope of our present study, but, as a hypothesis, it provides an impetus to further research in this area.

Perhaps more revealing with regard to informal Irish English are the results of an investigation by Murphy (2010), who used a corpus of casual conversations in southern Ireland (Limerick and Cork) featuring both males and females in three different age groups (20s, 40s and 70–80s). Unfortunately, the forms *or something* and *or something like that* were counted together, so no distinction in their uses could be investigated. The combined forms, as in *or something (like that)*, had the highest token count in the youngest group and were among the most frequent forms at every age. The other disjunctive forms (*or anything, or whatever*) were prominent throughout the data in female speech. Males produced a lot more tokens of *and all (that)*, not used at all by younger females, who preferred *and everything* at all ages. In keeping with patterns already noted in other Englishes, *and stuff (like that)* was only recorded among speakers in their twenties and *and things (like that)* was only recorded by those in the oldest group. When we try to match Murphy's (2010) frequency count in her Irish data with any of the sets listed in Table 7.5 (removing *and stuff* from the comparison), we find that her two most frequent forms *or something (like that)* and *and everything* are only found in the top three in American English. The very low token count of *and that* marks this variety as quite distinct from other varieties in England. Generally speaking, Irish English uses the same types of general extenders as the other varieties we've studied (but with different frequencies). There is, however, an occasional example (of a specific extender) that does have an Irish feel to it, as in (23) from O'Keeffe (2004: 9).

(23)   the ozone layer ***or some other one of these quare things up there in the sky***

[IrE, M, Adult]

We know that the use of general extenders in Scottish English was well established in the eighteenth century, as shown in (24), from the Robert Burns poem *A man's a man for a' that* (1795/1859), a well-known call for a more egalitarian society. The phonetic reduction of *all* remains a feature of the contemporary language, as illustrated in (25), just one of many examples in the work of Irvine Welsh (1994: 99–100). In the same source, there is a distinctive Scottish version, as in (26), of the negative polarity disjunctive form, typically *or anything like that* in other varieties, which has an emphatic sense indicating "hard to believe," as described earlier in Chapter 4. In this case, it incorporates a double negative.

(24) *What though on hamely fare we dine. Wear hoddin' grey,* ***an' a' that***

[ScotE, M, Adult, WC]

(25) *Naebody could run like John Deaf. Eh wis really strong* ***n aw***

[ScotE, M, Adult, WC]

(26) *John Deaf's hoose had fuck all in it; nae furniture* ***or nowt like that***

[ScotE, M, Adult, WC]

In an early quantified account of general extenders used by one speaker of Scottish English, Macaulay (1985: 112) found an overwhelming preference for *and that*, a finding that matches other studies of working-class speech, especially in northern England (e.g. Cheshire, 2007; Pichler and Levey, 2011). In Pichler and Levey's (2011: 469) study, *and that* accounted for more than half of the adjunctive forms recorded. They also reported uses of *or nowt like that* and *or owt like that* in their data from Berwick-upon-Tweed, a small English town that hasn't always been on the other side of the Scottish border. In (27) and (28) are examples of the "dialectal variants" *or owt like that* and *or summat*, identified by Tagliamonte (2016: 121) in her archival data from Maryport, another small English town near the border with Scotland. The overall structure of (28) is also dialectal and not common in other varieties.

(27) *she's a black belt and first dan* ***or summat***

[ScotE, M, Adult, WC]

(28) *cos he's not a fellow to mix with other men* ***or owt like that*** *or do anything* ***or owt***, *isn't Bob*

[ScotE, M, Adult, WC]

It may be that these variants, already low in frequency, will only remain in records of "conservative dialects" (Tagliamonte, 2016: 137) and that the incursion of new forms such as *and stuff* will take over, leading to a rapid loss of variation, as Denis (2017) documented in Toronto. Is this happening everywhere that *and stuff* goes? That is a research question that can only be answered through research on more current data.

7.9 What Is the Relevant Data?

As we prepare to undertake further studies to elicit more current data on social variation, it would help to have some agreement on what the relevant data-elicitation procedures should be or at least become much more cognizant of the fact that differences we encounter may be a by-product of how we collected a particular data set. One of the most obvious problems we have faced in the wide-ranging nature of previous research has been the basic non-compatibility of elicited data for any serious attempt at comparison, as Macaulay (2002) has pointed out with regard to data in a lot of discourse studies. In many cases, research has been undertaken using data sets that were collected for quite different purposes, such as the investigation of dialectal features among working-class speakers in northern England (Pichler and Levey, 2011), or the study of broadcast talk in a corpus from an Irish radio phone-in program, with a focus on different local topics, customs and cultural references (O'Keeffe, 2004). The discrepancy between resulting data sets can be revealed when spoken language collected in different periods is compared, as in Aijmer's (2002: 233) presentation of the large differences in frequency between English general extenders in the *London-Lund Corpus*, collected in the 1960–1970s, and the *Bergen Corpus of London Teenage Language* (COLT), collected in 1993. We might think we could look into these two collections and come away with quantified data showing how the language changed in the period between the two data sets. However, these corpora also differ in other ways, such as the participants, with older academics featured prominently in the first and young teenagers in the other, so we are not just looking at differences through time.

Data-elicitation procedures also differ substantially from one study to the next. The collection of the COLT data (Stenström *et al.*, 2002) was quite unlike any other, with teenagers being given recorders and sent off to record their everyday talk (and ending up with the talk of parents and teachers too). In contrast, Overstreet (1999) based her study on interactions among familiars that she knew (family and friends informally recorded), intentionally trying to collect data from individuals whose worlds of reference she would have insight into. In yet another contrast, the sociolinguists (e.g. Cheshire, 2007; Levey, 2012) collected their data through formal interview protocols involving non-familiars, specifically adult researchers interviewing teenagers and adolescents, a participation framework that may have had an effect of creating social distance. Cheshire (2007) recognizes those circumstances as having a potentially restrictive effect on the nature of the data and draws attention to the "extreme context-dependency" (2007: 161) of general extenders, a point that Pichler (2010) makes more generally in that "the extreme context-sensitivity of discourse features hampers cross-corpora comparability and generalizability" (2010: 567).

We are not sure what the best way forward might be, but it may be time to develop a less cavalier approach to what might count as appropriate methodology, particularly in the study of the sensitive area of social variation, in order that we are basing our findings on elicited material that everyone recognizes as relevant data for the research purpose. Having explored variation in general extender use among English speakers, we will turn, in the next chapter, to the study of possible equivalents in other languages.

8   In Different Languages

Extending our investigation of variation in general extender use, we will try to identify forms in different languages that fulfill similar roles to those identified so far, even if the linguistic expressions are not always similar. One area where we might expect to find some connection to aspects of English general extender use is in those languages that adopted expressions from English as a superstrate lexifier language, that is, in English Creoles. As Fischer and Rosenbach (2000: 6) have pointed out, "the development of Creoles presents an ideal field for the study of grammaticalization," so we might expect to find novel expressions that have emerged from the processes we described in Chapter 6.

8.1   English Creoles

When we look at the forms of general extenders in English Creoles, we find very distinct patterns in phonology and morphology that are quite consistent across varieties, though the forms that undergo modification may differ. In some Caribbean varieties, the phrase *and things* loses its plural affix and the interdental fricative /θ/ becomes an alveolar stop /t/, typically transcribed as *an ting* in the Creoles of both Barbados (Hickey, 2004; Rickford and Handler, 1994) and Trinidad (Youssef, 1993: 291). The reduced form of the conjunction (*an*) is a common effect of coarticulation in all spoken English varieties and not special to Creoles (cf. Yule, 2020: 50). In Hawai'i Creole English, we find the same pronunciation shift, with the voiceless alveolar stop /t/ in place of the standard interdental /θ/ within the expressions *or someting* and *and everyting*, but no examples of *ting* by itself and none with *an ting*. In some transcriptions, such as the representation of *eriting* in (1) from Meyerhoff (2006: 169), a pair of syllables (*an ev*) may be missing compared to the standard representation, as shown in Meyerhoff's translation.

(1)   *Dis spri jamp intu dis wan gai, fal awntu da graun **eriting***
      ("This spirit had jumped into this one guy, he (= the guy) fell onto the ground and everything")

151

The observation that there may be different representations of spoken forms by different researchers suggests that the full forms encountered in some transcriptions may not always be an accurate representation of what was actually said in the recording, a common problem encountered in attempts to analyze informal spoken data, no matter which variety is being studied (cf. Brown, 1990). Bearing this caveat in mind, we will take a close look at how general extenders have been represented and analyzed in two varieties of English Creoles.

8.1.1 Trinidad Creole

As far as we know, the first study of general extender use in a Creole was presented in Youssef (1993). In her pioneering study of *an ting* in Trinidad Creole, Youssef (1993) was able to demonstrate an important function of the expression in AIDS counseling sessions, where it was used by both the medical personnel and their patients. Youssef points out that these are discourses full of normally taboo topics, but also of cooperative uses of language to "obviate embarrassment" (1993: 298). In extract (2), the counselor uses *an ting* as part of a process of "attempting to break down the power differential conferred by their professional situation" (Youssef, 1993: 291). In this example, the counselor is appealing to shared background, saying *you know* three times and inviting the patient to think of relevant contexts, with *an ting* functioning as essentially another way of saying *you know*, all in an attempt to establish rapport. In (3), the counselor presents the information as if already shared, with *you know* (twice) bracketing his turn. The use of *an ting* here doesn't involve the addition of any more information. Rather, it has the interpersonal function of "marking solidarity" (Youssef (1993: 291). Youssef emphasizes "*an ting*'s double representation of solidarity, first as a Creole marker and second as a discourse feature entailing implicit shared knowledge" (1993: 291).

(2) But in case you pick up somebody **an ting** and intend having a sexual relationship you know (.7) you know you try to have safe sexual practices, you know

(3) You know well (.1) the AIDS virus could only spread (.2) through sex **an ting**. It can't spread by just touching somebody, you know

From the patients' perspective, this sense of solidarity may be what allows them to express highly personal information, as in (4), where Youssef describes the use of *an ting* (twice) as one of the devices used by a patient to create "male-to-male solidarity which he needed to support the confidence-sharing which he had entered into" (1993: 302).

(4) One night I wake up **an ting** (.1) an after (.) I get some signs **an ting** (2). And I wanted to find out why. I went to take a test.

8.1 English Creoles

In discussing (4), Youssef (1993: 302) points out that the "generalizers" (i.e. general extenders) are not contributing any additional content to what the speaker is communicating and might seem "redundant" if not recognized for their interpersonal function. In support of this very early insightful discourse-pragmatic perspective, Youssef (1993) describes another related use of *ting* in Trinidad Creole, to mark shared understanding through repetition, as in (5).

(5)   She go down the road an she **ting**, **ting**, **ting**, and she come back up

In Youssef's analysis, what *she* typically did "would be known by both speaker and hearer" (1993: 292) and hence the triple use of *ting* is not only functioning interpersonally, it is an iconic representation, echoic of not only the content, but also of a known sequence. Youssef (1993) describes other uses of *ting*, but doesn't go into detail regarding other types or functions of general extenders in Trinidad Creole. When Overstreet (2012a) investigates the use of general extenders in another Creole, Hawai'i Creole English, there is an opportunity to build on Youssef's (1993) specific focus on the adjunctive *an ting* and extend the analysis to a large number of forms and structures fulfilling a number of different functions.

8.1.2   Hawai'i Creole English/Pidgin

In Hawai'i Creole English, locally known as Pidgin among its speakers, we can look at records of the contemporary language to find general extenders at work. Unless otherwise indicated, the following examples are from an unpublished research report (Overstreet, 2012a) that was based on two sets of recordings of informal interviews involving Pidgin speakers, one from the early 1970s and the other from around 1990, involving some of the same individuals in both, in a corpus known as the *Kaipuleohone Digital Ethnographic Archive* (Berez, 2013). Other descriptions of Pidgin can be found in Sato (1991), Siegel (2000, 2008), Sakoda and Siegel (2003), Higgins and Furukawa (2012) and Drager (2012).

Although there has to be an element of speculation in proposing the earlier superstrate forms given here, we present them as a way of illustrating the types of regular phonological changes that are likely to have been involved in the creation of the contemporary forms. Recalling the study of the prosody of the long forms of English general extenders by Romero-Trillo (2015), if the structure has the demonstrative (*like that*) at the end, it attracts tonic stress, the part that would be heard best by earlier speakers of Pidgin, resulting in its eventual representation as *li'dat*, as in (6). When the structure has the demonstrative (*that kind*) near the beginning, it tends to attract tonic stress there, resulting in its representation in *dakine* near the beginning of the general extender, as in (7).

As illustrated in (6), both the voiced and voiceless versions of the interdental fricatives in the earlier forms become alveolars in the Pidgin.

(6)   *or some<u>th</u>ing /θ/ like <u>th</u>at /ð/ → or some<u>t</u>ing /t/ li'<u>d</u>at /ɾ/*

Although typically transcribed with "d," the pronunciation of the middle consonant in *li'dat* is actually best represented as a voiced alveolar flap, sounding not at all like /d/, but more like /ɾ/, close to the "r" sound in Spanish *pe<u>r</u>o* ("but").

In the adjunctive form shown in (7), we have substantial reduction overall, losing a preposition, with a typical final consonant cluster reduction in *ki<u>nd</u>* → *ki<u>ne</u>* (cf. Hickey, 2004: 333), as well as the consonant shift from interdental /ð/ to stop /d/.

(7)   *and <u>th</u>at ki<u>nd</u> of stuff/thing → an' <u>d</u>a ki<u>ne</u> (stuff)*

It is important to note here that both *li'dat* and *dakine* (as one word), as well as simply *kine*, are ubiquitous in Pidgin (Sakoda and Siegel (2003): 49–51), having become pragmatic markers with frequency and distribution similar to *y'know* and *like* in current American English conversation, as in (8) from Tonouchi (2001: 31), a contemporary author writing in Pidgin.

(8)   *I could feel myself getting all hot. And wuzn't **da kine** good **kine** hot, but **da kine** nervous **kine** hot*

In extract (9), also from a story by Tonouchi (2001: 13), the use of both *li'dat* and *dakine* in the teenage narrator's (Pidgin) speech prompts a reaction from Laurie, the girl he is with (who "speaks very well" and, of course, not Pidgin).

(9)   Narrator: *So, uh, we go head back **li'dat** befo' da bell ring ah, you know **da kine***
        Laurie: *Why do you talk funny sometimes?*

In (9), the two forms highlighted (which could feasibly be replaced by more standard general extenders in a translation) appear to be functioning as markers of intersubjectivity, signaling "you know what I mean," though not necessarily being heard that way by Laurie at that time. As with many basilectal features in Creoles generally, these two uses represent aspects of talk associated with less educated individuals, in contrast to Laurie's standard English, a distinction that is exploited by the writer.

In some cases, the expression *li'dat* is used like an oral punctuation mark, as described in Chapter 5, and illustrated in (10).

(10)   *There's a small village right outside (.) da camp **li'dat**. It's off limits **li'dat** (.) you cannot go down **li'dat***

8.1 English Creoles

When used in adjunctive extender constructions, *dakine* is frequently accompanied by *all*, as in (11), where *make* means "dead." The modifier *all* is also used with *stuff*, as in (12).

(11) So all da Hawaiians, dey come out night time. All dakine, make kine, you know, dey come outside, dey si:::ng, dey beat drums, dey blow conch she::lls **an' all dakine**

(12) he:h, cut around da cabinet **an' all dakine stuff**. I said, no can. I said, no can.

It may simply be the effect of *all* as an intensifier, but these general extenders with *dakine* seem to have an emphatic function similar to the uses of *and everything* and *and all that* described in Chapter 4. However, the uniquely Pidgin forms have not completely replaced those two phrases in a more acrolectal version of the Pidgin, used together in (13) for extra emphasis by a very aggravated local fisherman.

(13) an den da windsurfers come, dey just take ova everyting, den dey was (.) you know crossing ova whea us guys go diving **an all dat, an everyting**

Other familiar general extenders, with minor pronunciation differences, are sometimes used by Pidgin speakers, such as *or whatever* in (14), talking about cock fighting, without post-vocalic /r/, a frequent omission, also absent from *da supahvisahs*. There are two versions of *or anyting/or anykine* in (15) and (16), both mentioning the least that would be expected, similar to uses described in Chapter 4. These forms have relatively low frequency in the data sets studied. As we have generally found elsewhere in the English-speaking world, versions of *or something*, as in (17) and (18), are often the most common forms and they are used with much greater frequency in the later data.

(14) da people dat own da pla::ce, the um (.) what dey call dat, da supahvisahs **or whatevah** (.) dey match da birds

(15) He no moa phone **or anyting** da guy?

(16) Pi::lau da boy. Get all shit all around da yard. He no even – he no even cover da dirt **or anykine**

(17) and da watah cross da (.) uh road (.) just like s- river **or somtin'**

(18) I guess dat when they was taping, had one (.) one lady came by **or someting** foa tell you about one meeting **or someting li'dat** you see

One of the biggest changes in recordings of Pidgin from the 1970s to 1990 is the high token counts of *an' stuff* and *an' stuff li'dat* in the later data set versus zero in the earlier set. Interestingly, it is the longer form that is more frequent, as in (19) and (20).

(19) he started to forget tings **an' stuff li'dat**

(20) *Uh what – all dakine stories dey talk about is uh Eh my – my sons, dey play baseball now (.) tomorrow dey gotta go:: you know **an' stuff li'dat***

In (20), there is a noticeable clustering of pragmatic markers (*you know an' stuff li'dat*) at the end of the speaker's turn, echoing the (possibly tiresome) length of the stories about other people's children that he's being subjected to.

Although the longer form is not attested in our 1970s data set, it is recorded in earlier data referenced, transcribed and translated in Bickerton (1977: 336), as in the example shown in (21), cited in Siegel (2008: 261). We're not sure why the translation wasn't "and stuff like that."

(21) *so a figa a go fiks am ap, aftawdz, yu no – teik am dina **aen staf laidaet***
("so I figured I'd fix him up afterwards, you know, take him to dinner and that kind of thing")

In the last two examples, the inclusion of *you know/yu no* would support the idea that the speaker is using the accompanying adjunctive extenders with intersubjective function. In their detailed description of the uses of *li'dat* and *dakine*, Sakoda and Siegel (2003: 49–51) point to the intersubjective function as typical. In their analysis, it is this function that is most characteristic of the everyday uses of Pidgin, as in the following generalization.

Basically, *dakain* (*da kine*) can be used whenever you know that the person you're talking to will know what you mean. Its use emphasizes a bond of shared experience between people, and in this way epitomizes Pidgin.

This observation would not have been out of place in a description of *an ting* in Youssef's (1993) analysis presented earlier. It would seem that general extenders have a much stronger interpersonal role in Creoles. Whether this is always the case is a topic for further research.

8.2 Translation Equivalents

When we turn to the study of general extenders in other languages, we face a number of problems in the area of translation equivalents. Unlike lexical items, general extenders are not typically included in dictionaries, so we can't just look up a translation. We also must keep in mind that there may actually be no genuine translation equivalents. For example, the informality of expressions such as *and stuff* and *or something* in contemporary spoken English interaction may not have genuine equivalents in languages with different interactive norms. For current purposes, our solution has been to rely (most of the time) on the intuitions of the researchers whose examples, with translations, we cite.

In some cases, the formal similarities could be a guide, as when we see German *oder so* as English *or so*. There are limitations to this because functional similarities don't inevitably follow. The phrase *or so* has many more restrictions on its use than *oder so*, as described in Chapter 1. Turning to functional similarities, we find the Japanese all-purpose general extender-type expression *toka* ("and or"), mostly translated as "or something" (Watanabe, 2015), but sometimes translated as both "and so on" and "or something," with no formal distinction (Lauwereyns, 2002: 244). Yet similarity of function is how we decide that the two formally different expressions *and stuff* and *and that* are two versions of the same type of adjunctive extender (and *and you* is not), so functional correspondence is already built into our thinking about these expressions. Throughout the following sections, we will try to use our understanding of function to talk about translation equivalents for general extenders as they have been identified in research into a number of languages. We won't be able to cover the myriad of investigations into particular aspects of general extenders in a variety of languages and can only refer the reader to studies of Arabic (Farghal and Haggan, 2005), Danish (Jensen and Christensen, 2015), Japanese (Sunagawa *et al.*, 1998: 320, 413; Watanabe, 2015), and Slovene (Grzybek and Verdonik, 2014; Verdonik, 2015). We will offer detailed descriptions of general extenders in German, French, Swedish and Persian, but before that, we will report on smaller-scale studies involving Brazilian Portuguese, Spanish, Lithuanian and Russian.

8.3 Brazilian Portuguese and Spanish

Based on an observational study, Roth-Gordon (2007) described the uses of some general extenders in the Brazilian Portuguese of Rio de Janeiro, with *e tal* in (22) and *e péréré párárá* in (23) as examples of adjunctive forms. We include the author's translations and explanations: in (22) *em cima* ("on top") refers to possessing illegal drugs. The adjunctive form in (23) makes a similar rhythmic contribution to the utterance as *(et) patati patata* in Montreal French (Dubois, 1992), a variety we will investigate in a later section.

(22) *Dá geral nesse malandro aí. Vê se ele tá com alguma parade em cima **e tal***
("Search this bum here. See if he doesn't have something on top and all")

(23) *E o caboclo lá tava falando comigo **e péréré párárá**. Pode deixar.*
("And this guy there was talking with me and yada yada yada. Don't worry about it.")

In another observational study, Overstreet (2007) noted a high frequency of reduplicated sound-based forms such as *(e) bábábá, e bal bal bal* and *e tal tal tal*, this last expression being the equivalent of "and that, that, that." These are used as adjunctive forms. Overstreet (2007) also recorded disjunctive forms, typically beginning with *ou algo* ("or something"), as in (24) and (25).

(24)   *Tem algum principe (solteiro) por ai **ou algo assim**?*
       ("Is there a prince (single guy) out there or something like that?")

(25)   *Realmente, não existe nos EUA da forma como existe no Brasil. Também poderia ser performance bonus **ou algo parecido**.*
       ("Really, it does not exist in the USA in the same form as it exists in Brazil. It could also be a performance bonus or something similar.")

Despite their different forms, these Portuguese expressions seem to be fulfilling functions similar to general extenders we have identified in English, a point made in an earlier, more general study of discourse markers (Silva and Macedo, 1992).

Earlier studies of general extenders in Spanish, focusing on *y todo eso* ("and all that"), *o cosas así* ("or things like that") and *y tal* ("and such"), were presented by Cortés (2006, 2008), and a more recent report, tied to language education, was provided by Fernandez (2015). Describing the Spanish of Madrid, based on the *Corpus Oral de Referencia del Español Contemporáneo*, Fernandez reported an overwhelming prevalence of adjunctive forms over disjunctives, by a ratio of about nine to one, and a preference for short versions such as *y eso* ("and that") rather than long versions such as *y de todas estas series de cosas* ("and of all these series of things"). These are all adjunctive forms, with high-frequency examples illustrated in (26) and (27). Although *y tal* in (26) is translated by Fernandez in her Table 6 as "and such," not really a common contemporary English L1 form, it might be better rendered as "and that" or "and stuff."

(26)   *Bueno, pues, así, entra **y tal***
       ("So then, like that, he comes in and such")

(27)   *¿Ya no tiene mareos **y esas cosas**?*
       ¿Está major o peor?
       *¿De los mareos **y eso**?*
       ("She no longer has dizzy spells and those things?
       Is she better or worse?
       From the dizziness and that?")

A distinctive feature of Spanish, noted by both Cortés (2006) and Fernandez (2015), the source of (28), is a negative adjunctive form, beginning with *ni*, that is used to cancel the possibility of including other elements in a list. We can note that the negative general extender here is a right-hand bracket with *no sé* as a left-hand bracket in a construction that is familiar in English, as described in Chapter 5.

(28)   *lampiñas, no sé, o sea sin vello **ni nada de eso***
       ("hairless, I don't know, that is without hair, not anything like that")

Although much rarer, disjunctive forms such as *o algo* ("or something") and *o algo así* ("or something like that"), as shown in (29), are documented by Fernandez (2015) in her Table 7.

(29)   *Es que quería ... hacer encuestas **o algo así** a niños pequeños*
       ("It's just that I wanted to ... do surveys or something like that with small kids")

As we have pointed out with regard to their counterparts in English, Spanish general extenders, though singular, can attach to plural noun phrases and do not have to be utterance-final, as illustrated in (29).

Fernandez notes that these features of Peninsular Spanish are not necessarily the same as in South American varieties of Spanish, with *y tal* apparently used much less frequently among teenagers in Buenos Aires, Argentina. This would seem to be a fertile area for further research.

8.4   Lithuanian and Russian

In a study based on the *Corpus of Contemporary Lithuanian*, Ruzaitė (2010) identified a number of phrases that function like general extenders, noting that adjunctive forms vastly outnumber disjunctives. The most frequent form was *ir kiti* ("and other(s)"), followed by *ir panašiai* ("and the like"), sometimes reduced to *ir pan*, and *ir taip toliau* ("and so on"). This last form is often abbreviated in speech to *ir t. t.* in a way that is not found in English (i.e. we don't say "and s.n.," though we do write "etc."). Judging from the English equivalents listed by Ruzaitė (2010), the Lithuanian corpus seems to have mostly formal language, or alternatively, it may be that Lithuanians typically use general extenders in ways that sound formal to English speakers, though Ruzaitė (2018) describes some of the discourse variation that can be found in Lithuanian. Ruzaitė's (2010) study was less concerned with simply describing aspects of general extender usage and more focused on how translation between the two languages often results in the omission of general extenders, not because equivalents don't exist, but "due to the underestimation of the importance of vague language categories" (2010: 36).

Using the Business and Professional Spoken Language section of the *Russian National Corpus*, Malyuga and McCarthy (2018) analyzed the frequency of Russian general extenders ("vague category markers" in their analysis) compared to those found in a British corpus of business English. The two most frequent English forms were both disjunctive forms (*or something (like that)* and *or whatever*), yet the two most frequent Russian forms were adjunctive, exemplified in (30) and (31).

(30)   *U nikh v ofisakh, karty byli, instruktsii, kak upravliat' samoletom **i vse takoe***
       ("They had maps in their offices, and instructions on how to fly a plane, and everything")

(31) *Deistvitel'no, tam khimicheskie veshchestva i radioaktivnye veshchestva raspylili, izmerili, **i vse takoe procheye***
("Indeed, there were these chemical substances and radioactive substances that were diffused, measured, and all that sort of thing")

The authors translate these two general extenders as "and stuff" and "and stuff like that" (2018: 48), yet, given the formal nature of the business context, they might sound too informal. These "stuff" forms were low on the list of general extenders in the comparable corpus of business English used by the authors. We decided to use "and everything" and "and all that sort of thing," based on the observations that both of the Russian expressions contain the quantifier *vse* ("all"). In contemporary Russian, as shown in (30), the adjunctive form can be combined with plural noun phrases and, in (31), with verb phrases. In both these examples, the general extenders complete a three-part list. The next most frequent general extender in the Russian data was *et cetera*, also illustrated in a list-completing role. We are not sure if the formal nature of "business talk" in Russian is responsible for the "decisive predominance" of adjunctive forms (78.6%) over disjunctives (Malyuga and McCarthy, 2018: 50). Alternatively, it may be that adjunctive forms are simply more frequent in most languages, as seems to be the case, and English is the exception with its predilection for disjunctive forms in conversation. We will return to this issue later in the chapter. Whatever the reason, Malyuga and McCarthy conclude, with regard to the difference between their Russian and English adjunctive/disjunctive frequency counts, "there is no obvious explanation for this difference" (2018: 50). We can only treat this as another incentive for further research.

8.5 German

Terraschke (2007b) points out that "little research exists on the forms and functions of general extenders in German" (143), echoing Overstreet (2005: 1850), who had found only passing mention of some of the forms in Betten (1976) and Schwitalla (1997), who lists some of them as *lexikalische Gliederungssignale* ("lexical structuring signals"). The research reports we do have, Overstreet (2005), Overstreet *et al.* (2006), Terraschke (2007a, b) and Terraschke and Holmes (2007), are based on data from conversations involving educated middle-class speakers of Hochdeutsch, or standard German, recorded in Germany and the USA (Overstreet, 2005) and in New Zealand (Terraschke, 2007a). We suspect that there is likely to be variation in general extender form and function among different regional and social groups, as well as possibly in different registers, in German-speaking countries, but those are areas of research yet to be explored.

8.5 German

German speakers use a wide range of general extenders according to evidence recorded by Terraschke (2007a: 69), who lists twenty-one different adjunctive (*und* +) forms and seventeen different disjunctive (*oder* +) forms. However, most of those forms were used only once in the data while three forms dominate the frequency list, in this order: *oder so, und so, oder so was*. The frequency ordering of these three general extenders was exactly the same in Overstreet's (2005) earlier study, although the contexts were different geographically. However, the interactive contexts were similar, both involving conversations (not survey interviews), with the result that disjunctive forms were more frequent than adjunctives. The small set of forms in the same order is reported as the most frequently used by a German L1 group in a later study comparing L1 use and German L2 learner use in yet another different geographical location (Dippold, 2016). Cutting's (2015) investigation of German speakers' beliefs about vague language also listed the same three expressions in the same order as most frequent, from data collected in yet another different location.

The German general extender system involving three primary forms seems to be remarkably minimalist and consistent across varied contexts. In the two most common German general extenders *so* appears in the place of all these English translation equivalent forms: *something, anything, stuff, things, everything* and *that*. In the published reports we are reviewing here, no translation equivalents were provided for the German general extenders, which were simply repeated. We will take a different approach and try to include intuitively appropriate English versions of general extenders in the translations in order to capture the range of functions served by the German forms. We will present examples from two in-depth studies: (32), (33), (35) and (37) are from Terraschke (2007a) and (34), (36) and (38)–(43) are from Overstreet (2005).

The first three forms in terms of frequency are illustrated in (32)–(34). In (32), the speaker uses the disjunctive form *oder so* twice as she tries to explain her ineffective approach to exams. The vagueness of *oder so* here contributes to the sense in which this speaker was not very sure about what she was doing. The different grammatical contexts, positive and negative, prompt the use in translation of two different English general extenders for the same German expression (*oder so*).

(32) *genau weiß ich ich würd's einfach nich machen ich würd dann halt irgendwie zwei Wochen vorm Examen **oder so** anfangen zu lernen und würd's nicht schaffen **oder so***
("I know exactly I wouldn't do anything then I would start studying like two weeks before the exam or something and I wouldn't manage it or whatever")

In (33), with two uses of the adjunctive form *und so*, we suspect that the speaker is indicating that more could be said about each town. These uses are reminiscent of British English *and that*, which we have included here, but the typical American English adjunctive form *and stuff* could have served equally well as a translated equivalent.

(33)   *ich finde Hamburg eigentlich eine ganz gute Stadt so vom (.) von der Kultur und vom Stadtleben her **und so** von den äh Gruppen von den Leuten die da wohnen es ist ziemlich offen das finde also das Problem mit Jena **und so** also em ich mein das ist schon alles viel konservativer da unten*
("I think Hamburg is a pretty good city in terms of culture and city life and that the groups of people who live there it is quite open that's the problem I have with Jena and that so em I mean it is much more conservative down there")

Example (34) has the third most frequent form *oder so was*, which seems to convey something more than just *oder so*. We have suggested the long form *or something like that* as a translation, incorporating the sense of potential inaccuracy while indicating that one of the possibilities mentioned (*like that*) may be close to accurate.

(34)   *Ich glaub' die is irgendwie so im Brown oder Duke oder irgendwie so 'ne große Uni ehm an der (.5) Ostküste **oder so was***
("I think she's like at Brown or Duke or some like large University um on the (.5) east coast or something like that")

Among Terraschke's (2007a) university students, the fourth most frequent form, illustrated in (35), was *und so weiter*, a phrase associated with more formal spoken and written German, occurring minimally in Overstreet's (2005) data. In this case (35), the speaker is describing the extent to which he really feels he was cheated by the doctor in all aspects of his medical treatment, with *und so weiter* not simply indicating there was more (which could be translated by *and so on*), but marking the extreme nature of this treatment with the verb *abgeknöpft* ("unbuttoned," or colloquially "ripped off") and leading us to translate this use of the general extender as *and everything*.

(35)   *ich glaub ich wurde auch vom Arzt in in in Banjos verarscht also (.) der hat mir auch 'n Medikament und Behandlung **und so weiter** da (.) gut abgeknöpft*
("I think I got cheated by a doctor in Banjos as well also (.) he ripped me off with medicine and treatment and everything")

In Overstreet's (2005) data, the fourth most frequent form was another disjunctive phrase, *oder was weiß ich* (literally "or what do I know"), exemplified in (36), which appeared only once in Terraschke's (2007a) corpus.

(36)   *Da waren sie nicht so dafür, daß ich mich mit deutschen Buben oder Männern **oder was weiß ich** treffe*
("They weren't really in favor of me meeting with German boys or men or whatever")

8.5 German

In Overstreet's (2005: 1860) analysis, there is a dismissive element in this speaker's comment on her parents' opinions about what she should do, similar in tone to English *or whatever*. The self-deprecating nature of this phrase seems to carry a sense of "I'm no expert (on my parents' point of view)," as well as signaling that the information attached may not be accurately stated, but accuracy is not necessary. The disjunctive extender in (36) is not the only form that is uniquely German, as evidenced in the lengthy expression highlighted in (37).

(37)   *ist echt für mich (.) eine komplett neue Welt gewesen ich hab keine Ahnung gehabt wie man überhaupt Sätze konstruiert **oder sonst irgendwie was in der Richtung** macht*
("it really was a completely new world for me I had no idea how you even construct sentences or anything like that")

In (37), we have included in the translation the most likely equivalent ("or anything like that") in this context, which doesn't quite capture the sense of exaggeration that, according to Terraschke (2007a: 89), is being signaled here with the help of the long form *oder sonst irgendwie was in der Richtung* (literally "or otherwise like something in that direction") that accompanies the speaker's claim that he didn't know how to construct sentences. Terraschke explains that the general extender here "seems to implicate a whole range of potential problems with academic and writing skills" (2007a: 89) that the German speaker experienced on first arrival at the university in New Zealand. This is a good example of an individual creation with subjective function to represent the speaker's personal experience.

Another particularly German expression is illustrated in (38), with the conjunction *und* repeated to give an iconic sense of something continuing without end, similar to a translation equivalent in Persian presented later in example (68). We imagine that English speakers would use *and so on and so forth* or *et cetera et cetera* to capture this sense.

(38)   *Denn Pferde selbst zu haben kann sehr teuer werden – Veterinäre, weißt du, Tierarztkosten, und Futter, **und und und***
("Because having your own horses can become very expensive – Veterinarians, you know, veterinary costs, and feed and so on and so forth")

We should note the inclusion of *weißt du* in (38), used in a way that is very similar to its English translation "you know," both in terms of marking intersubjectivity as the basis for understanding what is being said and also as a left-hand bracket before the details of the costs, with the adjunctive extender as the right-hand bracket, a structural configuration described in Chapter 5. Another structuring function we identified in Chapter 5 is exemplified in (39) where *und so* is being used like a punctor. (*Alex* is "Alexanderplatz," an area in what was the former East Berlin.) The general extender *und so* in this case is added, almost like a reflex, after each clause in this speaker's explanation of the direction of her thinking. The common British phrase *and that*, as described in Macaulay (1985), would seem to be an appropriate translation.

(39)   *Ich hatte schon überlegt, ob ich nich' auszieh'* **und so***, weil alle meine Leute wohnen im Osten* **und so** *und ich arbeite ja am Alex* **und so**
("I had already considered whether I shouldn't move out and that, because all my people live in the East and that and I work like on Alex and that")

In example (40), while preparing for a trip, Ralf asks Peter if he has room in his luggage for some of Ralf's things. We include example (40) to illustrate two aspects of general extender use that are more typical of German than English. In the first line, the general extender has an adverb (*auch*) inside it, not a typical construction in English. Also, the pejorative term *Kram*, not unlike the American English "crap," provides the speaker with a way to minimize or downplay the potential imposition of his friend's request while indicating the nature of what he can accommodate.

(40)   Ralf: *Ungefähr diese Menge* **oder auch so**
            Peter: *Kleider* **und so Kram** *kann ich sicherlich noch hier rein tun*
            (Ralf: "About this amount or something (holds up some things)
            Peter: Clothes and crap like that I can still put in here for sure")

Also evident in (40) is the non-final position of the general extender in the utterance. The topicalization of the object noun phrase (*Kleider und so Kram*) results in a structure that is possible, without the subject–verb inversion, but fairly uncommon in English. The basic structure of German quite often puts general extenders in non-final position in clauses, and hence in utterances, as illustrated in examples (35), (36) and (37), where the verbs *abgeknöpft*, *treffe* and *macht* are each in clause-final position, following the general extender. The older idea that general extenders can be defined as "utterance-final" is not strictly true for English and is certainly inaccurate with regard to German.

As in the interpretation of *oder auch so* in (40), avoiding the impression of imposition is also the best interpretation of the way Hella structures her proposal in (41). There is a left bracket *Vielleicht* ("Maybe") and a right-bracket *oder so* around *am Wochenende* functioning as indicators associated with negative politeness as the speaker makes her suggestion tentative. Anna's response indicates that she didn't feel any imposition.

(41)   Hella: *Vielleicht am Wochenende* **oder so***, wenn ich dich anrufe. Hast du da-*
            Anna: *Ja, entweder dieses Wochenende oder nächtes Wochenende. Is' nicht so dringend*
            (Hella: "Maybe on the weekend or something, when I call you. Do you have-
            Anna: Yeah, either this weekend or next weekend. It's not so urgent.")

8.5 German

In (42), Robert is asking for information, but with vague hedging in *noch etwas mehr* ("something more") combined with *oder was* ("or what"), another disjunctive form reducing the sense of imposition inherent in his questioning. Then there is also the pragmatic marker *irgendwie* ("like") as a left-hand bracket before *gebunden* ("attached") with *oder so* as the right-hand bracket after it, all of which combine to make his questions sound a bit less demanding.

(42)   Robert: *Hm- weißt du denn über sein Privatleben noch etwas mehr,* **oder was***? Könnte sein, daß er schon irgendwie gebunden is* **oder so**
            Gisela: *Ne::, der hat keine Freundin*
            (Robert: "Do you know something more about his private life, or what? Could it be that he is already like attached or something
            Gisela: Nope. He doesn't have a girlfriend")

Finally, we would like to illustrate in (43) the German instantiation of a type of formulaic construction we identified in English in Chapter 4 ("X and everything, but Y"), where an interpretation of an idea is presented with a final adjunctive general extender (*und so*), then followed by a conjunction (*aber*) that indicates something contrary to that initial interpretation is actually the case.

(43)   Rosa: *Die deutschen Leute, die Amerika nur besuchen als Touristen, die schwärmen von den Amerikanern, nuh? Weil die Amerikaner so freundlich sind* **und so**
            Sissi: *Ja:*
            Rosa: <u>*Aber* wenn die die wirklich kennen würden-</u>
            Sissi: *Ja*
            Rosa: *mehr Schein als Sein*
            Sissi: *Ja, genau*
            (Rosa: "The German people who visit America as tourists, they rave about the Americans, huh? Because the Americans are so friendly and everything
            Sissi: Yeah:
            Rosa: But if they would really get to know them
            Sissi: Yeah
            Rosa: more appearance than existence (= appearances are deceiving)
            Sissi: Yeah, exactly")

Interestingly, in (43), Rosa doesn't actually state that Americans aren't always *freundlich*, but seems to depend on the addressee's recognition that the formulaic structure will imply this interpretation, together with an idiomatic phrase indicating that (initial) appearances can be deceptive. Judging by Sissi's reactions (*Ja, Ja, Ja, genau*), that implication is clearly understood.

There is no doubt that much more could be said about German general extenders, which remain an intriguing topic for further exploration. We will return to a consideration of their uses in the area of second language learning in Chapter 9.

8.6 French

As we saw in Chapter 7, many of the studies of general extenders, beginning with Dines (1980), have been concerned with the analysis of sociolinguistic variation. This is also true of two major studies of general extenders in French. In an early investigation of Montreal French, Dubois (1992, 1993) identified a number of differences in the use of some general extender-type phrases ("extension particles" in her analysis) tied to age and socioeconomic class. More recently, in a series of research reports, Secova (2011, 2014, 2017, 2018) investigated sociolinguistic variation in the use of general extenders in a corpus of Parisian French and compared her results with those from a matched corpus of London English, involving teenage (10–19-year-old) participants in a multicultural project. Perhaps surprisingly, there was relatively little similarity in the phrases identified as general extenders in the two French varieties. Secova (2014: 7) notes that some very common Montreal variants such as *des affaires comme ça* and *choses de même* (both translated as "things like that") as well as *toute l'affaire* and *tout le kit* (both translated as "and everything") were completely absent from her corpus. This observation is consistent with Dostie's (2009) study of discourse markers in Quebec French based on data from around 1970. Dostie (2009: 203) identified common discourse markers such as *coudon* ("hey, by the way") used in Quebec but not in the European varieties of French, and came to the conclusion that certain forms undergo grammaticalization "in one region but not necessarily in the other" (2009: 201). We have also noted this phenomenon in English varieties, with the grammaticalization of *and that* in (especially northern) British English, but not at all in American English (cf. Aijmer, 2013).

In the studies of the two French varieties, there were some similar findings. Women, especially "professional women," used more general extenders overall than men in both cities. Younger people used more, and more "derogatory forms," than older people, who tended to use a more limited range of forms, attached to a restricted type of antecedent (nominalizations and enumerations/lists).

In an earlier observational study of spoken French, Andrews (1989) noted the use *(.) comme ça* ("(pause) like that") by speakers to mark a completion point, at the end of a topic and/or turn. To us, this phrase seems to be functioning very much like a general extender. If it is a reduced form of any (or all) of the following *choses/trucs/quelque chose comme ça* ("things/stuff/something like that"), then it is another example of the modifier phrase (not the proform) being the focal point and the part that survives reduction. In spoken French there seems to be more attention paid to the modifier phrase in what Andrews calls "terminating devices" (1989: 193). In that respect, French and Hawai'i Creole English, with *li'dat*, have something in common.

8.6 French

In Montreal, Dubois also reported that professionals were more likely to use *et cetera* and *ainsi de suite* ("and so on"), but not *(et) patati patata*, an expression described as "continuing the intonational rhythm of a multiterm enumeration" (1992: 196), favored by working-class and younger speakers. English doesn't seem to have anything with quite the same rhythm. Working-class women, but not teenage speakers, also use *(puis) tout le kit*, translated as "and everything," an idiomatic phrase derived from "the whole kit and caboodle" (1992: 194). Although identified as more of a working-class expression, *affaires de même* is also found in the speech of the youngest (teenage) group in Dubois' (1992: 188) analysis, as illustrated in (44). We include the translations reported by the researchers after each example.

(44)　　*Je jouais au hockey pour le college, au hockey-salon au:: au hockey intérieur tu sais **des affaires de meme** tu sais des activités parascolaires là*
("I played hockey for the college, floor-hockey, inside hockey you know things like that you know extracurricular activities")

This young speaker adds *tu sais* ("you know"), a pragmatic marker assuming the addressee's acceptance, typically pronounced *tsé*, according to Vincent and Sankoff (1992: 215), as a bracket before and after the general extender structure and then at the end comes up with the lexicalized category that the *affaires* belong to. Like many of the examples in Dubois' (1992) report, the general extender form in (44) has no introductory conjunction, which may actually be a characteristic of the variety, as also illustrated in example (46). However, it is also possible in this variety to begin a general extender with two introductory conjunctions *et* and *puis*, as in (45). We feel that there is something missing in the translation of this example, because a literal translation "and then" doesn't seem appropriate, but it may just be that there is something about the combination *et puis* that just doesn't translate very well.

(45)　　*J'aime mieux le parler de campagne en Europe, le parler de Marseille **et puis ces choses-là***
("I prefer the speech of the countryside in Europe, the speech of Marseilles and those things")

Dubois (1992: 183) reports on a single example of a disjunctive form (*quelque chose comme ça*), as shown in (46) with no introductory conjunction, and records relatively low numbers in her token count of disjunctive forms (1992: 195), especially among younger speakers.

(46)　　*Il avait une cassure dans les reins, dans l'épine dorsale démanchée **quelque chose comme ça***
("He had a break near the kidneys, a dislocated spinal column something like that")

The observation that there were more adjunctive general extenders than disjunctive is also the case in Secova's (2011) study and is consistent with other (English-based) studies using sociolinguistic survey-interview data (e.g. Cheshire, 2007). However, this is where the similarities start to disappear. In terms of tokens of French disjunctive forms, Secova's (2011) data reveals an extremely low count relative to adjunctive forms and compared to a much higher count in the London data. It is not that a regular disjunctive form beginning with *ou* ("or") doesn't exist in French, as evidenced in (47), from Vincent and Sankoff (1992: 209), with their translation.

(47)   *quand on est marié **ou des affaires de meme***
       ("when you're married or something like that")

To put this scarcity of disjunctive tokens in perspective, rates of short disjunctive forms (out of all forms) were only 2.64 percent in Paris, yet 19.7 percent in London, and for longer forms, the difference was even greater, at 1.76 percent in Paris versus 25 percent in London (Secova, 2017: 8–9). These are unusually large differences, which may be related to some unknown variable not explored in the study. Secova (2017) comments in a note that this "is another relevant finding reflecting an interesting language-specific phenomenon" (2017: 8). But surely we are not to believe that speakers of Parisian French rarely hedge on accuracy or politeness in their spoken interactions? Or perhaps they use some linguistic means other than general extender structures for those functions? No answers to these questions have been offered (as far as we know) and the reported anomaly remains unexplained, as we also noted regarding Russian earlier.

Obviously, the characteristic general extenders among speakers of Parisian French must be adjunctive forms, and Secova (2014, 2017) points to the high frequency of one expression *et tout* (literally "and all"), which accounts for almost two-thirds (62%) of all tokens in teenage speech. Secova (2014) notes that "*et tout* is favored with zero referential value" and mostly among those "with lower education level" (2014: 15).

Among older speakers, those who are fifty and older, the phrase *et tout* only accounts for about 20 percent of the tokens while *et cetera* is used more often (about 40%). Perhaps because the Montreal data sets were from an earlier period (1971 and 1984), there are no instances recorded of the basic form *et tout*, though there are related forms such as *puis tout ça* ("and all that"), as in (48), from Dubois (1992: 191).

(48)   *Bien je faisais beaucoup de sports, de la gymnastique **puis tout ça***
       ("well I played a lot of sports, gymnastics and all that")

The use of *puis* (literally "then") to introduce adjunctive forms occurs quite often in the Montreal data, but not in Paris. It can also occur with longer forms, as in (49), also from Dubois (1992: 191).

8.6 French

(49)   *Il a commencé jeune. Il renflait de la colle,* **puis toutes sortes de choses comme ça**
("He started young. He sniffed glue, and all sorts of things like that")

In most of the Montreal data, there is a lot of transparency in the identifiability of constituents in the general extenders, making them relatively easy to compare, almost word for word, with their English counterparts, as just exemplified in (48) and (49). When we try to investigate the comparability of *et tout* in the Paris data, we are confronted with a range of equivalent English phrases in the translations provided by Secova (2017, 2018).

We have already noted in Chapter 1 an example from Secova's (2017: 10) data, repeated in (50), where a younger speaker used the expression *et tout* four times in an utterance in a way similar to a punctor.

(50)   *elle était souvent avec eux* ***et tout*** *elle s'asseyait sur leurs genoux tout ça* ***et tout*** *elle les calculait elle leur courait après* ***et tout*** *donc eux ils avaient l'habitude ils se sentaient ils se sentaient beaux frais* ***et tout***
("she'd hang out with them and stuff she'd sit on their knees all that and everything she was always after them and everything so they were used to it they felt- they felt handsome hot and everything")

In (50), the first use of *et tout* is translated as "and stuff," following a topical statement about one girl's behavior, then three times as "and everything" after each of the extreme aspects of the girl's actions. There is a clue in these (and other different) translations that may help us understand the remarkably high token count of *et tout* in the Parisian data. It is an "all-purpose" general extender for these young Parisians. It has become the dominant adjunctive form, which may be used almost like an automatic reflex, similar to the use of *and that* by Macaulay's (1985) Scottish miner, and the use of *and stuff* by a nurse in Overstreet's (1999) American English data, as discussed and exemplified in Chapter 5.

One particular discourse context that seems to attract the use of *et tout* is after reported speech, a context we have already analyzed in English as one that favors the disjunctive form *or something (like that)*, recorded as long ago as the early nineteenth century in the novels of Jane Austen (see Chapter 6). It may simply be that *et tout* has such extensive coverage of functions among younger Parisians that other forms, particularly disjunctive forms, are not needed as much. Additionally, as Secova (2018) points out, referencing Tannen (1986), much of the reported material may actually be constructed dialogue (not exact quotation) and "may be used for purely expressive and rhetorical purposes" (2018: 158). We noted a comparable use of English *and everything* in Chapter 4, and data from the studies of Levey (2012) and Wagner *et al.* (2016) also exhibit high frequencies of *and everything* in (excited, involved) talk of younger speakers interacting with each other.

170   8 In Different Languages

Secova (2018: 158, 170) focuses on this aspect of *et tout* in her data, with examples such as (51)–(53).

(51)   *au début de l'année moi je l'aimais pas parce que genre elle disait trop "euh ouais arrêtez de bavarder" **et tout***
("at the beginning of the year I didn't like her 'cos like she was always saying 'um yeah stop talking' and everything")

(52)   *j'etais là "pitié, pitié, pitié"* < *voix> j'etais en train de prier dans le tram **et tout***
("I was like 'please, please, have mercy' <voice> I was praying in the tram and everything")

(53)   *ils disent "monsieur vous vous prenez pour qui"* ***et tout nanana***
("they're saying 'sir who do you think you are' and everything blah blah")

Also included in (53) is *nanana*, listed as the third most frequent extender in Secova's (2018) French data, substantially more frequent than its translation equivalent *and blah blah (blah)*, but apparently used with a similar downgrading effect related to reported talk, as observed by Overstreet (1999: 138). This latter phrase is noticeably absent from Secova's (2018: 175) London data, where no comparable onomatopoeic forms are recorded. Once again we are looking at the development and use of a specific expression, with a specific function, in one variety of French (in Paris) that is substantially different from an equivalent expression *patati patata* found in another variety (in Montreal), and also unlike the comparable American English phrase *and blah blah (blah)* or any other phrase in the recordings of London English. The obvious point here is that variation in form can only be analyzed across varieties through the recognition of comparable functions (cf. Beeching, 2018).

As we have seen with *et tout*, there is no single corresponding form in English and we have to look at function in context in order to come up with a translation. For example, the appropriate translation of *et tout* after reported talk is not solved by equating it with *and everything* partly because this latter form is found in other contexts, such as (54), and also because other expressions are used after reported talk, as in (55). We can point out that *et tout* is translated in (54) as both *and that* and *and everything*, in neither case following reported talk, but in (55), after reported talk, *et tout* is translated as *and stuff*.

(54)   *il fait son footing **et tout** genre "pf pf pf"* <*imitation/gestures*> *les petits abdos **et tout***
("he does his jogging and that like 'pf pf pf' <imitation/gestures> little sit-ups and everything")

(55)   *je l'ai regardé comme ça (.) genre en mode "tu veux quoi"* ***et tout***
("I looked at him like that (.) like 'what do you want' and stuff")

Although they may have different lexical sources, the expressions *genre (en mode)* and its translation equivalent *like*, as illustrated in (55), are both used in a very similar way as left-hand brackets before the reported material, with the general extenders (*et tout, and stuff*) as right-hand brackets. The forms may differ, but the textual functions are very similar.

There are many more aspects of general extender use in French varieties, including French Creoles, that we have not touched on here and that await further, more detailed, research. Meanwhile, we will move on to see if general extenders in another European language exhibit comparable form–function relationships to those already discussed.

8.7 Swedish

In an Appendix that is part of Aijmer (1985: 387–89), there is a token count of general extenders ("terminating tags" in her analysis) in a corpus of spoken Swedish. There are more adjunctive than disjunctive forms. The most frequent form is *å så där* ("and so there"), which Aijmer translates as "and that," followed by *eller nånting* ("or some thing") and *å så* ("and so"). What is striking about Aijmer's Swedish data is a consistent pattern in which longer forms are more frequent than their shorter counterparts, already illustrated with *å så där* being more frequent than *å så*. Tokens of *å sånt där* ("and such there") are double those of *å sånt* ("and such") and both *eller nånting* ("or something") and *eller nåt sånt där* ("or something such there") are used more frequently than *eller nåt* ("or something"). Perhaps the speakers in these recordings were using more formal language, influenced by written norms. Or it may be that this data was collected at a time when shorter forms were simply not as popular as more established longer expressions.

Aijmer (1985: 389) points out that *å så* is used in combination with plural nouns, as in (56), and also with preposition phrases, as in (57), which may be evidence, along with the reduction in form, that this marker has grammaticalized in Swedish. Judging by its frequent use in later data from one speaker, briefly exemplified in (58) and analyzed more fully in Chapter 5, *å så* would seem to have gone through the grammaticalization process so thoroughly that it can be used as a punctor.

(56)   *det var faktiskt kul – utflykter **å så***
       ("it was actually great fun – excursions and so")

(57)   *dom är ju i 20-års åldern **å så***
       ("they are in their twenties and so")

(58)   *på dee sättet **å så** (.) och eh- mot nazister (.) mycke (.) **åå så** (.) mot fascism överhuvudtaget mot polisen mot- mot liksom mot (.) systemet **å så** (.) mer*
       ("in that way and so and eh- against Nazis a lot and so against fascism on the whole against the police against- against like against the system and so")

Example (58) is from data collected about twenty years later than the corpus used by Aijmer (1985) and presented as part of an investigation with a sociolinguistic approach in two papers by Winter and Norrby (2000) and Norrby and Winter (2002). They focus on the three most frequent general extenders ("discourse extenders" in their account) used by younger speakers (high school students) of Swedish. While fifty-four different forms were actually recorded, only three forms, exemplified and highlighted in this adapted extract (59) were analyzed. Here the speakers are all female, speaking with a lot of overlap and laughter, as they try to come up with appropriate scenarios for listening to a particular type of music.

(59) #1: *jaa eller när man dricker te **eller nånting***
 ("yeah or when you have tea or something")
 #2: *ja (.) mer*
 ("yeah, more")
 #3: *sitter hemma å läser tidningen **å sånt** liksom typ*
 ("sitting at home reading the paper and such sort of like")
 #2: *ja*
 ("yes")
 #1: *en sån kväll när man bara sitter hemma å gör ingenting*
 ("such an evening when you're sitting at home doing nothing")
 #2: *ja men-*
 ("yes but-")
 #3: *de e ganska (.) intet (.) sägande ändå*
 ("it's quite nondescript anyway")
 #4: *typ sitter (.) **å så***
 ("like sitting and so")

The most frequent form is *å så*, translated by Norrby and Winter (2002: 2) as "and so," not a typical expression in English, which might be better represented by "and that" or "and stuff." Next in frequency is the disjunctive form *eller nånting*, also recorded in the form *eller nåt*, which has a similar form and function to "or something." The third most frequent form is *å sånt*, translated here as "and such," a rather archaic phrase in English that might be better represented as "and (all) that." Alternatively, given the combination of pragmatic markers attached to the phrase here (*å sånt liksom typ*), both of which signal approximate similarity, we might prefer to translate this whole four-word phrase as another one favored by English-speaking teenagers: "and stuff like that." What the researchers observe about much of the type of interaction they recorded is the overlapping collaboration of the speakers, including the use of three general extenders by three different speakers in (59), as they "provide the scaffolding for the scenario" (2002: 5) being jointly created. Through this interactive process, the speakers establish their affiliations while "co-constructing their realities" (2002: 7).

There is one other general extender-type phrase included in the Swedish data (Winter and Norrby, 2000: 5) that is similar in form to a long English general extender, incorporating the word *grejerna* ("things"), as in (60).

(60)   *man ska i- bli vegetarian å man ska inte dööda djuren å man ska liksom (.) å alla dom där grejerna*
("you should n- become a vegetarian and you shouldn't kill the animals and you should like (.) and all those things")

The use of "and all those things" signals that there are a lot of issues involved here, which the speaker goes on to list at some length, punctuated by the more common shorter form *å så*, as discussed in more detail in Chapter 5. While English speakers have taken the lexical item "things" and incorporated it into general extenders with its referential meaning bleached out, Swedish speakers do not seem to have followed the same path, as evidenced by the infrequent use of *grejerna* in this way, which was also the case in Aijmer's (1985) corpus.

We will return to the use of general extenders in the language of Swedish speakers when we review their use of English as a second language in Chapter 9.

8.8   Persian

In their in-depth study of general extenders in Persian, Parvaresh *et al.* (2010, 2012) found that adjunctive forms were a lot more frequent than disjunctive ones. The shortest adjunctive form *væ inâ*, translated as "and stuff" and illustrated in (61), was by far the most frequent. Among other frequent adjunctive forms, the phrase *in hærf hâ* ("of such talks"), illustrated in (62), was part of the general extender, marking the "more" element in the Persian adjunctive form as meaning "more talk," a distinguishing feature not generally found in other languages investigated so far. Another noticeable feature of Persian general extenders is the frequent inclusion of the expression *nemidunæm* ("I don't know") within the general extender structure, as illustrated in (63). In English we find "I don't know/I dunno" as a bracket used with a general extender as another bracket, as described in Chapter 5, but not inside the structure of the general extender, making the form shown in (63) a distinct and characteristic feature of Persian general extender use. In citing examples, we will rely on the translations provided by the authors (Parvaresh *et al.* 2012: 266–71).

(61)   *pul væ ehsâsât væ inâ dorost*
("money and feelings and stuff are of course necessary")

(62)   *dærbâreje zehne bærtær vætæqvijæte hâfeze væ æz hærf hā*
("it's about the greater mind and improving the memory and of such talks")

(63)   âxe xeire særeš dæm æz væ fâdâri **væ nemidunæm æz in hærf hâ** mizæd hæmiše
("she was the sort of person who about loyalty and I don't know of such talks was always talking")

Although Persian general extenders are often clause-final, as in (62), a distinct feature is the frequency with which they are found in non-final position. As shown in (61), the general extender is part of the subject noun phrase and in (63) it is part of the object noun phrase in an embedded clause. Unlike English, with its Subject-Verb-Object word order, Persian is a language with Subject-Object-Verb word order, with the consequence that general extenders as part of the object noun phrase will typically be inside the clause.

Among disjunctive forms, the most frequent is *jā čizi* ("or something"), illustrated in (64) and noticeably in non-final position.

(64)   je mântoji *jā čizi* mixām bærdâræm
("An overcoat or something I want to buy")

A particular feature of Persian discourse is the use of a disjunctive extender "to express outrage and frustration" (Parvaresh *et al.*, 2012: 274), as illustrated in (65). In the typical pattern, a speaker repeats a word or phrase uttered by another speaker (that was considered offensive), followed by the disjunctive form *jā hærči* ("or whatever") to express outrage.

(65)   (bâ æsæbânijæt) â:::h begæm beheš? bæbæ? *jā hærči!*
((angrily) "Oh ye:::ah I should tell her? Sneak? Or whatever!")

However, in a different context, *jā hærči* is not translated as "or whatever." In (66), from Tayebi and Parvaresh (2014: 82), using a different transcription system, *ja harchi* is translated as "or anything," in keeping with its role in the formulaic disclaimer structure (*not* X *or anything, but* Y).

(66)   xodajish nemixam azijatet konam *ja harchi*, vali vaqe'an bajad kareto avaz koni
("God knows I don't want to bother you or anything, but you really must change your job.")

In (66), before expressing his opinion, the speaker disclaims any intention to be problematic, in a formulaic construction almost identical to that described for English in Chapter 4, with the same subjective function.

There are two adjunctive forms that seem to be commonplace in Persian spoken discourse but sound unfamiliar in translation to most English speakers. The translated version of *væ in væ un* in (67) as "and this and that" is not an impossible form in English (there are three examples recorded in the Canadian data of Tagliamonte and Denis, 2010: 363), but it is generally rare. The translation of *væ væ væ* in (68) as "and and and" is not a phrase used as a adjunctive extender in English, but is identical in form to *und und und,* an expression in German, as we saw in example (38) in an earlier section.

(67)   *goft ke "bijâ mæn ævæl bærât je vizâje kâr dorost mikonam miri xâredʒ (.) væ bæʔdešæm moqim miši" væ in væ un*
("He said, 'come I first arrange for a working visa, you'll go abroad (.) and you'll become a permanent resident' and this and that")

(68)   *šæb tâsobh xundæm væ væ væ væli âxæreš oftâdæm!*
("I didn't sleep the whole night and and and, but at the end I failed!")

This last exemplar, *væ væ vae*, is used in direct translation as "and, and, and" in the speech of Persian learners of English, according to Parvaresh *et al.* (2012). In Chapter 9, we will investigate the use of general extenders, familiar and unfamiliar, in the data collected from Persian learners, as well as learners from a variety of first-language backgrounds.

8.9   Highlighting Differences

Having described some features of general extender use in different languages, we can highlight some aspects of their use(s) that differ from those established for English. Most notably, only the reports on German seem to have a similar ratio of disjunctive to adjunctive forms as English. All the other research reports for the other languages we looked at record much higher numbers of adjunctive forms. We are not sure if this is an artifact of how data was collected or if we have uncovered some kind of cross-cultural difference(s) hitherto unnoticed. That difference is likely to be based on more than linguistic analysis and awaits further investigation.

Another notable difference is the absence, in many examples from other languages, of a nominal proform, such as *stuff* or *thing*, that characterizes English adjunctive extenders. Instead, other languages like German (*und so*) and Swedish (*å så*) have developed constructions without nominals. There are also structures, such as the equivalent of "and, and, and" in German and Persian, that have no counterpart in English. Most noticeably in French, there is frequently no conjunction introducing the general extender, an occasional aspect of English, though only typically at the end of an utterance and completing a turn, a restriction not found in French. In structural terms, English has a strong tendency to put general extenders in utterance-final position (though it is not an exclusive position), whereas both German and Persian, for different syntactic reasons, regularly include general extenders within utterances.

There are also aesthetic differences. Other languages have expressions functioning as adjunctive extenders that have a flowing rhythmic pattern not found in English. We noted *(e) pérére párárá* and *(e) bábábá* in Brazilian

Portuguese, *(et) patati patata* in Montreal French and *(et) nanana* in Parisian French. German also has an expression *und tralala*, described later in Chapter 9, that contains a (non-content) word with a similar three-beat melody. The closest English equivalent in our data seems to be *(and) blah, blah, blah*, consisting of a repeated (non-content) form in three syllables, yet almost always expressed with more of a staccato effect. We are not sure if we are witnessing some other underlying cultural differences being instantiated in the way speakers of different languages indicate that more could be said (when it is of little consequence), but that there are differences is not in doubt. The cross-linguistic study of general extenders has hardly begun.

9 In Learner Language and Language Teaching

One of the most consistent findings from studies of the spoken discourse of second language (L2) learners is the low frequency of pragmatic expressions used as discourse markers and pragmatic markers (Gilquin, 2008; Hasselgren, 2002; Müller, 2005; Shirato and Stapleton, 2007). Not only do L2 learners use small numbers of pragmatic expressions, they also typically use a more limited range compared to first language (L1) speakers (Fung and Carter, 2007). In the words of Romero-Trillo (2002), there is a form of "pragmatic fossilization" (2002: 769) that results from learning and relying on only a small set of discourse markers. While most of the research in this area has been undertaken with a focus on English as the L2, the same phenomenon has been reported from studies where a different L2 is the target. In Dippold's (2008) report on the use of hedges in argumentative discourse by advanced-level British students learning German as their L2, the learners used relatively few hedges in comparison with the frequent use by a group of German (L1) speakers. In Fernandez's (2013) case studies of students learning Spanish (L2), there were some individuals who used no general extenders at all and others who had a tendency to use two common general extenders, direct translation equivalents of their British English (L1) counterparts, and a restricted range of other forms.

9.1 Explaining Low Frequency

One simple explanation for the low frequency is that L2 learners have no idea that there are pragmatic expressions such as general extenders in language use. This doesn't mean that they don't use pragmatic expressions in their L1, but they may be completely unaware that they do so. They are not the only ones, as we discovered in the early 1990s when we were investigating the use of general extenders in the conversational data we were collecting. Many people, including English language teachers and professors of linguistics, not only appeared to be unaware of the existence of general extenders in their L1, but then after being told about them, claimed they personally didn't use such forms in their speech (despite empirical evidence to the contrary).

Those claims may provide another explanation for the low frequency of pragmatic expressions in the speech of learners. They may be tied to beliefs, conscious or not, that the use of vague language is indicative of vague thinking and certain vague linguistic expressions are only used by uneducated people. As Fernandez and Yuldashev note, with regard to the academic context, "vague language continues to be frowned upon as imprecise and therefore unsuitable for 'educated' speech and writing" (2011: 2624). The negative perception of the role of vague language applies to general extenders, as documented in Channell (1994: 120) and Overstreet (1999: 22). Consequently, we shouldn't be surprised if this underlying value system leads to an avoidance of the type of so-called "sloppy" language represented by pragmatic expressions. Most L2 speakers in our research are in educational settings where they are likely to absorb some version of the value system just described and develop a preference for (approved) written language forms such as *and so on* and *et cetera* and not for (disapproved) casual spoken forms such as *and that* and *and stuff*. Whether unrecognized at all, or recognized yet avoided, it would follow that certain pragmatic expressions would be predictably missing from L2 learner talk.

Another practical explanation for the low frequency of pragmatic expressions would be that many English L2 speakers don't perceive a need for them in most situations where they use the language. Often this follows from the nature of the discourse and/or the participants, as when English is used as a lingua franca, for example. When speakers of two different languages use English as their medium of interaction, according to Murray (2012), "discourse markers and particles appear to be relatively scarce" (2012: 321). It may be that such encounters are generally treated as more "transactional" by the participants, focused on information transfer involving "factual or propositional information" (Brown and Yule, 1983: 2). They may be less interested in developing "interactional" language skills that are more devoted to the social function of English in the development and maintenance of personal and professional relationships. In this scenario, the model of formal written English may be a more valued target than casual conversational English.

9.2 French Learners

Some support for this scenario comes from the research of De Cock (2004) and Aijmer (2015), who both reported on similar aspects of English L2 use among French L1 speakers. As we noted in Chapter 1, the French L1 students in De Cock's (2004) study used different frequencies of general extenders compared with an English L1 group of British students. The learners' two most frequent adjunctive forms were *and so on* and *et cetera*, which were virtually absent from the speech of the L1 group. They also preferred long forms (*and things like that*) and hardly used short forms (*and things*). They didn't use *and stuff* at all, unlike the L1 group, who used it frequently, along with *and things* and *and everything*. This split parallels the difference in distribution between formal and informal spoken language usage as reported by Overstreet and Yule (1997b) and Biber *et al.* (1999). The French L1 speakers were using expressions associated with academic English, both written and spoken, which was probably the primary input source in their learning environment.

In a comparison with speakers of other L1s, Aijmer (2015: 223) noted that the French L1 group's tendency to use longer forms (*and things like that, or something like that*) rather than short forms (*and things, or something*) was not matched by L1 speakers of Dutch, German or Swedish. Those French L1 speakers produced no examples with *or anything (like that)*, unlike the German L1 speakers and Swedish L1 speakers, but closer to the Dutch L1 group with a small number of such tokens. Interestingly, although the French L1 group used *and so on* a lot, they didn't use *or so* at all, unlike the German and Dutch L1 speakers, and more like the English L1 group. The overall impression from the analyses of data from that particular group of French L1 speakers was that their spoken English L2 sounded rather formal.

One effect of using more formal expressions in spoken interaction is that the English of L2 learners "may sound rather bookish and pedantic" (Channell, 1994: 21). De Cock also commented on the effect of the English expressions used by the French L1 speakers in interpersonal terms, pointing to "the impression of detachment and formality they will give in informal situations" (2004: 236). We already know, as detailed in Chapter 8, that the French language has a range of general extenders that are presumably familiar, in terms of form and function, to the students in De Cock's (2004) study, but those students were unable to extend their L1 pragmatic knowledge to the identification of appropriate equivalents in English. Building awareness of the appropriate use of pragmatic expressions has become more of a priority in recent approaches to teaching spoken English, as we will see in a later section.

9.3 Dutch Learners

In an in-depth investigation of English L2 general extender use among Dutch speakers (university students at an advanced proficiency level), Buysse (2014) analyzed their performance in interviews and compared their output with that of a matched group of British university students. Aijmer (2015) also reports on the frequency counts of English general extenders among Dutch L1 speakers. We should note that the amount of talk produced by the English L1 group in Buysse's (2014) study was substantially more than the L2 group. The ratio of general extender use, however, was virtually identical at about twenty-six tokens per ten thousand words. One of the most striking aspects of Buysse's

(2014: 218) results was a major difference in the numbers of adjunctive versus disjunctives in each data set. For the English L1 group, there were more adjunctive than disjunctive forms, whereas for the L2 group the relationship was reversed, with more disjunctive than adjunctive. A major reason for this difference was the very high use among the L2 group of *or something (like that)*, with more than half of those uses analyzed as approximations, attached to amounts, numbers and forms of lexical items. The L1 group had fewer tokens of *or something (like that)* overall and significantly fewer attached to forms of lexical items (Buysse, 2014: 232). As reported elsewhere (Overstreet, 2012b), the disjunctive phrase *or something (like that)* is learned early and used often by English L2 speakers, typically as a hedge indicating some uncertainty about accuracy in a way that is also common among English L1 speakers. However, as Buysse (2014) notes, using examples reproduced here as (1) and (2), *or something* may be used too often in contexts where English L1 users prefer another form (e.g. *or anything*) and not used enough when a less appropriate form is chosen (e.g. *or so*).

(1)   *we went there and em we never really ate in in er in a restaurant **or something***

In (1), the negative element (*never*) would normally prompt the use of *or anything* by English L1 speakers. This may not happen for Dutch L1 speakers because the basic grammatical distinction in English between *some* and *any* is not a feature of Dutch, as Buysse explains (2014: 231). Yet, for advanced learners, this basic distinction must be known already, so the problem is not that they haven't learned to distinguish English *some* and *any*, it is that they haven't transferred that learning to distinguish between *something* and *anything* in general extenders.

In Buysse's (2014: 233) examples, there are other situations where using *or something* would actually have been the more appropriate choice. As shown in (2), the Dutch L1 speaker used *or so* in a context where English L1 speakers would likely use *or something*.

(2)   *they're better in English but (.) when (.) like (.) there's a phone call **or so***

As we mentioned in Chapter 1, Dutch has a direct translation form (*of zo*) for *or so*, but the Dutch expression is much less restricted in its distribution, so when transfer occurs, it can result in an unfamiliar use of the English equivalent, as in (2).

In Buysse's (2014) report, the higher number of adjunctive forms in the English L1 data was as a result of more tokens of *and things (like that)*, *and stuff (like that)* and *and everything (like that)*. In particular, the British students used *and things (like that)* a lot compared to negligible instances in the data from the Dutch group, who were more likely to use *and stuff (like that)*, probably as a result of more media exposure to American English, according to Buysse

(2014: 221). More noticeable in the L2 data than the low token counts of adjunctive forms with *things* or *everything* is the relatively high count for *and so on*, ten times more frequent in the L2. As we've noted elsewhere, in De Cock's (2004) report, many English L2 speakers rely on this fixed expression, no doubt as a result of more exposure to academic register norms in their education. However, in a fine-grained analysis of the data, Buysse (2014) notes that the higher-frequency tokens of *and so on* in this study were partially the responsibility of two individuals for whom this phrase seemed to be a favorite, or "a pragmatic teddy bear," giving them security (Gilquin, 2008: 129), as cited in Buysse (2004: 219). We can illustrate this prevalent usage with an example in (3), adapted from Buysse (2014: 220).

(3)   *the journalists (.) would (.) er after seeing th- seeing (.) th- the press screening **and so on** would er (.) apply for erm (.) well would come to me and ask for interviews well via email **and so on** (.) and I had to eh arrange it with the distributors (.) with the m- film distributor distributors and the managers **and so on***

The three examples of *and so on* here are functioning not unlike the other filled (and unfilled) pauses as the speaker seems to be putting together the utterance while speaking and, like the pauses, could be omitted with little change in the content of what is being explained. In this sense, *and so on* is being used in a way similar to a punctor, as described in Chapter 5, though an unusual choice in spoken interaction, where *and that* or *and stuff* would be more typical.

Rather than focus only on inappropriate uses of general extenders by these Dutch L1 speakers, we can point to quite complex English structures with pragmatic function that appear to have been learned and put to appropriate use, as shown in (4), adapted from Buysse (2014: 223), describing the venue for a summer language course.

(4)   *it is a very nice place (.) with a swi- swimming pool and (.) great view **and everything** <u>but</u> it's very expensive to go there and the food is very expensive*

As described in Chapter 4, the formulaic construction (X *and everything but* Y) provides a means of presenting information that may give rise to expectations prior to giving "a justification for thinking contrary to those expectations" (Overstreet and Yule, 2002: 792). This Dutch L1 speaker has used the general extender *and everything* perfectly while expressing reservations about something one would be expected to be enthusiastic about.

9.4   German Learners

The most detailed study of German L1 speakers using English L2 general extenders was undertaken by Terraschke (2007a) and reported in Terraschke

(2007b, 2010) and Terraschke and Holmes (2007). That study analyzed data from German L1 speakers who were attending a university in New Zealand and hence were immersed in an English-speaking environment, perhaps accounting for their high-frequency use of *and stuff*, matching the output of the New Zealand English L1 speakers in the study. There were occasional expressions, such as *and the whole stuff*, that seemed to be the idiosyncratic creations of individual German L1 speakers, but these German learners mostly used adjunctive forms in ways comparable to the English L1 group, as illustrated in (5), from Terraschke (2007a: 99), where both *and stuff* and *or something* are used in ways similar to English L1 uses.

(5) L: *she used to be an alcoholic **and stuff** and she like really got attached to me like as if I was her best friend **or something***
 B: *oh no*
 L: *and then she got like really jealous of my boyfriend and like wouldn't let me see him anymore **and stuff***

The three uses of general extenders and the four uses of *like* (in a left-hand bracket each time) are very much in line with how English L1 speakers (who are the same age) use the expressions.

There were differences, however, with the English L1 group using *and things* quite frequently while the German L1 group produced none. Although there is a high-frequency German adjunctive general extender *und so*, a cognate of "and so," this phrase was rarely used in their English L2. One interesting, and melodic, transfer was the use of *und tralala*, as in (6), from Terraschke (2007a: 98).

(6) *so we kept on looking but we couldn't find anything so we we've sort of seen these so it was like oh that's cool (.) especially with the meaning and everything in it yeah like it it was quite something one ring forever intertwine them **and tralala***

Terraschke (2007a: 97) explains that the German L1 speaker in (6) is describing a special ring he and his partner found and completes his excited account with the transferred form. Terraschke's fine-grained analysis captures a feature of L1 transfer that is not normally noted, when she points out that the speaker "adopts English phonology when he articulates the extender, pronouncing the /r/ sound and the vowels in an un-German manner. This might indicate that he is not actually aware that he is using a non-standard form that is the product of L1 transfer" (2007a: 97). This represents another interesting way in which English L2 learners create their own personal uses of general extenders combining a phrase from the German L1 with pronunciation from the English L2.

While there were minor differences in the use of English adjunctive forms, a major difference was found in the German L1 group's preference for the disjunctive form *or so*, used even more than *or something*, which really seems to be an effect of transfer from the high-frequency German cognate *oder so*, as we noted in Chapter 1. Example (7) is from Terraschke (2007a: 112), illustrating a use of *or so* that would be unlikely in English L1 speech, but noticeably causes no problem for the interacting English L1 speaker, who echoes the German student's phrase (*quite formal*) and responds to the novel use of the general extender without confusion or comment.

(7) V: *okay okay it's like quite formal **or so**?*
     G: *yeah it can be quite formal*

As we suggested in Chapter 1, the English form *or so* appears to have become an all-purpose disjunctive general extender for European speakers of English as a lingua franca and its high frequency among these German L1 speakers may be occurring without any sense of inaccurate or inappropriate usage with regard to standard varieties of English.

Terraschke (2007a) notes a few other features that seem specific to the German L1 speakers, such as a liking for *this* instead of *that* in long disjunctive forms, as in *or something like this*, but the overall impression is that the speakers in her study were able to use general extenders in their English L2 without much difficulty or misunderstanding.

9.5 Swedish Learners

When we are introduced to the investigation of the English L2 of Swedish L1 speakers, we are advised that "advanced Swedish learners of English have a good command of English grammar and lexis," but that they "may overuse or underuse certain devices" (Aijmer, 2004: 173–74). Among these devices are general extenders, which were not used with very high frequency in Aijmer's (2004) study of Swedish L1 speakers of English L2. Like many other English L2 speakers, the Swedish L1 group seemed to overuse *or something*, with a token count three times higher than in the English L1 database used for comparison. However, although used a lot, *or something* is not used inappropriately and is well placed in the examples cited, as in (8), from Aijmer (2004: 186).

(8) *When you- going to a room and there's a short video sequence – of <u>like</u> one person **or something** and that's I like that kind of art*

The structure in (8) is very similar to an English L1 pattern, where *or something* is used as a right-hand bracket with *like* as the left-hand bracket, as analyzed in Chapter 5. Also similar to contemporary English L1 usage is the coordination of *or something* with a noun phrase *one person* with "human" reference (and not the "non-human" literal reference of *some thing*), a genuine disjunctive

184   9 In Learner Language and Language Teaching

extender usage. Another example, in (9) from Aijmer's (2004: 186) report, provides evidence of proficiency in the use of the negative polarity phrase *or anything*.

(9)   *er yeah I guess (.) but not like the ordinary stuff <u>like you know</u> Rembrandt* ***or anything***

In (9), we can see *or anything* used structurally, filling the right-hand bracket, with a cluster of pragmatic markers (*like you know*) in the left-hand bracket. Aijmer (2004) interprets many of the Swedish L1 group's use of markers as indicative of a speaker's potential communication problems and sees the kind of bracketing we've just described as part of a solution to those problems while maintaining fluency, as in the following conclusion: "clustering of markers was another characteristic feature of learner language with the function of filling a space in conversation" (2004: 188).

Surprisingly, one expression (*and so on*) that learners often overuse was completely missing from the first Swedish L1 group's token count (2004: 178), yet it was the most frequent adjunctive form in the English L1 database used for comparison. However, we now realize that the English database used in this study, the *London-Lund Corpus* (Svartvik and Quirk, 1980), contains a lot of formal spoken language variants. When Aijmer (2015) reports on a later analysis of another group of Swedish L1 speakers, *and so on* has a high frequency count but hardly appears at all in the comparable English L1 corpus. In this reanalysis, the preference for *and so on* is treated as a preference for a more formal variant over less formal variants such as *and things* (Aijmer, 2015: 224). It is worth noting that in the token counts, the combination of the numbers of the short form *and things* together with the long form *and things like that* actually has a higher frequency than *and so on*, and, though not used as frequently as in the comparable English L1 data, appears to be used in a similar way, as illustrated in (10) from Aijmer (2015: 229).

(10)   *London is a bit too big it's nice to be there <u>like</u> a couple of days **or something** (.) is- it's too big and is er people are stressed **and things** (.) em Brighton is a bit more relaxed*

As we pointed out in Chapter 6, it is a common feature of contemporary English usage to have *and things* connected to an adjective (e.g. *stressed*), as in (10), and not restricted to another noun phrase. This speaker also knows how to make use of a left-hand bracket *like* in combination with a right-hand bracket *or something*. Features like these in the spoken English of the Swedish L1 group are analyzed in terms of greater fluency and, indeed, the examples presented by Aijmer (2015) exhibit fewer hesitations, pauses and false starts than those in Aijmer (2004). One of the clearest indicators that the Swedish L1 group's use of general extenders approaches similarity with that of the comparable English L1 group is the near equal count for both *and stuff* and *and stuff like that*, two phrases that are either missing from the token counts of other L1 groups (e.g. French) or used with low frequency (e.g. Dutch and German) in comparable corpora (Aijmer, 2015: 223). Aijmer describes "striking similarities in terms of the preferences for short forms over long forms" (2015: 219) between the English L2 data from the Swedish group and the English L1 data.

These results suggest that at least some members of the Swedish L1 group have become proficient users of English general extenders. However, we must remain aware of the fact that in Aijmer's (2015) corpus of fifty interviews involving Swedish L1 speakers, there were ten interviews in which zero general extenders were recorded. This is a reminder that L2 learning is ultimately something that individuals do, and some are better at it than others. The aggregating of tokens to represent the language of groups has the potential to seriously misrepresent the performance of any individual within that group.

9.6 Persian Learners

Most studies of English L2 use of general extenders, as we have just illustrated, are based on European languages, but, in a remarkably original study, Parvaresh *et al*. (2012) provide a detailed report on general extenders used by Persian (L1) speakers of English L2. In Chapter 8, we noted that word order in Persian (SOV) frequently results in general extenders inside the structure of utterances and not just in final position, yet there were no examples in the research report of this type of syntactic structure being transferred to their English L2 utterances. However, they do transfer fixed phrases.

In the English L2 data, the speakers use more adjunctive forms than disjunctive and, as we mentioned in Chapter 1, they have a tendency to transfer features from phrases in their L1 to create novel English L2 forms. As we noted there, the Persian expression *væ væ væ* is directly rendered in their English L2 speech as "and, and, and," not a phrase used by English L1 speakers. Other direct (word-for-word) transfers are shown in (11), from *væ in væ un*, and (12) from *væ in čiz hâ*, both examples from Parvaresh *et al*. (2012: 266).

(11) *he's sort of you know, em, stingy! I don't like him honestly! Always talks about his friend, em, how good she is (laughs)* **and this and that**

(12) *Iranian people do not have the capacity to watch western movies, listen to foreign music,* **and such things**

The expression *and such things* is not unknown in (the history of) English L1 usage though it does have a rather old-fashioned sound. Adjunctive forms that refer to more "talk," as in *væ æz in hærf hâ* ("and of such talks") are not directly transferred, but are a likely source of the Persian L1 speakers' most frequent general extender in their English L2, "and blah blah blah," as illustrated in (13), from Parvaresh *et al.* (2012: 268).

(13)   *We should be loyal to translator (.) and at the same time, em, for example, em to the reader, the ethics,* **and blah, blah, blah**

The general extender *and blah, blah, blah* is recorded in Overstreet's (1999) American English data, but is completely missing from token counts in most other studies, so it is not the most familiar general extender for most English L1 speakers. In addition, this form is typically used with a downgrading type of expressive meaning, usually reserved for even more talk that the speaker indicates is irrelevant (cf. Overstreet, 1999: 146), as illustrated in Chapter 4. If those Persian L1 speakers do not intend to be interpreted as expressing a negative attitude to the attached material, then *and stuff* or *and everything* might be better choices of general extender than *and blah, blah, blah* in utterances such as (13). Finding ways to help English L2 learners make better general extender choices has been a goal of those advocating explicit teaching of pragmatic expressions used by English L1 speakers.

More intriguing are examples including *or these kind of things* and *and all the things*, as shown in (14), from Parvaresh *et al.* (2012: 266), used with some frequency, and even as part of the subject noun phrase on occasion.

(14)   *You know, I think, documents, notes,* **and all the things** *should be in good, I mean, safe places*

Among the examples of Persian L1 data listed (with translations) in Table 1 of Parvaresh *et al.* (2012: 264), there are no morphological elements equivalent to the English words "these" and "all," so the utterances containing these forms are not direct transfers from the L1. Moreover, the two phrases just described are not attested in English L1 studies of general extenders, so they are not forms learned from the L2. These are novel phrases created by the Persian L1 speakers as interlanguage forms, developed among themselves during English L2 interaction with each other, we assume. It may be that in contexts where English is learned as a foreign language, where there is little or no interactive contact with English L1 speakers, students take the opportunity to develop their own versions of general extenders. We might say that these students have something in common with others who use English as a lingua franca, not constrained by an adherence to external English L1 norms, but free to create expressions that serve their local communicative purposes. We will return to this topic, but first we should take note of another effect that can be observed when English (L1) speakers, whose general extenders have fairly simple morphology, attempt to use equivalent forms in a language that is a little more morphologically complex.

9.7 English Learners

While the focus of most studies on L2 learning involving general extenders has been on English, we have also noted occasional attempts to investigate the L2 learning experiences of English (L1) speakers. Fernandez (2013) reported on a research project tracking British English (L1) students learning Spanish (L2) during extended stays in Spain, noting that, while on study abroad, "learners often have access to much more linguistic variety, including forms that are not always considered appropriate for the language classroom" (2013: 326). Near the beginning of their experience, the English (L1) learners tended to use Spanish general extender forms that were direct translation equivalents of their typical L1 versions, as in *o algo (asi)* ("or something (like that)") and *y todo (eso)* ("and all (that)"). These phrases were not the most typical expressions used by Spanish (L1) speakers in a control group. Their high-frequency phrases were *y nada* ("and nothing") and *y eso* ("and that"), with relatively few disjunctive phrases recorded. Although the English (L1) students' production of L2 forms increased during their stay and included a much wider range of forms, many of their Spanish (L2) general extenders look like interlanguage forms. The students faced (and many failed to acquire) some features of longer general extenders in Spanish that were problematic (unlike their English counterparts). Nouns, even those used as proforms, and pronouns are marked for both number and gender, and both number and gender agreement are required within phrases in Spanish. Fernandez (2013: 302) presents some really revealing examples of adjunctive extender structures that were used by the English (L1) students while failing to include Spanish grammatical agreement, as in the two phrases reproduced in (15).

(15)   *y otros cosas* ("and other [masculine] things [feminine]")
         y cosas como eso ("and things [feminine] like that [masculine]")

Clearly there is more that has to be learned by English (L1) speakers attempting to use Spanish adjunctive extenders, at least in terms of formal accuracy, than would be the case in the opposite direction.

Despite these issues, Fernandez (2013) reports that the study-abroad experience had a positive effect in terms of some of the students' overall Spanish (L2) learning. Dippold (2016) reported a generally similar outcome from an investigation into the effect on the German (L2) use of general extenders by a group of English (L1) students during a study-abroad year. There were two interesting aspects of the German (L2) uses of general extenders reported by Dippold (2016). The most proficient group taking part increased their use of *oder so* and *oder so was*, the two most common disjunctive forms of the German (L1) speakers in a control group, while less proficient learners either used no disjunctive forms or produced a low-frequency German expression that was a literal translation of their most common L1 form: *oder etwas* ("or something"). A more intriguing finding was an effect we might describe as "unlearning," in which the most common form used by the lower-level students, *und so weiter* ("and so forth"), was not used at all by the higher-level learners, who had adopted *und so* as their favored adjunctive form, in line with German (L1) usage. We might speculate here that, for some learners, one expression that was learned from a textbook (*und so weiter*) was replaced during the study-abroad experience with another (*und so*) that is more common in everyday usage. The integration factor supported by a study-abroad experience was also argued to have a very positive effect on the use of interpersonal markers, including general extenders, in Grieve's (2011) study of German (L1) students in Australia.

9.8 English as a Lingua Franca

In Chapter 1, we speculated that the disjunctive extender *or so*, with relatively low frequency and restricted collocation requirements in English L1 usage, had become more frequent in the use of English as a lingua franca among European speakers. We suggested that cognates in German (*oder so*) and Dutch (*of zo*) had prompted speakers to transfer the unrestricted collocations into their use of the similar English form. Interestingly, in data presented in Hüttner (2009: 289), during a conversation in English with two German L1 speakers, a Chinese L1 speaker produced the form *or so*, as in (16), when talking about how a teacher's behavior had changed.

(16) *I mean her personality (.) her attitude changed very easy because she was so kind of strict **or so***

The linguistic context in (16) is not one that would normally occasion the use of *or so* (e.g. there is no numerical reference), so we may be witnessing an expanded use of this expression in English as a lingua franca beyond only speakers of European languages.

Investigating general extenders in English as a lingua franca requires a willingness to recognize different forms or not to find any at all, similar to the search for formulaic language (Kecskés, 2007: 193; MacKenzie, 2014: 94). In some recorded data they are almost completely absent. For example, in about nine pages of transcribed conversations presented in Jenkins (2014: 175–99), we found only two general extenders, one each from the interviewer and an interviewee. It may be that, in this case, the speakers of English as a lingua franca, international graduate students in a British university, were trying to avoid using casual language in interaction with an English L1 speaker/researcher in an academic context, especially if the L1 speaker was hardly using any. We might see this as evidence that English as a lingua franca is not something fixed that international speakers have as an alternative variety of English, but instead "is a variable way of

9.8 English as a Lingua Franca

using it" Seidlhofer (2011: 77) that is sensitive to context. When all speakers in an interaction are using English as a lingua franca, we may be able to find greater use of pragmatic expressions overall and general extenders in particular.[1]

In the most comprehensive study of general extenders in English as a lingua franca, Metsä-Ketelä (2016) analyzed recorded interactions among international students attending universities in Finland, among whom English was the lingua franca. There are examples of *or so*, but its frequency is relatively low compared to *or something (like that)*, the most common disjunctive form(s) in the data. We don't know if the token count included the variant *or something like this*, as in (17), from (2016: 333).

(17)   *you have these these er labels that say that it's a they are happy eggs or they are free eggs or they are free chickens' eggs **or something like this***

In (17), the speaker is trying to come up with an appropriate English expression (probably "free range eggs") and indicates the possible inaccuracy with the general extender, using *this* instead of *that*, creating another form that is a possible English phrase, but one that isn't used by English L1 speakers very often. It was noted in the English L2 of German L1 speakers in Terraschke's (2007a) study, so we may be witnessing an expanding use of this disjunctive variant in English as a lingua franca.

The high frequency of *or something* variants may also be due to an infrequent use of *or anything (like that)*, no examples of which were presented in Metsä-Ketelä's (2016) report. A clear example of *or something* being used where *or anything* might be expected in English L1 is illustrated in (18), from Smit's (2009: 208) study of English as a lingua franca in an international hotel management program.

(18)   *I don't think I would choose to study medicine in English **or something** but . . . hotel management I would*

What is striking about example (18) is the complexity of the syntactic structure of the utterance, with hypothetical modal verbs in embedded clauses plus object fronting and ellipsis, indicating a strong command of English grammatical structure, yet accompanied by an unexpected phrase as the (optional) general extender. This is a reminder that even advanced-proficiency English language users may not be aware of how pragmatic markers such as general extenders are normally used in English L1. It may be, of course, that the distinction in English L1 usage between *or something* and *or anything* is not treated as relevant among speakers of English as a lingua franca and *or anything* may end up with a reduced role or no role at all.

One of the most interesting disjunctive phrases in Metsä-Ketelä's (2016: 335) excellent array of examples is *or things (like that)*, as illustrated in (19).

(19) *they are er going to school once or twice a weekly or erm every six weeks for two weeks **or things like that***

When we look at token counts of general extenders in reports from English L1 in use, we tend not to find the word *things* in disjunctive phrases, so the example in (19) illustrates a distinct feature of English as a lingua franca, that is, the creation of novel expressions that look and sound like English L1 phrases, but that, on close inspection, are slightly different. This phenomenon is in line with MacKenzie's (2014) observation that "English as a lingua franca speakers exploit unused latent possibilities of English" (2014: 2).

Of course, some expressions are clearly novel forms, not found in databases of spoken English L1, that fulfill a clear textual function, as in (20), where the phrase *such things*, with no conjunction, signals the completion of a turn. It is also in the position of a right-hand bracket with *I don't know* as the left-hand bracket. As we noted in Chapter 1, the expression *I don't know* is the most frequent three-word phrase in Mauranen's (2012) data. Example (20) is from Shaw et al.'s (2009: 186) study involving international exchange students at universities in Sweden and Denmark.

(20) *just to improve my English, definitely, to meet some people, mmm, I don't know, get to know another country, **such things***

We have already noted the use of *such* in a general extender (*and such things*) by a Persian L1 speaker earlier and, in the translation (*and such*) of Swedish *å sånt* in Chapter 5. Is it possible that the speaker in (20) had acquired the *such* element from familiarity with the Swedish expression? We know that *such* was an integral part of some early forms of English general extenders, as described in Chapter 6, so we may find it has been resurrected among speakers of English as a lingua franca.

The most frequent adjunctive form in Metsä-Ketelä's (2016) data is *and so on* by a large margin. We have noted before that use of this phrase is normally limited to formal registers, written and spoken, in English L1 usage, yet it has almost unlimited distribution in English as a lingua franca. In Mauranen's (2012) analysis of the most common three-word phrases in her database, *and so on* was fifth in the top ten of frequent expressions, yet, in a comparable database of English L1 speech, it wasn't in the top ten at all. For Mauranen (2012), this adds to the impression (along with the frequency of *I don't know*) that, in English as a lingua franca, speakers are able to make use of vague language forms. One source of the high frequency of *and so on* is identified by Metsä-Ketelä (2016) in terms of a tendency among speakers of English as a lingua franca to add redundancy. In the case of exemplifying, speakers are often very explicit through a combination of the general extender in the right-hand bracket with *for instance* in a left-hand bracket, as in (21), from Metsä-Ketelä (2016: 340).

9.8 English as a Lingua Franca

(21)   *that still leaves a lot of say diversity because it includes <u>for instance</u> Serbo-Croats erm and Turkish and Moroccans **and so on***

Metsä-Ketelä (2016) makes the point that either *for instance* or *and so on* alone would have been sufficient to accomplish the communicative purpose, but with the combination, "the speaker makes the example more explicit and thus enhances comprehension" (2016: 340).

Another insight from Metsä-Ketelä's (2016) detailed investigation is the frequency with which adjunctive extenders are used when one speaker brings a paraphrase of previous discussions to a close prior to opening up a new direction/topic or asking a question, as illustrated in (22) from Metsä-Ketelä (2016: 342).

(22)   *now that we've been the last two days we've been discussing all these open source software issues **and things like that** how would you describe the situation of er open source software and this kind of development in Uzbekistan*

Mauranen (2012: 177) makes a similar point about how structured turns of the type in (22) are part of the argumentative discourse found in academic genres. While these speakers of English as a lingua franca are constructing their contributions to the ongoing interaction, they often use the more explicitly cohesive long forms (with *like that*), as in (22). Using longer forms tends to create an impression of greater formality, a known preference in the academic context.

In this brief review of general extenders in English as a lingua franca, we have found evidence of sophisticated structural organization of utterances and larger discourse segments, yet this is often not matched by a comparable level of expertise in the selection of established general extenders. If we think of general extenders as fitting into the same class as words and phrases in the lexicon, not the grammatical structure, of English as a lingua franca, then we can account for their absence among some speakers (like unknown vocabulary) and the creative use by others taking advantage of the open class (like new words or new forms of existing words). It is the creative use of language that is the most fascinating aspect of English as a lingua franca, "for it enables its users to express themselves more freely without having to conform to norms which represent the sociocultural identity of other people" (Widdowson 2004: 361). We anticipate a lot more research into the very interesting uses of pragmatic markers, including general extenders, in English as a lingua franca in the future. We will also no doubt witness an increase in attempts to work out how to introduce greater pragmatic awareness earlier in language education so that those speakers of English as a lingua franca can develop more confidence in their pragmatic awareness to accompany their well-developed structural knowledge.

9.9 In Language Teaching

Although, as researchers, we may find the new and different expressions used in English as a lingua franca interestingly innovative and intriguing to study, we should keep in mind that "English as lingua franca is an applied linguist's term: most users probably just think they are speaking English" (MacKenzie, 2014: 2). In fact, they mostly want to speak an established variety of English (L1) and may not display any enthusiasm for the idea of English as a lingua franca. MacKenzie reports becoming keenly aware of this when he introduced aspects of the lingua franca to a group of students in Switzerland who were planning to become English (L2) teachers: "they looked at me in horror and disbelief and asserted that they wanted to achieve near-native competence" (2014: 158). Programs and materials designed to help them achieve that goal have traditionally been devoted to grammar and vocabulary, with an emphasis on the written language, but in recent years they have tried to incorporate more spoken language activities, with a resulting interest in how to develop learners' pragmatic competence in interaction.

During the 1990s, the English (L2) teaching field experienced a number of changes that were mostly the outcome of new ideas emerging from the widespread adoption of communicative approaches. One of those ideas was that the use of spoken English depended on being aware of aspects of meaning creation that were tied to an understanding of the pragmatics of interaction, in addition to a knowledge of grammar and vocabulary. One problem with this idea was that most learners already had a lot of experience with their own pragmatics of interaction, at a subconscious level, resulting in the frequent transfer of L1 forms and their possible misinterpretation. From the beginning, the method believed to be the best solution to this problem was based on explicit attention to the analysis of difference: a pragmatic contrastive analysis. This is succinctly expressed by Terraschke and Holmes: "identifying areas of socio-pragmatic contrast where L1 transfer may cause problems for second language learners may assist in reducing instances of cross-cultural misunderstanding" (2007: 198). The impetus to increase pragmatic awareness among learners was the subject of a lot of articles and edited collections advocating pragmatics instruction (e.g. Schmidt, 1993; Bouton, 1994; Bardovi-Harlig, 1996; Kasper and Schmidt, 1996; Rose and Kasper, 2001). The early focus was on speech acts and the identification of politeness routines, which were clearly different among speakers of different L1s. As Koutlaki (2002) pointed out, what seems face-threatening in the act of making an offer in one culture may actually be face-enhancing in another. As more aspects of the pragmatics of spoken English were identified through research, it became clear that learners in educational contexts were not going to "pick up" appropriate pragmatic routines and that they would need focused instruction to raise their pragmatic awareness. This was certainly the case with the use of general extenders, which,

9.9 In Language Teaching

as we noted at the beginning of this chapter, were probably invisible (and unheard) as far as most teachers and learners were concerned. An early proposal regarding the introduction of general extenders into the spoken language materials used in the L2 classroom was put forward in Overstreet and Yule (1999), developed through occasional workshops with educators in the USA, Japan and Brazil (Overstreet, 2001, 2007) and presented as a few ideas for teaching in Overstreet (2012b) and Overstreet *et al.* (2006).

One practical suggestion that had already been circulating was the development of tasks designed to present (and lead to discussion of) pragmatic expressions in the students' L1 alongside comparable expressions (i.e. pragmatic equivalents) in the target L2, especially in a foreign language context where students share an L1 (Eslami-Rasekh, 2005). More specifically, Evison *et al.*, referring to VCMs ("vague category markers," or general extenders), proposed creating "comparisons between native speaker VCM usage and that by non-native expert users" (2007: 155). To that end, Overstreet (2012b) described an exercise to create a three-way comparison between the most frequent general extenders produced by learners in their L1, in their L2, and in those produced by a relevant group of L1 speakers of that target L2. We can illustrate this in action with a small sample of material that was designed for use with Persian (L1) speakers to help them realize how their preferred adjunctive forms in English (L2) might be unduly influenced by their L1 and were not the most typical English (L1) forms, as shown in (23).

(23)	Persian L1	English L2	English L1
	væ inâ	*and blah, blah, blah*	*and stuff*
	væ æz in hærf hâ	*and so on*	*and everything*

These examples are from Parvaresh *et al.* (2012) and Overstreet (2012b), whose English L1 examples here are from American English, which, judging from the choice of expressions, was also the target L2 for these learners. (Other target varieties have different high-frequency forms, as detailed in Chapter 7.) Presented with these examples, the Persian learners can be made aware of the fact that, in their English L2, they are mostly using either an extremely informal, and potentially negative, phrase (*and blah, blah, blah*), or a fairly formal phrase (*and so on*), used a lot by professors, not students (Simpson, 2004), while L1 speakers are using different phrases that have higher frequency in the everyday interactions of American English speakers. With the addition of examples from an English L1 corpus to illustrate typical contextualized uses of the target forms, learners can be provided with opportunities to become aware of the discrepancy between their (earlier use of) more specialized phrases and the English phrases more often used in those contexts.

The acquisition process assumed to be stimulated by this type of exercise is based on the psychological constructs of "noticing" and paying "attention" to focused details of the target in order that some understanding of their meaning or function is learned (Schmidt, 2001). After all, we can't process what we don't understand. Carter and McCarthy propose explicit "'noticing' tasks built around conversational extracts" (2004: 81), based on the assumption that "attention, noticing and awareness play an important role in any language acquisition" (Spöttl and McCarthy, 2004: 193). More details of this approach based on the use of an English (L1) corpus are presented in O'Keeffe *et al.* (2007).

In the following tables, we try to illustrate how direct attention and noticing can be fostered, using English (L1) data, in Tables 9.1, 9.2, and 9.4, and samples of English (L2) data, in Table 9.3. An important element in the "noticing" process is directing the student's attention to the contrast between what they have been saying (i.e. specific phrases used inappropriately) and what they are going to say in the future (i.e. more appropriate phrases). We hope that exercise C in Table 9.3 is a small, but exemplary, step in that direction. Table 9.4 may be best used with more experienced students because it requires some close attention to the contexts in which the different general extenders might naturally be used.

If we were to ask teachers to treat exercises of the type shown in Tables 9.1–9.4 as guides to making their own versions to suit their own situations, we would include some basic information about the two classes of general extenders. We would add that the common meaning of all disjunctive general extenders (Table 9.1) is that there are other possibilities, implicating approximation and implying potential inaccuracy.[2] The different versions indicate that there are different kinds of other possibilities, including the minimum expected in a situation. The common meaning of all adjunctive general extenders (Table 9.2) is that there is more (that could be mentioned).[3] The different versions indicate that there are different kinds of "more." The sentences presented in Table 9.3 are mostly versions of examples already noted in this chapter, only adapted for pedagogical purposes in an English (L2) learning exercise.[4] The examples in Table 9.4 represent a more difficult pedagogical exercise and come from a variety of published sources.[5] The biggest assumption in asking learners to do exercises like these is that at some later time those learners will find an opportunity to make use of one of these prefabricated solutions to a local communicative challenge and feel confident that they know exactly what to say.

9.9 In Language Teaching

Table 9.1 *Disjunctive general extenders: a basic learning exercise*

General extender	Typical uses: indicating that "there are other possibilities," approximating
or so	after information containing numbers, measurements and time expressions only
or anything	after information containing a negative (e.g. *n't, no, not, never*), and indicating a minimum that would be expected
or whatever	after information that may be incomplete or that allows another interpretation, but the "other" is not considered relevant
or something	after information that may be incorrect or that allows another valid interpretation or contains an invitation or request
or something like that	after information that is marked as being close to accurate, especially when trying to remember names, words and phrases

Task A. Choose the best disjunctive phrase from the set of five above to fill each space.

1 *The old house was about a mile _____ from the village.*
2 *I know what he's up to. Does he think I'm stupid _____?*
3 *He's so unpleasant and he never smiles _____. I feel sad for him.*
4 *So what if he has long hair and a beard _____. Can he do the job?*
5 *They're very rude, they don't say "Please" or "Thank you" _____.*
6 *Did you hear that noise last night? It was like a cheap firework _____.*
7 *She lives alone in a small flat and has no close family or friends _____.*
8 *I can't remember his new wife's name. It's Jane, or Jill, or Julie, _____.*
9 *It's too hot in here. Could you switch on the fan or open the window _____?*
10 *I think her research area is climate studies or environmental humanities _____.*
11 *They can have the old magazines or newspapers _____. It doesn't matter to me.*
12 *The meeting should only last an hour _____ and we'll be finished for the week.*
13 *I can't believe it. It's my birthday and he hasn't called or even sent me a card _____.*
14 *It was a really large building. I don't know the word. Palace? No, edifice, I think. It was an edifice _____.*

Table 9.2 *Adjunctive general extenders: a basic learning exercise*

General extender	Typical uses: indicating that "there is more"
and stuff	after information that is treated as familiar (informal)
and so on	after information or a quote that could continue, often in a list (formal)
and everything	after information that is surprising or extreme (informal), or indicating a maximum that might be expected
and blah, blah, blah	after information in reported speech or writing, more of which is considered not important or having negative value (informal)
and things like that	after information naming specific elements, often in a list

Task B. Choose the best adjunctive phrase from the set of five above to fill each space.

1 *They called him "Dummy" _____ that weren't very nice.*

Table 9.2 (*cont.*)

General extender	Typical uses: indicating that "there is more"

2 *Her older brother was super smart and went to Harvard _____.*
3 *Most visitors to London want to see Big Ben, Buckingham Palace _____.*
4 *We were kind of bored there, like you know, we just sat around _____.*
5 *It can lead to other problems, such as pneumonia and bronchitis _____.*
6 *They put on an amazing show. They had a bonfire and fireworks _____.*
7 *We were put off by the way Tina bragged about herself all the time, "I'm the best, the most wondrous, _____."*
8 *They'll give you this form, you know, and you have to sort of fill it out _____.*
9 *It's the kind of shop that sells small ornaments, cheap rings and earrings _____.*
10 *The cover includes information about the file such as its size, history _____.*
11 *It was such a shock. Someone had broken in and gone through all the drawers, pulling stuff out _____.*
12 *He had a long laundry list of complaints, how he has to do everything and we do nothing _____.*
13 *Remember how simple life was in the 90s, before we had mobile phones and email _____?*
14 *I mean, he's good-looking and filthy rich _____, but I couldn't stand him.*

Table 9.3 *General extenders: a correction exercise*

Task C. The general extenders in these sentences are used in unusual ways. Can you identify the unusual forms and suggest more appropriate replacements?

1 *Is it quite formal or so?*
2 *It seems like they don't have any stress or so.*
3 *I have to study, I mean, memorize things and, and, and.*
4 *They're called happy eggs or free eggs or something like this.*
5 *We went there and we never really ate in a restaurant or something.*
6 *They're better at answering in English when there's a phone call or so.*
7 *I don't know what it is called. We'll call it like umbrella species or whatever.*
8 *I'd like to travel to meet other people and get to know another country, such things.*
9 *It's important to remember the translators, their political views and blah, blah, blah.*
10 *Then she really got jealous of my boyfriend and wouldn't let me see him anymore and so on.*
11 *I think that documents, personal papers, and all such things should be kept in a safe place.*
12 *If I remember correctly, they offer the class twice a week, or for two weeks every six weeks, or things like that.*
13 *Most people here do not have the ability to watch western movies, listen to foreign music and such things.*
14 *It is a very nice place with a swimming pool and a great view and blah, blah, blah, but it's very expensive to go there.*

9.9 In Language Teaching

Table 9.4 *General extenders: a testing exercise*

or so	*and so on*	*stuff like that*
an' shit	*Whatever*	*and everything*
or what	*and things*	*or something like that*
and that	*or anything*	*and all that sort of thing*
and stuff	*or something*	

Task D. Choose one phrase from those listed above to fill each space. Use each form once.

1. *It doesn't matter. I don't care.* _____.
2. *I haven't had anyone for the last three months* _____.
3. *(about betting) You never told me if you won or lost* _____.
4. *Are you doing anything tonight? Do you want to go out* _____?
5. *(about decorating) There's no money and they need paint* _____.
6. *He must have been born in eighteen fifty-eight* _____, *I suppose.*
7. *They'd like to pluck your eye out and pull your arm outta socket* _____.
8. *I'd like to do it. I mean I really want to do it. I'm not being funny* _____.
9. *I don't think it's a Berwick word, moggy. You hear it on the telly* _____.
10. *(on her birthday) Everybody was really nice to me and I got a nice present* _____.
11. *(about a professor) He was terrible, terrible, so abstruse, he does sound changes* _____.
12. *It's in that prayer that we always recite, you know, "Our father who art in heaven,* _____."
13. *We used to play hide-and-seek a lot and hopscotch, baseball, and we would swim all the time, you know,* _____.
14. *I'm recovering from several days of strange meals and drinks* _____.

10 Reflections and Projections

In the preceding chapters we have tried to provide a comprehensive review of what we have learned about general extenders from earlier research, together with some new observations on their forms and functions in contemporary languages. The recognition of multiple functions has allowed us to combine earlier ideas such as set-marking with later proposals based on (inter)subjectivity to produce three distinct types of communicative function fulfilled by general extenders: referential, interpersonal and personal. An additional textual function has been explored here in detail for the first time. In order to look at how each of these functions is instantiated in terms of good exemplars, we treated them separately in individual chapters. Yet, in everyday use, we might expect general extenders to be used with more than a single function on any occasion.

10.1 Multiple Functions

Two detailed illustrations of the multifunctionality of general extenders (*an' stuff, or something like that*) in spoken American English can be found in Overstreet (1999: 148–51). In some more recent work, where researchers have shared detailed transcriptions of their data, we can find general extenders being used with at least two functions at the same time. We will analyze examples of this multifunctionality in English and French. In the extract in (1), from Nikolaou and Sclafani (2018: 256), with their transcription, a woman (T) is talking about her experiences as a foreign student in Athens during 2009.

(1)   T: it was <u>like</u> really around the time when there was a lot of um (..)
       I: Riots *[and stuff]*
       T: *[Attacking **and stuff**]* and <u>like</u> bombs, and tear bombs **and stuff**

Both speakers use *and stuff* in phrases with referential function identifying the kind of event being described, with the implication that there was more going on than is said, even if speaker T may not be able to come up with the most accurate terms. An additional implication is that they both seem willing to assume shared knowledge about what would be going on in such an event. At

10.1 Multiple Functions

the same time, *and stuff* occurs in the overlapping contributions of both speakers, marking a similarity of thought and communicative support, indicators of interpersonal function. In the contribution of speaker T, *and stuff* also serves as a right bracket with another pragmatic marker *like* in the left bracket twice, to create the beginning and end of her two conjoined descriptions, giving the forms a textual function as well. The forms used in those bracketing pairs (*like . . . and stuff*) at the time would also indicate that the speaker is probably younger and American (correct on both counts), giving them a social marking "function" too.

We have also tried to describe analogous uses of general extenders in different languages and offer extract (2), with Secova's (2017: 2) translation from French, as further exemplification of their use in the structuring of text as well as accompanying the expression of the speaker's point of view, which we have analyzed as the personal, or subjective function of general extender use.

(2)   *en fait (.) les filles elles venaient vers moi (..) et <u>genre</u> et <u>genre</u> je les ai vues arriver vers moi **et tout** (.) et après j'ai vu lui il arrivait (..) et <u>genre</u> je l'ai regardé comme ça (..) <u>genre en mode</u> "tu veux quoi" **et tout** (..) et après dès que j'ai vu qu'il allait ouvrir la bouche je fais "casse toi"!*
("actually (.) the girls were coming towards me (..) and like and like I saw them coming towards me and everything (.) and then I saw him coming (..) and like I looked at him like that (..) like 'what do you want' and everything (..) and then as soon as I saw that he was going to open his mouth I go 'piss off'!")

The expressions *genre* and *genre en mode* are used in a way that is very similar to English *like* in its pragmatic marker function and *et tout* is the most frequent general extender in Parisian French, as analyzed in Chapter 8. As the speaker reconstructs the event in (2), she recreates the scene, beginning with her awareness of the arrival of the females, bracketed by *genre . . . et tout*, then with the same grammatical structure (without brackets), the arrival of the male, followed by her bracketed (*genre en mode . . . et tout*) confrontational question, building to the climax of the event, her indication of how she feels about him. There is no discernible referential function for *et tout* here, but it adds intensity to what is being said each time. The clue of intensity marking leads us to a personal function, which together with a distinct textual function, allows us to analyze what is said in (2) in terms of two (or more) simultaneous functions.

The recreated scene in (2) is based on the speaker's perspective and contains only her two utterances in the event, using the double bracket with *et tout* to focus on her question, making the whole utterance serve a strongly personal function, expressing how she felt. Secova (2018: 164), in an insightful observation about her data sources, comments that "when speakers quote themselves" in a retelling, they are adding vividness to an account, as indeed is the case in (2). In fact, this text is restructured to represent a vivid personal experience. After the first attempt at setting the scene, the "orientation," the speaker changes course. She repeats the same information, but with a major change to make "self" the subject (*je*). She then continues to be the first-person subject of all the main verbs in her turn. It's all about *moi*. All other participants in the event are represented in grammatically subordinate roles. In addition, following Secova's (2014) analysis, and noting the frequent use of *et tout*, plus the use of a pejorative expression (*casse toi*), we would suspect that the speaker is younger, less educated and working class (all correct), resulting in a social marking "function" in this case as well as in (1).

We hope that the analysis of these two extracts will provide some guidance when others try to connect general extender form and function in other texts and contexts. Rather than simply summarize what we covered in the earlier chapters, we would like to encourage new research by introducing some novel (or previously neglected) forms of general extenders and different perspectives on their uses that might reward more attention in the future.

10.2 Utterance Position

One of the most persistent, and misleading, elements in definitions of general extenders is that they are "utterance-final" or even "sentence-final" (Tagliamonte, 2012: 258). As indicators that a list, a topic, or a turn, or even all three together, are "complete," adjunctive forms have a natural position at the end of utterances to mark that completion. In a language with Subject-Verb-Object word order, English speakers often attach general extenders to noun phrases functioning as objects as the final constituent in an utterance. However, those objects are not always in final position, as illustrated in (3) from Tagliamonte (2016: 122), where a preposition phrase follows the list of objects, and in (4), from Cheshire (2007: 177), where the same adjunctive form (*and things*) comes before the end of a subordinate clause that is followed by the main clause, resulting in a general extender in a position quite distant from the end of the utterance.

(3)   *my granny would go out and get parsley and leeks and kale **and things** out the garden for soup*

(4)   *but maybe if like parents have given permission **and things** first, they probably like might think "why am I saying that?" you know*

The general extender may also on occasion attach to a verb, as in (5), from Mauranen (2004: 184), where the disjunctive form is actually inside the verb phrase. Mauranen (2004: 185) also includes an example where the disjunctive form is inside a noun phrase, as in (6).

(5) *if they wanted to apply **or something like that** for funding then it'd be a good idea*

(6) *usually it's about a dozen **or so** people meeting once a month*

In example (7), from Aijmer (2002: 245), *and everything* is part of an object noun phrase (but not at the end of the clause), and *or something* is part of a subject noun phrase (and also not in final position).

(7) *I got my coat **and everything** caught under me and a young postman **or something** got up and I thought ooh this is grand*

The use of *or something* as part of the subject in (7) is worthy of notice since some commentators (Channell, 1994: 134; Palacios Martínez, 2011: 2454) have actually claimed that it cannot happen. Those opinions notwithstanding, we have been able to identify multiple uses of general extenders as part of subject noun phrases from early in the historical record (i.e. in *OED Online*), as in (8)–(10), as well as in the twentieth century, illustrated in the American English examples in (11) and (12), and the British English examples in (13) from Aijmer (2002: 50) and (14) from Pichler and Levey (2011: 446) in more recent studies. The early examples often occur with passive verbs.

(8) *if money **or sum oþer þing** be ʒeven to hem*

[1475 (a1400) *Apol. Lollard Doctr.* (1842) 11 OED]

(9) *an instrument in an house whereon garments **and other things** be hanged*

[1565–73 T. COOPER *Thesaurus Pegasus* OED]

(10) *A release is an instrument whereby estates, rights, titles, entries, actions, **and other things** be sometimes extinguished*

[1594 W. WEST *Symbolaeogr.: 2ⁿᵈ Pt.* §466 OED]

(11) *Walking **and things like that** are the only sane modes of getting about*

[1909 David Graham Phillips *The Fashionable Adventures of Joshua Craig; A Novel* COHA]

(12) *You think, Elsie, that school and that play **and stuff like that** are important*

[1935 Mark Schorer *House Too Old* COHA]

(13) *I think if I just sort of take you round and show you where central services **and so on** are*

(14) *We found that eh stuff **and that** was dearer for a while*

Note that in example (11), the adjunctive form is not only part of the subject, but also cannot be omitted without creating an ungrammatical structure

(*Walking are ...), illustrating a point made earlier in Chapter 1 that general extenders are not always syntactically optional.

These examples contain an eclectic group of general extender forms, so it isn't possible to say that only certain forms can be part of a subject noun phrase. What they do represent is an aspect of English general extender use that has not been given any sustained attention, providing a fairly open research topic at this time. Even if such structures turn out to have small token counts, we should acknowledge their existence and include them in an attempt to calculate the ratio of utterance-final to non-utterance-final positions of general extenders in different corpora. The result would have an impact on claims regarding the nature of right-periphery phenomena in English (cf. Traugott, 2012, 2016).

As we have noted already, there are other languages where a general extender form in non-final position is quite normal, either because of a different basic word order such as Subject-Object-Verb, illustrated in (15) from Persian, with the translation of Parvaresh *et al.* (2012: 266), or because of word order constraints in grammatical constructions, as in German, shown in (16), with Terraschke's (2007a: 62) translation.

(15) âxe xeire særeš dæm æz væfâdâri **væ nemidunæm æz in hærf hâ** mizæd hæmiše
("She was the sort of person who about loyalty and I don't know of such talks was always talking")

(16) ich würd dann halt irgendwie zwei Wochen vorm Examen **oder so** anfangen zu lernen
("then I would start studying like two weeks before the exam or something")

We suspect that, as we expand our investigations to other languages with different types of morphology and different word order patterns, we will discover greater versatility in the positions where general extenders are used than those determined so far, mostly on the basis of English language studies.

10.3 Associative Plurals

Going beyond English language data, there is a type of grammatical structure that is reported to be common in Asian, African, Australian and Pacific languages, according to Daniel and Moravcsik (2000), but not in European languages generally and not hitherto identified as a structure in English. The structure is described as an associative plural and is defined in the following way by Moravcsik (2003: 470).

Associative plurals will be taken to be constructions whose meaning is "X and X's associate(s)," where all members are individuals, X is the focal referent, and the associate(s) form a group centering around X.

10.3 Associative Plurals

Moravcsik (2003: 469) illustrates this grammatical feature with the example in (17), from Japanese. In this case, *Tanaka* is the focal referent and *-tachi* is the associative plural marker, attached to the noun and signaling, as in the translation here, reference to a group of people associated with him.

(17)   *Tanaka-**tachi*** ("Tanaka and his family or friends or associates")

We had noticed a similar structure in Hawaiian, as illustrated in (18) and (19), from Pukui and Elbert (1986: 217), where the focal referent is always human. The structure, though not the actual morpheme (*mā*), appears to have been carried over into Hawai'i Creole English/Pidgin, as in (20), from Tonouchi (2001: 32).

(18)   *Hina **mā*** ("Hina and her husband, friends")

(19)   *Ke ali'i **mā*** ("The chief and his retinue")

(20)   *she axed me wea my mom **guys** went*
        ("she asked me where my mom and her group went")

The use of *guys* here is not the only morpheme used to mark a group of associates in Pidgin because we have also heard the form *dem* ("them"), as in *Bev-dem*, referring to a woman named *Bev* and her group of friends. In (18)–(20), and in some other examples we have noted, the associative plural morpheme functions like an enclitic. That also seems to be the best grammatical analysis of the way some adjunctive forms are used as associative plural markers. We will return to this point, but first we should note that English has a tendency to lexicalize associative plurals, as in (21) and (22), from the late twentieth century (*OED Online*), which are specific extenders, both used as part of the subject noun phrase. Yet, there are occasional examples of general extender-type phrases with a proform that appear to be functioning as associative plurals, as in (23), from a novel by Nick Hornby (2001).

(21)   *Mitch **and his crowd** didn't flip for jazz, but he'd come on strong with the bingos.*

(22)   *Kozo **and his gang** threw a barbecue as a 'sayonara' present.*

(23)   *I'm like one of those American comic-book guys. Spiderman **and all them**.*

These last three examples are from written sources, but we can illustrate the same general extender function in spoken data. The utterances in (24), from Stenström *et al.* (2002), and (25), from Levey (2007), contain references to focal referents and groups associated with them, using the adjunctives *and that* and *and all that*.

(24)   *Where did Chantal **and that** go?*

(25)   *Well normally like boys think football's a boy game cause David Beckham **and all that** are boys*

In both these examples, the adjunctive forms are part of a subject noun phrase indicating the focal referent, and used as specific extenders for groups of people. This novel grammatical structure seems to have become quite common in British English, not only in the forms in (24) and (25) from young speakers in London, but also in other related forms. Example (26) is also from Stenström *et al.* (2002: 102), who actually list six tokens of *and all that lot* in their data. Example (27) is from Evison *et al.* (2007: 144), who list seven examples of that adjunctive structure in their token counts.

(26)   *What pissed me off is, is he's hanging about with Pierre **and that lot** now right*

(27)   *I was sitting with Jim **and that lot***

From these examples, we can see that the focal referent noun phrase is typically a proper noun naming an individual, but it can be other nouns that have a definite referent. In British English, the forms that we have identified as functioning as associative plural markers are *and that*, *and all that*, *and that lot* and *and all that lot*, or, in the form of a structural template: *and (all) that (lot)*. Since those phrases are not at all common as general or specific extenders in American English, we may have to look at other adjunctive forms that might be marking associative plurals in that variety, possibly in expressions such as *Jay-Z **and all them*** and *LeBron **and all them***, prompts for an interesting future research project.

There is another adjunctive extender-type expression functioning as an associative plural marker that we have identified in English, or rather, in a Latin expression used in a very limited register of English. It is an abbreviation used in bibliographic references such as Overstreet *et al.* (2006) that translates as "and others." This translation might lead us to label *et al.* as an adjunctive general extender. However, remembering Harvey Sacks' aphorism, "By etcetera we mean there are others, but not any others" (Sacks, 1992: 246), we have to interpret *et al.* in the same way and recognize the very narrow range of reference that is indicated here by "others" (i.e. other co-authors). This makes it a highly specific extender and, in this particular example, involving two female co-authors, it is *et aliae* ("and others, feminine") that is being abbreviated.

10.4   An Apparent Anomaly

In Chapter 6, we traced a path of development from *and things* to the later form *and things like that*. We speculated that, like other long forms, *and things like that* is used to indicate a more cohesive tie with its antecedent, giving it a distinct and separate function from the short form. That function seems to

10.4 An Apparent Anomaly

have been needed less among the speakers recorded in the *London-Lund Corpus* during the 1970s because the short form is used twice as often as the long form in the two studies reported in Aijmer (1985, 2002). In that time and place, *stuff*-variants were very rare. When we look at data where *stuff*-variants are frequent, such as the American English examples collected by Overstreet (1999) in the early 1990s, tokens of the short form *and stuff* are very frequent and long forms are rare. A similar relationship exists with *or something*, the short form, reported to be used more than ten times as often as the long form, *or something like that*, by Overstreet (1999), and more than five times as often in Aijmer (1985, 2002). To corroborate this pattern, we can point to a relatively high token count for *and everything* while the long form with *like that* is very rare in both British and American data sets. In summary, there is a distinct pattern in which short general extenders are used much more frequently than their longer counterparts.

Cheshire (2007) reported a similar pattern, with a dominant short form *and stuff* in data from all three of the English towns studied. However, although the short form *and things* was used more often than its long counterpart in the two towns in southern England, the token counts from the town further north revealed the opposite pattern, with the long form *and things like that* used more often. We might initially treat this anomaly as potentially another example of how southern British English differs from northern British English and assume that the different pattern is tied to some kind of regional dialect feature. This may be the case, but there seems to be another factor involved. Cheshire (2007: 164) reports a very clear difference in the use of *and things* according to the socioeconomic class of the speaker. In the southern towns, middle-class speakers use *and things* quite frequently, yet there are zero instances recorded among working-class speakers in those towns. There are fewer tokens of *and things* in the northern town and they are split between the middle and working classes. In the northern town, *and that* is the most frequent short form, especially among the working class. As we noted in Chapter 7, this southern middle class–northern working class divide in Britain has a number of linguistic correlates.

The strong preference for *and that* among working-class speakers in the north is supported by Macaulay's (1985) Scottish data and also by Pichler and Levey's (2011) data from another northern English town. Macaulay (1985) records no examples of *and things*, but does list a few examples of *and things like that*. Pichler and Levey (2011) actually report more tokens of *and things like that* than the short form *and things*. This is really an anomaly. Could it be that, in northern Britain, the short phrase *and that* is so dominant that another short form such as *and things* is excluded, but the long form *and things like that* continues to serve a different function, not fulfilled by *and that*? This might be one way of explaining the apparent anomaly. We should also remain aware of the possible desire among many in the north not to sound like someone who is southern middle class.

In a sociolinguistically less sensitive domain, we can observe another example of the dominance of one expression, in the case of *and so on* in formal spoken language, which has been used to the virtual exclusion of all the longer forms of other adjunctive phrases for a long time in a particular role (cf. Aijmer, 1985). When one dominant form, typically short, loses its exclusionary status, the process can be described as "lexical replacement" (Tagliamonte and Denis, 2010: 332). In Tagliamonte and Denis' (2010) Canadian data, the long form *and things like that* is recorded more than twice as often as the short form, showing that the apparent anomaly in Pichler and Levey's (2011) relative frequencies is not limited to northern Britain. Tagliamonte and Denis discuss the possibility that *things*-variants have been subject to lexical replacement by *stuff*-variants, a tendency confirmed by Denis (2017). This development would account for a reduction of *things*-variants overall, but doesn't, by itself, explain why the long form with *things* would be so much more frequent. It may be that there is a tendency in this type of lexical replacement for only short forms to replace short forms, so that *and stuff* replaced *and things*, while the long form with *and things like that* was not replaced. This would mean that it isn't simply the lexical item *things* that is being replaced by *stuff*, but it is the short phrase with *things* that is being replaced by another short phrase with the same conjunction. In a later study of American English, Wagner *et al.* (2015) reported that *and things like that* was the second most frequent adjunctive form while *and things* didn't make the top five in terms of frequency. (Only the five most frequent forms were listed.) The pattern in North American studies of the past two decades involves a different dominant adjunctive form *and stuff*, but with more tokens of the long form *and things like that* than *and things*, it is very similar to what we found in those British areas where *and that* is the dominant form.[1]

The implication in the use of lexical replacement as an explanation of the patterns being described is that, at an earlier time, the lexicalized phrase being replaced must have been more frequent. We might see the reports from Aijmer (1985, 2002), using British English data collected in the 1970s, as supporting this idea in terms of the earlier higher frequency of *and things*. It should follow that older speakers would be more likely to have used *things*-variants. When Stenström *et al.* (2002) compared vague expressions in the speech of teenagers and adults recorded in London during the 1990s, they found that older speakers used *things*-variants more than three times as often as the younger group. In another study investigating general extender use among older people, "collected in relic dialect areas and from conservative speakers," Tagliamonte (2016: 126) also found that those older speakers who were being interviewed used *things*-variants much more frequently than *stuff*-variants. (We noted, however, that the younger interviewers did not accommodate and remained dedicated to *stuff*-variants.)

Our hypothesis for explaining the apparent anomaly of *and things like that* being more frequently used than *and things* in recent studies is based on a process of lexical replacement whereby a short phrase, such as *and things* that was used more often in the past, loses its place to another short phrase, such as *and stuff*, yet the longer counterpart *and things like that* continues to be used with a distinct function. That is an idea that could be investigated more thoroughly in more recent data.

10.5   And/or elsewhere

There are quite a few phrases functioning as extenders that seem to have escaped the attention of researchers up to now, including us, and represent new territory waiting to be explored. Many of these phrases involve the word *else*. Their distribution and function await more detailed study of contemporary spoken English, but we will identify a variety of expressions in this section to illustrate the many variants of general and specific extenders with *else*. One of the most interesting expressions is *elsewhere*, virtually unchanged since Old English (*elles hwær*), which can be used to convey not only "addition," but also "alternative," with the result that it can be used in both adjunctive and disjunctive constructions, as in (28) from the fifteenth century, and (29), from a bit later, in early examples from British English. American English examples from the nineteenth century are cited in (30) and (31).

(28)   *It is granted that the risshbotes ("rush boats") at the Flete **and elsewhere** in London shall be taken into the hands of the Camberlain*

[1419 H.T. Riley *Memorials London* (1868) 676 OED]

(29)   *if you plant onelie one rowe by the sides of your field hedges **or elsewhere**, it will be inough*

[1600 R. Surflet tr. C. Estienne & J. Liébault *Maison Rustique* III xliiii 51 OED]

(30)   *a series of great peace meetings was held in New York **and elsewhere***

[1811 David Low Dodge *War inconsistent with the religion of Jesus Christ* COHA]

(31)   *he opened up upwards of six hundred bodies at the Hotel Dieu **or elsewhere***

[1822 *North American Review*: July 1822: 132–63 COHA]

If we were to paraphrase *elsewhere* in (28)–(31), we would likely say "other places," helping us identify these phrases as specific extenders. However, having identified an earlier form of *else* as *elles*, as in (32), cited in Carroll (2008: 26), we can find it in a phrase from earlier in Middle English that seems to function more like an adjunctive extender.

208   10 Reflections and Projections

(32)   *Mete and drink **and mani þing elles***
("Food and drink and many thing(s) else")

[c1330 (?a1300) *Arch. & M.* MED]

Recognizing another variation in the form as *els* in the historical record allows us to identify phrases with indefinite pronouns that are closer to modern versions of general extenders, as in (33) and (34), both from the sixteenth century, and not long after, find the modern spelling taking over, as in (35) and (36)

(33)   *the other example of children, which flatter their parents to get money, **or something els***

[1581 Stefano Guazzo tr, George Pettie *The ciuile conuersation* EEBO]

(34)   *without respecte either of parish, home charge, debt, **or anything els***

[1599 John Rainolds and Alberico Gentili
Th'overthrow of stage-playes EEBO]

(35)   *Phisitians found y^t he had there a glandule by wearing of armes **or something else***

[1656 R. WHITLEY in E. Nicholas *Nicholas Papers* (1897) III. 263 OED]

(36)   *Muskets to shoot Bullets without powder, **or anything else***

[1678 N. WANLEY *Wonders Little World* III. xliv §28. 227/2 OED]

These four examples are disjunctive forms, all of which are non-specific. There are also adjunctive forms, as shown in (37)–(41). The phrase *and every thing els*, with each constituent separate, can be found early in the seventeenth century, as in (37), and later in the same century, with the indefinite pronoun in its more recognizable form, as in (38). By the mid nineteenth century, the expression is subject to word-play, as in (39), indicating that it was well established at that time.

(37)   *Assuredly their name, estate, liberty **and every thing els** is precious to him*

[1632 William Gouge *The saints sacrifice* EEBO]

(38)   *they began to make war at a distance, and send armies into Sicily they lost their liberty **and everything else***

[1680 Niccolò Machiavelli *The Works of the famous Nicholas Machiavelli* EEBO]

(39)   *The abundant variety of "Shows," Theatrical, Musical, Ethiopical, Zoological, **and everything else-ical***

[1866 *Era* 14 Jan. 10/1 OED]

10.5 *And/or elsewhere*

The negative adjunctive form dates back to at least the mid sixteenth century, as in (40) with *els*, and already has the modern spelling before the end of that century, as in (41), emphasizing the message that "there is not more" involved.

(40)   *his disciples, who hauynge geuen ouer all care of wordily matters attended onely to the gospel **and nothing els***

[1548 Desiderius Erasmus *The first tome or volume of the Paraphrase of Erasmus vpon the Newe Testamente* EEBO]

(41)   *we doe find that by faith **and nothing else** we are justified*

[1592 Lancelot Andrewes *The wonderfull combate (for Gods glorie and mans saluation)* EEBO]

We can also find examples with the sense of "another person" (or not) with *somebody, everybody* and *nobody* from the seventeenth century, as in (42)–(44).

(42)   *It seems the Old Seal was under age too, for this he had a bul, but whether from the Pope, **or somebody else**, is the question*

[1650 George Walker *Anglo-Tyrannus, Or the Idea of a Norman Monarch* EEBO]

(43)   *and to let him **and everybody else** see*

[1695–1701 *The case of the brine-pits* EEBO]

(44)   *All pull him in Fourth. It must be Litus man, **and nobody else***

[1667 Abraham Bailey *The spightful sister* EEBO]

We can exemplify the continued use of these expressions with clearly human reference in later data, such as (45)–(47), but they are relatively low-frequency forms in PDE.

(45)   *And then you **or somebody else** will buy up and plot this land*

[1915 C. J. Galpin in *Res. Bull.* (Agric. Exper. Station Univ. Wisconsin No. 34. 33 OED]

(46)   *I don't care what Douglas **or anybody else** says or pamphletizes*

[1925 D. H. Lawrence *Let.* 26 May (1962) II 841 OED]

(47)   *Thus a differentiation arises between ourselves, the we-group or in-group, **and everybody else**, or the others-groups, out-groups*

[1906 W. G. Sumner *Folkways* i. 12 OED]

We should also note that in the earlier records prior to 1700, such as EEBO (*Early English Books Online*), there are no examples of any disjunctive forms with *someone, anyone* and *everyone* plus *else*. In the *OED Online*, those forms are nineteenth- and early-twentieth-century entries, though with relatively low frequency. These particular forms are also attested in American English in the nineteenth century, as shown in (48)–(50).

(48)   *I dare not tell him **or anyone else** the cause*

[1832 John Howard Payne *Woman's Revenge* COHA]

(49)   *unless it is necessary to prevent them from killing or badly injuring us **or someone else***

[1894 Martha Finley *Elsie at the World's Fair* COHA]

(50)   *to the surprise of himself **and everyone else**, the wearing apparel was thrown into the air*

[1904 Arnold Hague *The Yellowstone National Park* COHA]

The exception in this group is *and no one else*, which appears much earlier in the historical record, as in (51), though the phrase *and none else* (with human reference) is more frequent in the historical record from this time, as illustrated in (52), with a variant (*and none other*) also included. Tracking down different types of extenders constructed with *other* is definitely an area for future research.

(51)   *I'm satisfied she loves me **and no one else***

[1698 Young lady *The unnatural mother the scene in the kingdom of Siam* EEBO]

(52)   *Yea, to be a King and Priest in one person as he was, **and none else**; to typifie that glorious priviledge to belong to thee **and none other***

[1651 George Abbot *Brief notes on the whole book of Psalms* EEBO]

In addition to the phrases exemplified so far, we can point to other examples of specific extenders that have not been the subject of research, mainly because of low token counts (we assume) in the type of data investigated in earlier studies. Among the specific extenders related to place, we have also noted *or somewhere (else), or anywhere (else), or wherever (else), and everywhere (else)*, and *and nowhere else* (in which *else* doesn't seem to be optional). Other expressions that have long histories are *and much else* and *and much more*, which often function as adjunctive extenders.

We will end this section as we began by drawing attention to another pair of adjunctive and disjunctive extenders that are based on the same form: *what* as a pronoun plus *else*. Expressions with these components can be found in sixteenth-century uses, typically as part of a clause, that are not clearly general extender uses. Much clearer examples are in use during the seventeenth century, as in (53) and (54).

(53)   *as Mettalls, Plants, Beasts,* **and what else** *is remarkable at the Indies*

[1604 E. GRIMESTON tr. J. de Acosta *Nat. & Morall Hist. Indies* OED]

(54)   *Fire-eyed dragons,* **or what else** *therein doth dwell*

[1642 H. MORE *Platonica* sig. I4 OED]

While *and what else* doesn't appear to be in widespread use currently, it may still be a feature in the speech of some individuals. The example in (55), with *goodness knows* functioning like an intensifier, is from an interview on CNN (March 14, 2015) with Britain's Prince Charles about a recent visit to California.

(55)   *It was a great opportunity to see all sorts of interesting projects there, farmers markets* **and goodness knows what else**

We don't know if this example of an adjunctive form is a characteristic feature of the Prince's idiolect, a matter that could be resolved, no doubt, through further study. It is noticeable that the sociolinguistic studies reported in Chapter 7 were concerned with differences in general extender use according to social class in Britain, but they did not include any data from the upper class. That would seem to be a jolly interesting topic for future research.

We suspect that there are other *else* expressions, no doubt used with low frequency, in addition to those in examples (28)–(55), that can be described as general and specific extenders, yet have not been the subject of research, not only into their special forms, but also what special functions they serve. In this respect, at this time, this area of research is wide open.

Before leaving this section, we should note that in some of these examples, (28), (45), (46), (53) and (54), the extender is attached to the subject noun phrase, an aspect of usage that we have already identified as worthy of more careful scrutiny.

10.6   Lists and the Like

Within the study of the functions of general extenders in Chapter 2, we noted that their position at the end of lists typically allowed us to recognize the referential category being implicated. However, apart from Jefferson (1990), there really has been no dedicated attempt to investigate this relationship or to identify the specialized forms that are used as "list completers" (Jefferson, 1990: 67). (This is not to say that there have not been other studies of lists (e.g. Lerner, 1994; Schiffrin, 1994; Masini *et al.*, 2018).) We have noted that *et cetera* and *and so on* are often used after lists to indicate that "more" examples exist. This is particularly true in contexts involving formal spoken language, as illustrated in data from Cucchi's (2007) analysis of debates in the parliament of the European Union. Extract (56), from Cucchi (2007: 10), contains a lengthy list, each component providing specific examples in support of the rather abstract category expressed by *their situation in life*, and completed with *and so on*.

(56) *Progress will hopefully take the competition out of the allocation of funding and other resources to social partners representing people who, because of their situation in life – physical, mental, social, ethnic, employment or lack of employment **and so on** – need the support of the wider community.*

The extended list in (56) would not fit in with Jefferson's (1990) interest in studying "three-partedness" in list construction. Given this limitation, alternative analytical criteria would seem to be needed in not only the investigation of general extenders in list construction, but also in the identification of different types of lists.

Although we have illustrated the use of a range of adjunctive forms at the end of lists (in Chapter 2), there are certain expressions that seem to be specialized list completers. Actually, we should think of them more as "listing completers," because the speaker or writer uses them to signal an end to the listing activity while the implication of the adjunctive form is that the speaker's list is not in fact complete. In general, when used as part of a list, adjunctive general extenders (e.g. *and so on*) have a paradoxical double function: they simultaneously signal that the list continues and that it is at an end. The continuation signal says that "there is more" and the end signal says that the speaker is at a completion point.

In addition to *et cetera* and *and so on*, Aijmer (2002: 239) identifies two adjunctive forms, described as "tags" here, that are associated with list construction.

Some tags were strongly preferred in the list function. Almost half of the examples of *and things* had the function of list completers (20 examples) and it was the only function of *and the rest (and all the rest (of it))*.

The expression *and all the rest of it* is also more typically found among older speakers, as we noted in Chapter 7, but its usage has not received much attention beyond the simple observation that it is a six-word lexical bundle (quite rare), used to complete lists by older speakers (of British English).

Another expression that we have not previously studied, and that awaits a more detailed investigation, is the adjunctive phrase *and the like*, as illustrated in the following examples from the *OED Online*. In the earliest recorded uses, we find phrases with *other* and *soch* most common, as in (57) from the fifteenth century and (58) from the sixteenth century, with a version closer to the modern structure (59) developing not long after. Ortega-Barrera (2012) provides a description of a range of general extender-type expressions (including *and*

10.7 A New Linguistic Category

the like) "which occur at the end of enumerations" (2012: 223) in a corpus of early English recipes. In the contemporary language, as exemplified in (60) and (61) from *The Economist* (May 30, 2020: 24), the phrase continues to be used as a listing completer, and one that has a tendency to occur with relatively long lists.

(57)   *Sokynge grownde, as sandy grownde,* **and other lyke**

[c1440 *Promptorium Parvulorum* 463/2 OED]

(58)   *The dedes of ye flesh are manifest, which are these: dronkennes, glotony* **and soch like**

[1535 Bible (Coverdale) Gal. v. C OED]

(59)   *There were also a secte called Manichæi, who not onely refused flesh, but also egges, milke & chese,* **and the lyke**

[1556 M. HUGGARDE *Displaying of Protestantes* f. 19 OED]

(60)   *Happily, we are no longer permitted to discriminate against gender, sexuality, race, religion, disability* **and the like**

(61)   *They are vulnerable because they depend most on revenue from students; others find ways to hire out campuses for conferences, raise research funds, earn bequests* **and the like**

While there may be different types of lists (of things, actions, concepts, activities), the functions of the final adjunctive expression are generally the same. Looking at *and the like* in (59), we can see that it fulfills the basic function of indicating "there is more," signaling that the referential list is incomplete, yet simultaneously signaling that the current listing activity is complete. That is, a referential function and a textual function are realized at the same time. Under normal circumstances, another function of *and the like*, tied to intersubjectivity, is to signal to the addressee that familiarity with the implicated category is being assumed (not guaranteed), on the basis of similar knowledge. The phrase *and the like*, like other general extenders, is obviously multifunctional, but is it also a social marker? That sounds like another research question.[2] We would encourage a fresh approach to the study of general extenders in lists with a broader perspective than the earlier work.

10.7 A New Linguistic Category

In our early research on spoken American English, we created the term "general extender" as a category label to describe a large number of similar types of expressions that were being used by speakers in similar ways. Earlier studies had focused narrowly on their use as "set-markers" or "category-identifiers" (Dines,

1980; Channell, 1994), which, we were able to demonstrate, represented only one of their multiple functions. We chose a more neutral term with regard to form and function and investigated their wide range of functions in some detail in Overstreet and Yule (1997a,b) and Overstreet (1999). Comparing the relatively small token counts of expressions from that early research (Overstreet and Yule, 1997b: 253) with the extensive numbers in Tagliamonte and Denis (2010: 362–63) and Pichler and Levey (2011: 469–71), it has become clear that the category is extremely productive, with a large inventory of variants. What constrains the use of a particular variant at any time is the speaker's perspective on the occasion of speaking and all the socio-pragmatic factors involved in spoken interaction, some of which we have explored in the preceding pages.

Many of those expressions identified as general extenders have deep historical roots, as we demonstrated in Chapter 6, so the linguistic category they instantiate is not new. What is new has happened at the level of naming the category as an addition to the metalanguage of the discipline. We have noted that the term "general extenders" is now commonly used in the literature, for example in a textbook on pragmatics (Archer *et al.*, 2012) and a monograph on pragmatic markers (Beeching, 2016), and can be included alongside "comment clauses" and "question tags" in a list of linguistic categories that Traugott (2016: 26) investigated.

Much work on pragmatic markers in the history of English has been devoted to expressions used clause-initially at "left periphery." By contrast, this study provides an account in broad outlines of the incremental development of pragmatic markers in clause-final "right periphery" position. Particular attention is paid to the rise of comment clauses, question tags, general extenders, and retrospective contrastive markers.

We hope that our contribution in these pages will be helpful in future investigations of topics such as "right periphery markers" and the range of other research topics we have suggested throughout.

Notes

1   Introduction

1. In our earlier studies (Overstreet and Yule, 1997a, b; Overstreet, 1999), we focused fairly narrowly on our own database of American English, which continues to be one of our primary sources. Our other primary sources are the German and Hawai'i Creole English databases referenced mainly in Chapter 8. However, the expansion of studies involving other varieties of English and other languages in the last twenty years has provided us with a wealth of examples (our secondary sources), as in (1)–(12), allowing us to illustrate the widespread use of the expressions. Those sources: (1) is from the *Corpus of English Dialogues 1560–1760* (Kytö and Culpeper, 2006), cited in Tagliamonte and Denis (2010: 364); (2) from Stenström *et al.* (2002: 101); (3) from Winter and Norrby (2000: 4); (4) from Tagliamonte and Denis (2010: 350); (5) from Murphy (2010: 98); (6) from Aijmer (2002: 235); (7) from Meyerhoff (1992: 68); (8) from Macaulay (1985: 114); (9) from Palacios Martínez (2011: 2453); (10) from Pichler and Levey (2011: 450); (11) from Overstreet (1999: 91); (12) from Salinger (1951: 1).
2. In every study reporting detailed lists of general extender forms in a corpus, there is always a high number of hapaxes, forms that occur only once (from Greek, *hapax legomenon*, "said once"). In some cases, the hapaxes actually outnumber other forms that were used twice or more. In Pichler and Levey's (2011: 469–71) impressively detailed report, there were eighty-five different forms of general extenders in their corpus and, of these, more than half (forty-six) were hapaxes. This is evidence of a highly open and productive category that provides a way for speakers to make individual and innovative choices while accomplishing the communicative functions we describe.
3. Some of the conjunction-less long forms, those involving versions with *what*, have been described as "bare *what*-GEs" by Brinton (2020).

5   Textual Function and Turn Construction

1. Occasionally we find commentary on the low status of general extenders, as in this extract from a novel, *Lucy Carmichael*, cited in the *OED Online*.

    "Aren't they engaged **or something**?"
    "I don't know what you mean by **or something**. It's a vulgar slipshod phrase."
    [1951 MARGARET KENNEDY *Lucy Carmichael* II. iii 100 OED]

216   Notes to pages 92–100

2. The terms "left bracket" and "right bracket" are not perfect because they clearly relate to visual position on a page, that is, in the transcript of speech, not the stream of speech. It would be preferable to have technical terms that match the linear nature of speech production better. From the analysis of syllabic structure, we could borrow the terms "onset" (to replace "left") and "coda" (to replace "right") and extend their uses to the structure of parts of utterances. Technically, that would be better. However, the left-right terminology is likely to continue because it is so firmly entrenched and has more recently been incorporated into another technical distinction between left and right periphery. (See note 3.)
3. We have focused on general extenders in combination with other pragmatic markers in the internal structure of utterances. Other analytic frameworks focus on the beginning and end of utterances, what we might think of as the "outer edges" because they are described as the "left periphery" and "right periphery." There have been a number of studies of specific expressions, typically adverbs, which can have different functions in the two different positions (Watts, 1989; Traugott, 2012, 2016; Beeching and Detges, 2014; Beeching, 2015; Haselow, 2015; Hancil et al., 2015). Beeching (2016: 43) discusses those different functions:

> there is a demonstrable tendency for items which appear in the left periphery to be discourse-structuring (linking the previous turn to the ensuing one) and for those on the right periphery to be modalising (commenting subjectively or intersubjectively on what has just been uttered).

This description contains an account of the functions of right-periphery items that matches our analysis of general extenders in Chapters 3 and 4. Although they do not fully fit the periphery-based profile, the position(s) and function(s) of general extenders would seem to be a perfect topic for further investigation in periphery analysis.

6   Historical Development and Change

1. This chapter would not have been as comprehensive in its coverage, nor as accurate in its analysis, without the generous support and advice of Laurel Brinton.
2. The expression *or thereabouts* is another fixed form, with an original sense of being near to a location that extended to being near to an amount, as in (1), a number (2), a date (3) and then to other things like age (4) and time (5) later. Remarkably, this general extender, functioning as an approximation indicator, has been fixed in an Old English structure (*þær onbutan*) for almost seven hundred years, and like *or so*, its nearest functional counterpart, is more often found in formal language.

   (1) *I wyl that man lyue in . . . tribulacion fyue thousand yere **or neyhe ther aboutes***

   [1413 Pilgr. Sowle (1483) IV. XVII 64 OED]

   (2) *They had assocyed to the number of dcc persons **or thereabouts***

   [1441 in T. Stapleton *Plumpton Corr.* (1839) Introd. 57 OED]

   (3) *Cyrus was borne in the hundreth yere **or there aboutes** after the death of Esaie*

   [1561 T. NORTON tr. J. Calvin *Inst. Christian Relig.* I viii f. 17 OED]

(4) *At the age of fourteen **or thereabouts**, the front rows of lace-holes may be omitted*

[1871 *Figure Training* 34 OED]

(5) *I'll call for you tomorrpw morning at eight, **or thereabouts***

[1917 E. FERBER *Fanny Herself* x. 176 OED]

3. The absence of punctuation in many of the early corpora can create a problem for identifying some phrases appropriately, *and so on* in particular. The most common version in the fifteenth and sixteenth centuries, as evidenced in EEBO, occurs at the beginning of a clause and would be better punctuated as *and so, on a certeyn night*, for example, with *on* introducing various kinds of preposition phrases, not part of an adjunctive extender. The phrase *And so* seems to be a common discourse marker at the left periphery during this period.
4. One of our reviewers pointed out a connection between our analytic approach and that found in Construction Grammar. General extenders are certainly examples of "learned pairings of forms and functions" (Goldberg, 2019: 2), according to one definition of constructions. We can speculate that the development of the phrase *or something* in the past, for example, resulted in a new form (short disjunctive extender) with a new function (accuracy hedge) which would seem to fit the characterization of constructionalization as "the creation of new form (new) – meaning (new) (combinations of) signs" (Traugott and Trousdale, 2013: 22). On the basis of similar revisions to form (additional modifier phrase) and function (more cohesive), the expression *or something like that* seems to have undergone "constructional change" (Traugott, 2015: 53) at least, if not full constructionalization, some time in the late nineteenth century. We hope that this speculative note will encourage a more thorough investigation of the connection by those with more expertise in this area.

7 Social Marking and Variation

1. We must acknowledge our debt to the published work of Michael McCarthy and his colleagues at the universities of Nottingham and Limerick, referenced throughout this section, for much of what is currently known about general extender use in these formal contexts.
2. The expressions and their ordering in Table 7.5 do not match those in Table 4.7 in Aijmer (2013: 137). Aijmer's results are based on the *International Corpus of English* (ICE), which seems unreliable, given the extremely low token counts for Canada, for example (2013: 133), when compared with the numbers for Toronto English in Tagilamonte and Denis (2010). The numbers in ICE also don't match our counts of adjunctive versus disjunctive forms in British English, based on studies referenced in this chapter. We created Table 7.5 based on these and studies of other varieties as an indication of the appropriate ordering of the most frequent forms.

9 In Learner Language and Language Teaching

1. While Seidlhofer (2011) describes English as a lingua franca very generally as "any use of English among speakers of different first languages for whom English is the

communicative medium of choice, and often the only option" (2011: 7), most of the reported research has involved fairly advanced-proficiency users of the language (e.g. Mauranen, 2012). MacKenzie (2014) has a long list of professional contexts, "international politics, diplomacy, international law, business, the media, tertiary education and scientific research," where speakers use English as a lingua franca and seems to downplay the relevance of other types of interactions, such as those involving tourists who use "a very simple form" (2014: 2). Consequently, our discussion of the relevant research on general extenders in English as a lingua franca is limited to its use in professional contexts, mainly in the academic world, involving speakers who have presumably already spent substantial amounts of time studying English L2, and it shows. At the moment, we can make no claims about general extender use in other situations involving less proficient speakers of English as a lingua franca.
2. Table 9.1: Suggested answers

   1 *or so*, 2 *or something*, 3 *or anything*, 4 *or whatever*, 5 *or anything*, 6 *or something*, 7 *or anything*, 8 *or something like that*, 9 *or something*, 10 *or something like that*, 11 *or whatever*, 12 *or so*, 13 *or anything*, 14 *or something like that*
3. Table 9.2: Suggested answers

   1 *and things like that*, 2 *and everything*, 3 *and so on/and things like that*, 4 *and stuff*, 5 *and things like that/and so on*, 6 *and everything*, 7 *and blah, blah, blah*, 8 *and stuff*, 9 *and things like that*, 10 *and so on/and things like that*, 11 *and everything*, 12 *and blah, blah, blah/and so on*, 13 *and stuff, and things like that*, 14 *and everything*
4. Table 9.3

   These examples have been adapted from data referenced in this chapter. Examples 1, 10 are from Terraschke (2007a), 2, 5, 6, 14 from Buysse (2014), 3, 9, 11, 13 from Parvaresh *et al.* (2012) and 4, 7, 8, 12 from Metsä-Ketelä (2016). Suggested replacements: 1 *or something*, 2 *or anything*, 3 *and so on / and everything*, 4 *or something like that*, 5 *or anything*, 6 *or something*, 7 *or something like that*, 8 *and stuff/and things like that*, 9 *and so on / and things like that*, 10 *and stuff/or anything*, 11 *and everything/and things like that*, 12 *or something like that*, 13 *and things like that/or anything like that*, 14 *and everything*
5. Table 9.4

   These examples have been adapted from the following sources. Example 1 is from Brinton (2017), 2, 4, 5, 6 are from Aijmer (2002), 3, 7 from Overstreet (1999), 8, 10, 11 from Stenström *et al.* (2002), 9 from Pichler and Levey (2011), 12 from Overstreet and Yule (2019, notebook entry), 13 from Tagliamonte and Denis (2010), 14 from Aijmer (2018).

   Suggested answers: 1 *Whatever*, 2 *or so*, 3 *or what*, 4 *or something*, 5 *and stuff*, 6 *or something like that*, 7 *an'shit*, 8 *or anything*, 9 *and that*, 10 *and everything*, 11 *and all that sort of thing*, 12 *and so on*, 13 *stuff like that*, 14 *and things*

10 Reflections and Projections

1. When we look at the historical record in COHA, we find increasing token counts for *and things* throughout the nineteenth century and into the early part of the twentieth century, reaching a high point in the 1920s, after which there is a steady decline in numbers. As for the long form *and things like that*, there are relatively few tokens in the nineteenth century, but, beginning around 1910, the frequencies increase

substantially. We have noted this increase in other long general extenders with the modifier *like that* during the same period.

2. We have focused on the adjunctive version, but the disjunctive version also had a role in earlier periods, with examples such as the following from 1600:

> *to lift our hands to heauen, to beate our breasts* **or the like**
> [1600 George Abbot *An Exposition vpon the prophet Ionah* EEBO]

Tracing the path of the disjunctive version (in its various forms) and identifying any other functions performed would seem to be another topic for future research.

References

Adolphs, S., S. Atkins and K. Harvey (2007). Caught between professional requirements and interpersonal needs: Vague language in healthcare contexts. In J. Cutting (ed.) *Vague Language Explored*. Basingstoke, UK: Palgrave Macmillan. 3–20.
Aijmer, K. (1985). What happens at the end of our utterances? The use of utterance-final tags introduced by *And* and *Or*. In O. Togeby (ed.) *Papers from the Eighth Scandinavian Conference of Linguistics*. Copenhagen: Copenhagen University, Institut für Philologie. 366–89.
Aijmer, K. (2002). *English Discourse Particles*. Amsterdam: John Benjamins.
Aijmer, K. (2004). Pragmatic markers in spoken interlanguage. *Nordic Journal of English Studies* 3: 173–90.
Aijmer, K. (2013). *Understanding Pragmatic Markers*. Edinburgh: Edinburgh University Press.
Aijmer, K. (2015). General extenders in learner language. In N. Groom, M. Charles and S. John (eds.) *Corpora, Grammar and Discourse*. Amsterdam: John Benjamins. 211–33.
Aijmer, K. (2018). Positioning the self in interaction. In K. Beeching, C. Ghezzi and P. Molinelli (eds.) *Positioning the Self and Others*. Amsterdam: John Benjamins. 177–95.
Aijmer, K. and A.-M. Simon-Vandenbergen (2011). Pragmatic markers. In J. Zienkowski, J.-O. Östman and J. Verschueren (eds.) *Discursive Pragmatics* Amsterdam: John Benjamins. 223–47.
Amador-Moreno, C., K. McCafferty and E. Vaughan (eds.) (2015). *Pragmatic Markers in Irish English*. Amsterdam: John Benjamins.
Andrews, B. (1989). Terminating devices in spoken French. *International Review of Applied Linguistics in Language Teaching* XXVII: 193–216.
Archer, D., K. Aijmer and A. Wichmann (2012). *Pragmatics. An Advanced Resource Book for Students*. Abingdon, UK: Routledge.
Ariel, M. and C. Mauri (2019). An "alternative" core for *or*. *Journal of Pragmatics* 149: 40–59.
Austen, J. (1813). *Pride and Prejudice*. Whitehall, London: Thomas Egerton.
Austen, J. (1814). *Mansfield Park*. Whitehall, London: Thomas Egerton.
Austen, J. (1818). *Persuasion*. London: John Murray.
Bailey, R., J. Robinson, J. Downer and P. Lehman (1975/1994). *Michigan Early Modern English Materials*. Ann Arbor, MI: University of Michigan.
Ball, C. and M. Ariel (1978). Or something, etc. *Penn Review of Linguistics* 3: 35–45.
Bamford, J. (2004). Gestural and symbolic uses of the deictic here in academic lectures. In K. Aijmer and A.-B. Stenström (eds.) *Discourse Patterns in Spoken and Written Corpora*. Amsterdam: John Benjamins. 113–38.

References

Barbieri, F. (2012). "Another god called Allah or something": General extenders and register variation in American talk. Paper presented at the *1st Discourse-Pragmatic Variation and Change Conference*, Salford, UK.

Bardovi-Harlig, K. (1996). Pragmatics and language teaching: Bringing pragmatics and pedagogy together. *Pragmatics and Language Learning* 7: 21–39.

Bardovi-Harlig, K. (2001). Evaluating the empirical evidence for instruction in pragmatics. In K. Rose and G. Kasper (eds.) *Pragmatics in Language Teaching*. London: Routledge. 13–32.

Barron, A. and K. Schneider (2009). Variational pragmatics: Studying the impact of social factors on language use in interaction. *Intercultural Pragmatics* 6: 425–42.

Barsalou, L. (1983). Ad hoc categories. *Memory and Cognition* 11: 211–27.

Beeching, K. (2002). *Gender, Politeness and Pragmatic Particles in French*. Amsterdam: John Benjamins.

Beeching, K. (2016). *Pragmatic Markers in British English*. Cambridge: Cambridge University Press.

Beeching, K. (2018). Metacommenting in English and French: A variational pragmatics approach. In K. Beeching, C. Ghezzi and P. Molinelli (eds.) *Positioning the Self and Others*. Amsterdam: John Benjamins. 127–53.

Beeching, K. and U. Detges (2014). *Discourse Functions at the Left and Right Periphery*. Amsterdam: John Benjamins.

Berez, A. L. (2013). The digital archiving of endangered language oral traditions: Kaipuleohone at the University of Hawai'i and C'ek'aedi Hwnax in Alaska. *Oral Tradition* 28: 261–70.

Betten, A. (1976). Ellipsen, Anakoluthe und Parenthesen. *Deutsche Sprache* 2: 207–30.

Biber, D., S. Johansson, G. Leech, S. Conrad and E. Finegan (1999). *Longman Grammar of Spoken and Written English*. London: Longman.

Biber, D., S. Conrad and V. Cortes (2004). If you look at ... Lexical bundles in university teaching and textbooks. *Applied Linguistics* 25: 371–405.

Bickerton, D. (1977). *Change and Variation in Hawaiian English*, Volume 2: Creole Syntax. Honolulu, HI: Social Sciences and Linguistics Institute, University of Hawai'i.

Bilmes, Jack. (2015). *The Structure of Meaning in Talk: Explorations in Category Analysis*. Volume I: Co-categorization, contrast and hierarchy. www2.hawaii.edu/~bilmes/structure_of_meaning.pdf.

Bouton, L. (1994). Conversational implicatures in a second language: Learned slowly when not deliberately taught. *Journal of Pragmatics* 22: 157–67.

Boxer, D. (1993). *Complaining and Commiserating*. New York: Peter Lang.

Boye, K. and P. Harder (2012). A usage-based theory of grammatical status and grammaticalization. *Language* 88: 1–44.

Brems, L. and K. Davidse (2010). The grammaticalisation of nominal type noun constructions with *kind/sort of*: Chronology and paths of change. *English Studies* 91: 180–202.

Brezina, V. and M. Meyerhoff (2014). Significant or random? A critical review of sociolinguistic generalizations based on large corpora. *International Journal of Corpus Linguistics* 19: 1–28.

Brinton, L. (1996). *Pragmatic Markers in English: Grammaticalization and Discourse Functions*. Berlin: Mouton de Gruyter.

Brinton, L. (2017). *The Evolution of Pragmatic Markers in English*. Cambridge: Cambridge University Press.

Brinton, L. (2020). The rise of *what*-general extenders in English. Unpublished manuscript.

Britain, D. (1992). Things and that in Porirua: An analysis of set-marking tags. *Presentation at a department seminar*, Victoria University at Wellington, New Zealand (cited in Stubbe and Holmes, 1995).

Brontë, C. (as C. Bell) (1847). *Jane Eyre*. London: Smith, Elder and Company.

Brotherton, P. (1976). *Aspects of the Relationship between Speech Production, Hesitation Behaviour and Social Class*. Ph.D. dissertation University of Melbourne (cited in Dines, 1980).

Brown, G. (1990). *Listening to Spoken English*, 2nd edn. London: Longman.

Brown, G. (1998). Context creation in discourse understanding. In K. Malmkjaer and J. Williams (eds.) *Context in Language Learning and Language Understanding*. Cambridge: Cambridge University Press. 171–92.

Brown, G. and G. Yule (1983). *Discourse Analysis*. Cambridge: Cambridge University Press.

Brown, P. and S. Levinson (1987). *Politeness*. Cambridge: Cambridge University Press.

Burns, R. (1795/1859). *The Complete Works of Robert Burns*. Boston: Phillips, Sampson and company.

Buysse, L. (2014). We went to the restroom or something: General extenders and stuff in the speech of Dutch learners of English. In J. Romero-Trillo (ed.) *Yearbook of Corpus Linguistics and Pragmatics 2014: New Empirical and Theoretical Paradigms*. Cham, Germany: Springer. 213–37.

Bybee, J. (2003). Mechanisms of change in grammaticalization: The role of frequency. In B. Joseph and R. Janda (eds.) *The Handbook of Historical Linguistics*. Oxford: Blackwell. 602–23.

Caffi, C. (2009). Metapragmatics. In J. Mey (ed.) *Concise Encyclopedia of Pragmatics*, 2nd edn. Oxford: Elsevier.

Carroll, R. (2007). Lists in letters: NP-lists and general extenders in early English correspondence. In I. Moskowich-Spiegel and B. Crespo-Garcia (eds.) *Bells Chiming from the Past*. Amsterdam: Rodopi. 37–53.

Carroll, R. (2008). Historical English phraseology and the extender tag. *Selim* 15: 3–37.

Carter, R. and M. McCarthy (2004). Talking, creating: Interactional language, creativity and context. *Applied Linguistics* 25: 62–88.

Carter, R. and M. McCarthy (2006). *Cambridge Grammar of English*. Cambridge: Cambridge University Press.

Channell, J. (1994). *Vague Language*. Oxford: Oxford University Press.

Cheepen, C. and J. Monaghan (1990). *Spoken English: A Practical Guide*. London: Pinter.

Cheng, W. (2007). The use of vague language across spoken genres in an intercultural Hong Kong corpus. In J. Cutting (ed.) *Exploring Vague Language*. New York: Palgrave Macmillan. 161–81.

Cheng, W., C. Greaves and M. Warren (2005). The creation of a prosodically transcribed intercultural corpus: The Hong Kong Corpus of Spoken Language (Prosodic). *ICAME Journal* 29: 5–26.

Cheshire, J. (2005). Syntactic variation and beyond: Gender and social class variation in the use of discourse-new markers. *Journal of Sociolinguistics* 9: 479–508.

Cheshire, J. (2007). Discourse variation, grammaticalisation and stuff like that. *Journal of Sociolinguistics* 11: 155–93.

References

Cicourel, A. (1974). *Cognitive Sociology*. New York: Free Press.

Cieri, C., D. Graff, O. Kimball, D. Miller and K. Walker (2004–2005). *Fisher English Training Speech Parts 1 and 2 Transcripts*. Philadelphia, PA: Linguistic Data Consortium.

Clancy, B. (2015). "Hurry up baby son all the boys is finished their breakfast." Examining the use of vocatives as pragmatic markers in Irish Traveller and settled family discourse. In C. Amador-Moreno, K. McCafferty and E. Vaughan (eds.) *Pragmatic Markers in Irish English*. Amsterdam: John Benjamins. 229–47.

Clancy, B. and M. McCarthy (2014). Co-constructed turn-taking. In K. Aijmer and C. Ruhlemann (eds.) *Corpus Pragmatics: A Handbook*. Cambridge: Cambridge University Press. 430–53.

Corbett, G. (2000). *Number*. Cambridge: Cambridge University Press.

Corbett, G. and M. Mithun (1996). Associative forms in a typology of number systems: Evidence from Yu'pik. *Journal of Linguistics* 32: 1–17.

Cortés, L. (2006). Los elementos de final de serie enumerativa del tipo *y todo eso, o cosas así, y tal*, etc. Perspectiva interactiva. *Boletín de lingüística* 18(26): 102–29.

Cortés, L. (2008). *La Serie Enumerativa en el Discurso Oral Español*. Madrid: Arco Libros.

Cotterill, J. (2007). "I think he was kind of shouting or something": Uses and abuses of vagueness in the British courtroom. In J. Cutting (ed.) *Vague Language Explored*. Basingstoke, UK: Palgrave Macmillan. 97–116.

Craig, R. and K. Tracy (1983). *Conversational Coherence: Form, Structure, and Strategy*. Beverly Hills, CA: Sage.

Cucchi, C. (2007). An investigation of general extenders in a corpus of EU parliamentary debates. Paper (Number 242) presented at the *Corpus Linguistics Conference* CL 2007, University of Birmingham, UK.

Cutting, J. (ed.) (2007). *Vague Language Explored*. Basingstoke, UK: Palgrave Macmillan.

Cutting, J. (2015). Dingsbums und so: Beliefs about German vague language. *Journal of Pragmatics* 85: 108–21.

Daniel, M. and E. Moravcsik (2000). The associative plural. In M. Haspelmath, M. Dryer, D. Gil and B. Comrie (eds.) *The World Atlas of Language Structures (WALS)* Oxford: Oxford University Press. 150–53.

Davies, M. (2008). *Corpus of Contemporary American English: 5670 Million Words, 1990-Present*. www.english-corpora.org/coca/.

Davies, M. (2010). The Corpus of Contemporary American English as the first reliable monitor corpus of English. *Literary and Linguistic Computing* 25: 447–64.

Davies, M. (2012). Expanding horizons in historical linguistics with the 400-million word Corpus of Historical American English. *Corpora* 7: 121–57.

De Cock, S. (2004). Preferred sequences of words in NS and NNS speech. *Belgian Journal of English Language and Literatures*, New Series 2: 225–46.

Dehé, N. and K. Stathi (2016). Grammaticalization and prosody: The case of *sort/kind/type of* constructions. *Language* 92: 911–47.

Denis, D. (2011). Innovators and innovation: Tracking innovators and stuff in York English. *University of Pennsylvania Working Papers in Linguistics* 17: 61–70.

Denis, D. (2017). The development of *and stuff* in Canadian English: A longitudinal study of apparent grammaticalization. *Journal of English Linguistics* 45: 157–85.

Denis, D. and S. Tagliamonte (2016). Innovation, *right*? Change, *you know*? Utterance-final tags in Canadian English. In H. Pichler (ed.) *Discourse-Pragmatic Variation and Change in English*. Cambridge: Cambridge University Press. 86–112.

De Smet, H. (2010). Grammatical interference. In E. Traugott and G. Trousdale (eds.) *Gradience, Gradualness and Grammaticalization*. Amsterdam: John Benjamins. 75–104.

Dines, E. (1980). Variation in discourse – "and stuff like that." *Language in Society* 1: 13–31.

Dippold, D. (2008). Reframing one's experience: Face, identity and roles in L2 argumentative discourse. In M. Pütz and J. Neff-van Aertselaer (eds.) *Developing Contrastive Pragmatics: Interlanguage and Cross-Cultural Perspectives*. Berlin: Mouton de Gruyter. 131–53.

Dippold, D. (2016). *The Acquisition of General Extenders by L2 Learners of German*. Unpublished manuscript.

Dostie, G. (2009). Discourse markers and regional variation in French: A lexico-semantic approach. In K. Beeching, N. Armstrong and F. Gadet (eds.) *Sociolinguistic Variation in Contemporary French*. Amsterdam: John Benjamins. 201–14.

Drager, K. (2012). Pidgin and Hawai'i English: An overview. *International Journal of Language, Translation and Intercultural Communication* 1: 61–73.

Drew, P. (2014). CA in sociolinguistics. In J. Holmes and K. Hazen (eds.) *Research Methods in Sociolinguistics*. Oxford: Wiley Blackwell. 230–45.

Du Bois, J., W. Chafe, C. Meyer, S. Thompson, R. Englebretson and N. Martey (2000–2005). *Santa Barbara Corpus of Spoken American English, Parts 1–4*. Philadelphia, PA: Linguistic Data Consortium.

Dubois, S. (1992). Extension particles, etc. *Language Variation and Change* 4: 179–203.

Dubois, S. (1993). Les particules d'extension dans le discours: Analyse de la distribution des forms et patati patata. *Revue Québécoise de Linguistique Théorique et Appliquée* 11: 21–47.

Eckert, P. (1997). Age as a sociolinguistic variable. In F. Coulmas (ed.) *Handbook of Sociolinguistics*. Oxford: Blackwell. 151–67.

Ediger, A. (1995). *An Analysis of Set-Marking Tags in the English Language*. Ph.D. dissertation, University of California Los Angeles.

Ephron, N. (1983). *Heartburn*. New York: Random House.

Erman, B. (1992). Female and male usage of pragmatic expressions in same-sex and mixed-sex interaction. *Language Variation and Change* 4: 217–34.

Erman, B. (1995). Grammaticalization in progress: The case of *or something*. In I. Moen, H. Simonsen and H. Lødrup (eds.) *Papers from the XVth Scandinavian Conference of Linguistics*. Oslo: University of Oslo, Department of Linguistics. 136–47.

Erman, B. (2001). Pragmatic markers revisited with a focus on *you know* in adult and adolescent talk. *Journal of Pragmatics* 32: 1337–59.

Erman, B. and U.-B. Kotsinas (1993). Pragmaticalization: The case of ba' and you know. *Studier I Modern Språkvetenskap*. New Series 10. Acta Universtatis Stockholmiensis. Stockholm: Almqvist and Wiksell. 76–93.

Eslami-Rasekh, Z. (2005). Raising the pragmatic awareness of language learners. *ELT Journal* 59: 199–208.

References

Evison, J., M. McCarthy and A. O'Keeffe (2007). "Looking out for love and all the rest of it": Vague category markers as shared social space. In J. Cutting (ed.) *Vague Language Explored*. London: Palgrave Macmillan. 138–57.

Fairclough, N. (1992). *Discourse and Social Change*. Cambridge: Polity Press.

Farghal, M. and M. Haggan (2005). The tag and everything revisited: The case of *u-kulši* in Arabic. *Multilingua* 24: 399–412.

Farr, F. and E. Riordan (2015). Turn initiators in professional encounters. In C. Amador-Moreno, K. McCafferty and E. Vaughan (eds.) *Pragmatic Markers in Irish English*. Amsterdam: John Benjamins. 176–202.

Fernandez, J. (2013). A corpus-based study of vague language use by learners of Spanish in a study abroad context. In C. Kinginger (ed.) *Social and Cultural Aspects of Language Learning in Study Abroad*. Amsterdam: John Benjamins. 299–331.

Fernandez, J. (2015). General extender use in spoken Peninsular Spanish: Metapragmatic awareness and pedagogical implications. *Journal of Spanish Language Teaching* 2: 1–17.

Fernandez, J. and A. Yuldashev (2011). Variation in the use of general extenders and stuff in instant messaging interactions. *Journal of Pragmatics* 43: 2610–26.

Finegan, E. (1995). Subjectivity and subjectivisation: An introduction. In D. Stein and S. Wright (eds.) *Subjectivity and Subjectivisation*. Cambridge: Cambridge University Press. 1–15.

Fischer, O. and A. Rosenbach (2000). Introduction. In O. Fischer, A. Rosenbach and D. Stein (eds.) *Pathways of Change: Grammaticalization in English*. Amsterdam: John Benjamins. 1–37.

Fung, L. and R. Carter (2007). Discourse markers and spoken English: Native and learner use in pedagogic settings. *Applied Linguistics* 28: 410–39.

Gilquin, G. (2008). Hesitation markers among EFL learners: Pragmatic deficiency or difference? In J. Romero-Trillo (ed.) *Corpus and Pragmatics: A Mutualistic Entente*. Berlin: Mouton de Gruyter. 119–49.

Goffman, E. (1959). *The Presentation of Self in Everyday Life*. New York: Doubleday.

Goffman, E. (1974). *Frame Analysis*. New York: Harper & Row.

Goldberg, A. (2019). *Explain Me This*. Princeton, NJ: Princeton University Press.

Greenbaum, S. (ed.) (1996). *Comparing English Worldwide: The International Corpus of English*. Oxford: Clarendon Press.

Grice, P. (1975). Logic and conversation. In P. Cole and J. Morgan (eds.) *Syntax and Semantics 3: Speech Acts*. New York: Academic Press. 41–58.

Grieve, A. (2011). *Adolescent Identity and Pragmatic Marker Acquisition in a Study Abroad Context*. Ph.D. dissertation, University of Melbourne.

Grzybek, P. and D. Verdonik (2014). General extenders: From interaction to model. In V. Jesenšek and P. Grzybek (eds.) *Phraseology in Dictionaries and Corpora*. Maribor, Budapest: Bielsko-Biala. 113–30.

Guthrie, A. (1994). *Quotative Tense Shift in American English Authority-Encounter Narratives* M.A. thesis, California State University, San Bernadino, California.

Halliday, M. (1970). Language structure and language function. In J. Lyons (ed.) *New Horizons in Linguistics*. London: Penguin Books.

Hancil, S., A. Haselow and M. Post (2015). *Final Particles*. Berlin: De Gruyter.

Handford, M. (2010). *The Language of Business Meetings*. Cambridge: Cambridge University Press.

References

Haselow, A. (2015). Left versus right periphery in grammaticalization. In A. Smith, G. Trousdale and R. Waltereit (eds.) *New Directions in Grammaticalization Research*. Amsterdam: John Benjamins. 157–86.

Hasselgren, A. (2002). Sounds a bit foreign. In L. Breivik and A. Hasselgren (eds.) *From the COLT's Mouth ... and Others: Language Corpora Studies in Honour of Anna-Brita Stenström*. Amsterdam: Rodopi. 103–23.

Heine, B. (2003). Grammaticalization. In B. Joseph and R. Janda (eds.) *Handbook of Historical Linguistics*. Oxford: Blackwell. 575–601.

Heine, B., U. Claudi and F. Hünnemeyer (1991). *Grammaticalization: A Conceptual Framework*. Chicago, IL: Chicago University Press.

Heine, B. and T. Kuteva (2005). *Language Contact and Grammatical Change*. Cambridge: Cambridge University Press.

Hickey, R. (2004). English dialect input to the Caribbean. In R. Hickey (ed.) *Legacies of Colonial English*. Cambridge: Cambridge University Press. 326–59.

Higgins, C. and G. Furukawa (2012). Styling Hawai'i in Haolewood: White protagonists on a voyage of self discovery. *Multilingua* 31: 177–98.

Hofland, K. A. Lindebjerg and J. Thunestvedt (eds.) (1999). *ICAME Collection of English Language Corpora*. The HIT Centre: University of Bergen. http://icame.uib.no/ceecs/index.htm.

Holmes, J. (1990). Hedges and boosters in women's and men's speech. *Language and Communication* 10: 185–205.

Hopper, P. (1991). On some principles of grammaticization. In E. Traugott and B. Heine (eds.) *Approaches to Grammaticalization*, Vol. 1. Amsterdam: John Benjamins. 17–35.

Hopper, P. (2010). Grammaticalization. In L. Cummings (ed.) *Encyclopedia of Pragmatics*. London: Routledge. 180–82.

Hopper, P. and E. Traugott (2003). *Grammaticalization*, 2nd edn. Cambridge: Cambridge University Press.

Hornby, N. (2001). *How to Be Good*. New York: Riverhead Books.

Huddleston, R. and G. Pullum (2002). *The Cambridge Grammar of the English Language*. Cambridge: Cambridge University Press.

Husserl, E. (1929/1977). *Formale und Tranzendentale Logik*. The Hague: Martinus Nijhoff.

Hüttner, J. (2009). Fluent speakers – fluent interactions: On the creation of (co)-fluency in English as a lingua franca. In A. Mauranen and E. Ranta (eds.) *English as a Lingua Franca*. Newcastle, UK: Cambridge Scholars Publishing. 274–97.

Jefferson G. (1990). List-construction as a task and resource. In G. Psathas (ed.) *Interaction Competence*. Lanham, MD: University Press of America. 63–92.

Jenkins, J. (2014). *English as a Lingua Franca in the International University*. Abingdon, UK: Routledge.

Jensen, T. and T. Christensen (2015). Extending in time and space: General extenders in Danish. Paper presented at the *International Conference on Language Variation in Europe*. Leipzig, Denmark: Universität Leipzig.

Jucker, A., S. Smith and T. Lüdge (2003). Interactive aspects of vagueness in conversation. *Journal of Pragmatics* 35: 1737–69.

Kärkkäinen, E. (2003). *Epistemic Stance in English Conversation*. Amsterdam: John Benjamins.

Kasper, G. (1997). The role of pragmatics in language teaching education. In K. Bardovi-Harlig and B. Hartford (eds.) *Beyond Methods: Components of Language Teacher Education*. New York: McGraw-Hill. 113–16.

Kasper, G. (2001). Four perspectives on L2 pragmatic development. *Applied Linguistics* 22: 502–30.

Kasper, G. and R. Schmidt (1996). Developmental issues in interlanguage pragmatics. *Studies in Second Language Acquisition* 18: 149–69.

Kecskés, I. (2007). Formulaic language in English lingua franca. In I. Kecskés and L. Horn (eds.) *Explorations in Pragmatics*. Berlin: Mouton de Gruyter. 191–218.

Keizer, E. (2007). *The English Noun Phrase*. Cambridge: Cambridge University Press.

Kleiner, B. (1998). Whatever – Its use in "pseudo-argument." *Journal of Pragmatics* 30: 589–613.

Koester, A. (2007). "About twelve thousand or so": Vagueness in North American and UK offices. In J. Cutting (ed.) *Vague Language Explored*. Basingstoke, UK: Palgrave Macmillan. 40–61.

Koutlaki, S. (2002). Offers and expressions of thanks as face threatening acts: tæ'arof in Persian. *Journal of Pragmatics* 34: 1733–56.

Kozman, M. and J. Swales (2008). *Vague Language in Academia*. Unpublished manuscript, University of Michigan.

Kristeva, J. (1966/82). *Desire in Language*. New York: Columbia University Press. (Originally published in French as *Sémiotikè*.)

Kurath, H., S. Kuhn, J. Reidy and R. Lewis (eds.) (1952–2001). *Middle English Dictionary*. Ann Arbor, MI: University of Michigan Press. http://quod.lib.umich.edu/m/med/.

Kurylowicz, J. (1965). The evolution of grammatical categories. In J. Kurylowicz (ed.) (1976) *Esquisses linguistique*, Vol. 2. Munich: Fink. 158–74.

Kytö, M. and J. Culpeper (2006). *Corpus of English Dialogues 1560–1760*. Helsinki: University of Helsinki Press.

Labov, W. (1972). *Sociolinguistic Patterns*. Oxford: Blackwell.

Labov, W. (1994). *Principles of Linguistic Change, Volume 1: Internal Factors*. Oxford: Blackwell.

Labov, W. (2006). *The Social Stratification of English in New York City*, 2nd edn. Cambridge: Cambridge University Press.

Lakoff, G. (1972). Hedges: A study in meaning criteria and the logic of fuzzy concepts. In *Papers from the Eighth Regional Meeting of the Chicago Linguistic Society*. Chicago, IL: Chicago University Press. 183–228.

Lakoff, R. (1975/2004). *Language and Woman's Place* (revised edn.) New York: Oxford University Press.

Lakoff, R. (1990). *Talking Power*. New York: Basic Books.

Lauwereyns, S. (2002). Toka "or something" in Japanese spoken discourse. In Y. Shirai, H. Kobayashi, S. Miyata, K. Nakamura, T. Ogura and H. Sirai (eds.) *Studies in Language Sciences*, Vol. 2. Tokyo: Kurosio Publishers. 299–312.

Lehmann, C. (1985). Grammaticalization: Synchronic variation and diachronic change. *Lingua e Stile* 20: 303–18.

Lerner, G. (1994). Responsive list construction. *Journal of Language and Social Psychology* 13: 20–33.

Levey, S. (2007). *The Next Generation: Aspects of Grammatical Variation in the Speech of Some London Preadolescents*. Ph.D. dissertation, Queen Mary University of London.

Levey, S. (2012). General extenders and grammaticalization: Insights from London preadolescents. *Applied Linguistics* 33: 257–81.
LoCastro, V. (2012). *Pragmatics for Language Educators*. Abingdon, UK: Routledge.
Macaulay, R. (1985). The narrative skills of a Scottish coal miner. In M. Görlach (ed.) *Focus on: Scotland*. Amsterdam: John Benjamins. 101–24.
Macaulay, R. (1991). *Locating Dialect in Discourse*. Oxford: Oxford University Press.
Macaulay, R. (2002). You know, it depends. *Journal of Pragmatics* 34: 749–67.
MacKenzie, I. (2014). *English as a Lingua Franca*. Abingdon, UK: Routledge.
Malyuga, E. and M. McCarthy (2018). English and Russian vague category markers in business discourse: Linguistic identity aspects. *Journal of Pragmatics* 135: 39–52.
Margerie, H. (2010). On the rise of (inter)subjective meaning in the grammaticalization of *kind of/kinda*. In K. Davidse, L. Vandelanotte and H. Cuckyens (eds.) *Subjectification, Intersubjectification and Grammaticalization*. Berlin: Mouton de Gruyter. 315–48.
Masini, F., C. Mauri and P. Pietrandrea (2018). List constructions: Towards a unified account. *Italian Journal of Linguistics* 30: 49–94.
Matthews, P. (2007). *Oxford Concise Dictionary of Linguistics*, 3rd edn. Oxford: Oxford University Press.
Mauranen, A. (2004). "They're a little bit different . . . ": Observations on hedges in academic talk. In K. Aijmer and A.-B. Stenström (eds.) *Discourse Patterns in Spoken and Written Corpora*. Amsterdam: John Benjamins. 173–98.
Mauranen, A. (2008). *The Corpus of English as a Lingua Franca in Academic Settings*. Helsinki: ELFA. www.helsinki.fi/elfa/elfacorpus.
Mauranen, A. (2012). *Exploring ELF: Academic English Shaped by Non-Native Speakers*. Cambridge: Cambridge University Press.
Mauri, C. and A. Sansò (2018). Linguistic strategies for ad hoc categorization: Theoretical assessment and cross-linguistic variation. *Folia Linguistica* 52: 1–35.
McCarthy, M. (2020). Vague language in business and academic contexts. *Language Teaching* 53: 203–14.
McCarthy, M. and R. Carter (2002). This that and the other: Multi-word clusters in spoken English as visible patterns of interaction. *Teanga* 21: 30–52.
McColm, D. and G. Trousdale (2019). Whatever happened to *Whatever*? In N. Yáñez-Bouza, E. Moore, L. van Bergen and W. Hollman (eds.) *Categories, Constructions and Change in English Syntax*. Cambridge: Cambridge University Press. 81–104.
McSparran, F. (ed.) (2006). *Middle English Compendium: Corpus of Middle English Prose and Verse*. http://quod.lib.umich.edu/c/cme/.
Meillet, A. (1912/1958). L'évolution des forms grammaticales. *Scientia* 12. Reprinted in A. Meillet *Linguistique Historique et Linguistique Générale*. Paris: Champion. 130–48.
Metsä-Ketelä, M. (2016). Pragmatic vagueness: Exploring general extenders in English as a Lingua Franca. *Intercultural Pragmatics* 13: 325–51.
Meyerhoff, M. (2006). Topics from the tropics (Hawai'i). In W. Wolfram and B. Ward (eds.) *American Voices*. Oxford: Blackwell. 165–71.
Miskovic-Lukovic, M. (2009). "Is there a chance that I might kinda sort of take you to dinner?" The role of pragmatic particles *kind of* and *sort of* in utterance interpretation. *Journal of Pragmatics* 41: 602–25.
Moravcsik, E. (2003). A semantic analysis of associative plurals. *Studies in Language* 27: 469–503.

References

Müller, S. (2005). *Discourse Markers in Native and Non-Native English Discourse.* Amsterdam: John Benjamins.

Murphy, B. (2010). *Corpus and Sociolinguistics: Investigating Age and Gender in Female Talk.* Amsterdam: John Benjamins.

Murray, N. (2012). English as a lingua franca and the development of pragmatic competence. *ELT Journal* 66: 318–26.

Nikolaou, A. and J. Sclafani (2018). Representations of self and other in narratives of return migration. In K. Beeching, C. Ghezzi and P. Molinelli (eds.) *Positioning the Self and Others.* Amsterdam: John Benjamins. 241–62.

Norrby, C. and J. Winter (2002). Affiliation in adolescents' use of discourse extenders. In C. Allan (ed.) *Proceedings of the 2001 Conference of the Australian Linguistic Society.* www.als.asn.au.

O'Keeffe, A. (2004). "Like the wise virgins and all that jazz": Using a corpus to examine vague categorization and shared knowledge. *Language and Computers* 52: 1–26.

O'Keeffe, A. (2006). *Investigating Media Discourse.* Abingdon, UK: Routledge.

O'Keeffe, A., M. McCarthy and R. Carter (2007). *From Corpus to Classroom: Language Use and Language Teaching.* Cambridge: Cambridge University Press.

O'Keeffe, A., B. Clancy and S. Adolphs (2011). *Introducing Pragmatics in Use.* Abingdon, UK: Routledge.

Ortega-Barrera, I. (2012). A diachronic discussion of extenders in English remedies found in the Corpus of Early English Recipes (1350–1850). In H. Sauer and G. Waxenberger (eds.) *English Historical Linguistics 2008.* Vol. II: Words, Texts and Genres. Amsterdam: John Benjamins. 223–36.

Overstreet, M. (1999). *Whales, Candlelight and Stuff Like that: General Extenders in English Discourse.* New York: Oxford University Press.

Overstreet, M. (2001). *Increasing Pragmatic Awareness.* Unpublished material from a workshop presented at Nagoya Institute of Foreign Studies, Nagoya, Japan.

Overstreet, M. (2005). And stuff, und so: Investigating pragmatic expressions in English and German. *Journal of Pragmatics* 37: 1845–64.

Overstreet, M. (2007). *Cross-linguistic pragmatic analysis.* Unpublished material from a workshop presented at the Federal University of Espírito Santo, Vitória, Brazil.

Overstreet, M. (2010). Metapragmatics. In J. Cutting (ed.) *The Pragmatics Encyclopedia.* Abingdon, UK: Routledge. 266–68.

Overstreet, M. (2011). Vagueness and hedging. In G. Andersen and K. Aijmer (eds.) *Pragmatics of Society.* Berlin: Mouton de Gruyter. 293–318.

Overstreet, M. (2012a). General extenders in Hawai'i Creole English. Paper presented to *Da Pidgin Coup*: Charlene Junko Sato Center for Pidgin, Creole and Dialect Studies, University of Hawai'i.

Overstreet, M. (2012b). Pragmatic expressions in cross-linguistic perspective. *Applied Research in English* 1(2): 1–13.

Overstreet, M. (2014). The role of pragmatic function in the grammaticalization of English general extenders . *Pragmatics* 24: 105–29.

Overstreet, M. (2015). Metapragmatics. In C. Chapelle (ed.) *The Encyclopedia of Applied Linguistics.* Online: Wiley-Blackwell.

Overstreet, M. and G. Yule (1997a). Locally contingent categorization in discourse. *Discourse Processes* 23: 83–97.

Overstreet, M. and G. Yule (1997b). On being inexplicit and stuff in contemporary American English. *Journal of English Linguistics* 25: 250–58.

Overstreet, M. and G. Yule (1999). Fostering pragmatic awareness. *Applied Language Learning* 10: 1–13.

Overstreet, M. and G. Yule (2001). Formulaic disclaimers. *Journal of Pragmatics* 33: 45–60.

Overstreet, M. and G. Yule (2002). The metapragmatics of *and everything*. *Journal of Pragmatics* 34: 785–94.

Overstreet, M., J. Tran and S. Zietze (2006). Increasing pragmatic awareness: Die Vagheit der Sprache und so. *Die Unterrichtspraxis/Teaching German* 39: 24–29.

Palacios Martínez, I. (2011). I might, I might go I mean it depends on money things *and stuff*: A preliminary analysis of general extenders in British teenagers' discourse. *Journal of Pragmatics* 43: 2452–70.

Palacios Martínez, I. and P. Núñez Pertejo (2015). "Go up to Miss Thingy," "He's probably like a whatsit or something." Placeholders in focus. The differences in use between teenagers and adults in spoken English. *Pragmatics* 25: 425–51.

Parvaresh, V., M. Tavangar and A. Rasekh (2010). General extenders in Persian discourse: Frequency and grammatical distribution. *Cross-Cultural Communication* 6(3): 18–35.

Parvaresh, V., M. Tavangar, A. Rasekh and D. Izadi (2012). About his friend, how good she is, *and this and that*: General extenders in native Persian and non-native English discourse. *Journal of Pragmatics* 44: 261–79.

Pichler, H. (2010). Methods in discourse variation analysis: Reflections on the way forward. *Journal of Sociolinguistics* 14: 561–608.

Pichler, H. and S. Levey (2010). Variability in the co-occurrence of discourse features. *Language Studies Working Papers* 2: 17–27.

Pichler, H. and S. Levey (2011). In search of grammaticalization in synchronic dialect data: General extenders in northeast England. *English Language and Linguistics* 15: 441–71.

Poos, D. and R. Simpson (2002). Cross-disciplinary comparisons of hedging: Some findings from the Michigan Corpus of Academic Spoken English. In R. Reppen, S. Fitzmaurice and D. Biber (eds.) *Using Corpora to Explore Linguistic Variation*. Amsterdam: John Benjamins. 3–23.

Poutsma, H. (1904–1926). *A Grammar of Late Modern English*. Groningen: P. Noordhoff.

Pukui, M. and S. Elbert (1986). *Hawaiian Dictionary*, revised and enlarged edn. Honolulu, HI: University of Hawai'i Press.

Quirk, R., S. Greenbaum, G. Leech and J. Svartvik (1972). *A Grammar of Contemporary English*. London: Longman.

Rickford, J. and J. Handler (1994). Textual evidence on the nature of early Barbadian speech, 1676–1835. *Journal of Pidgin and Creole Languages* 9: 221–55.

Romaine, S. and D. Lange (1991). The use of *like* as a marker of reported speech and thought: A case of grammaticalization in progress. *American Speech* 66: 227–79.

Romero-Trillo, J. (2002). The pragmatic fossilization of discourse markers in non-native speakers of English. *Journal of Pragmatics* 34: 769–84.

Romero-Trillo, J. (2015). Understanding vagueness: A prosodic analysis of endocentric and exocentric general extenders in English conversation. *Journal of Pragmatics* 86: 54–62.
Rommetveit, R. (1974). *On Message Structure*. London: John Wiley.
Rosch, E. (1975). Cognitive representations of semantic categories. *Journal of Experimental Psychology* 104: 192–233.
Rose, K. (2005). On the effects of instruction in second language pragmatics. *System* 33: 385–99.
Rose, K. and G. Kasper (eds.) (2001). *Pragmatics in Language Teaching*. Cambridge: Cambridge University Press.
Roth-Gordon, J. (2007). Youth, slang, and pragmatic expressions: Examples from Brazilian Portuguese. *Journal of Sociolinguistics* 11: 322–45.
Ruzaité, J. (2010). Translation equivalents of vague language items: A study of general extenders in a parallel corpus. *Studies about Languages* 16: 33–38.
Ruzaité, J. (2018). General extenders and discourse variation: A focus on Lithuanian. *International Journal of Corpus Linguistics* 23: 467–93.
Sacks, H. (1992). *Lectures on Conversation*, Vol. 1. Oxford: Blackwell.
Safina, C. (2002). *Eye of the Albatross*. Holt Paperbacks.
Sakoda, K. and J. Siegel (2003). *Pidgin Grammar*. Honolulu, HI: Bess Press.
Salinger, J. D. (1951). *The Catcher in the Rye*. Boston, MA: Little, Brown and Company.
Sankoff, G. (2018). Language change across the lifespan. *Annual Review of Linguistics* 4: 297–316.
Sato, C. (1991). Sociolinguistic variation and attitudes in Hawai'i. In J. Cheshire (ed.) *English Around the World: Sociolinguistic Perspectives*. Cambridge: Cambridge University Press. 647–63.
Scheibman, J. (2002). *Point of View and Grammar*. Amsterdam: John Benjamins.
Schiffrin, D. (1987). *Discourse Markers*. Cambridge: Cambridge University Press.
Schiffrin, D. (1994). Making a list. *Discourse Processes* 17: 377–406.
Schleef, E. (2008). The "lecturer's OK" revisited: Changing discourse conventions and the influence of academic division. *American Speech* 83: 62–84.
Schmidt, R. (1993). Consciousness, learning and interlanguage pragmatics. In G. Kasper and S. Blum-Kulka (eds.) *Interlanguage Pragmatics*. Oxford: Oxford University Press. 21–42.
Schmidt, R. (2001). Attention. In P. Robinson (ed.) *Cognition and Second Language Instruction*. Cambridge: Cambridge University Press. 3–32.
Schutz, A. (1932/1967). *The Phenomenology of the Social World*. (Translated by G. Walsh and F. Lehnert). Evanston, IL: Northwestern University Press.
Schutz, A. (1962). *Collected Papers Volume 1* (edited by Arvid Broderson). The Hague: Martinus Nijhoff.
Schwitalla, J. (1997). *Gesprochenes Deutsch*. Berlin: Erich Schmidt.
Secova, M. (2011). *Discourse-Pragmatic Features of Spoken French: Analysis and Pedagogical Implications*. Ph.D. dissertation, Queen Mary University, London.
Secova, M. (2014). "*Je sais et tout mais* ... " might the general extenders in European French be changing? *Journal of French Language Studies* 24: 281–304.
Secova, M. (2017). Discourse-pragmatic variation in Paris French and London English: Insights from general extenders. *Journal of Pragmatics* 114: 1–15.

References

Secova, M. (2018). Direct speech, subjectivity and speaker positioning in London English and Paris French. In K. Beeching, C. Ghezzi and P. Molinelli (eds.) *Positioning the Self and Others*. Amsterdam: John Benjamins. 155–75.

Seidlhofer, B. (2011). *Understanding English as a Lingua Franca*. Oxford: Oxford University Press.

Shaw, P., T. Caudery and M. Petersen (2009). Students on exchange in Scandinavia: Motivation, interaction ELF development. In A. Mauranen and E. Ranta (eds.) *English as a Lingua Franca*. Newcastle, UK: Cambridge Scholars Publishing. 178–99.

Shirato, J. and P. Stapleton (2007). Comparing English vocabulary in a spoken learner corpus with a native speaker corpus: Pedagogical implications arising from an empirical study in Japan. *Language Teaching Research* 11: 393–412.

Siegel, J. (2000). Substrate influence in Hawai'i Creole English. *Language in Society* 29: 197–236.

Siegel, J. (2008). *The Emergence of Pidgin and Creole Languages*. Oxford: Oxford University Press.

Silva, G. and A. Macedo (1992). Discourse markers in the spoken Portuguese of Rio de Janeiro. *Language Variation and Change* 4: 235–49.

Simpson, R. (2004). Stylistic features of academic speech: The role of formulaic expressions. In U. Connor and T. Upton (eds.) *Discourse in the Professions*. Amsterdam: John Benjamins. 37–64.

Skelton, J. (1988). The care and maintenance of hedges. *ELT Journal* 42: 37–42.

Smit, U. (2009). Emic evaluations and interactive processes in a classroom community of practice. In A. Mauranen and E. Ranta (eds.) *English as a Lingua Franca*. Newcastle, UK: Cambridge Scholars Publishing. 200–24.

Spöttl, C. and M. McCarthy (2004). Comparing the knowledge of formulaic sequences across L1, L2, L3 and L4. In N. Schmitt (ed.) *Formulaic Sequences*. Amsterdam: John Benjamins. 191–225.

Stenström, A.-B. (2011). Pauses and hesitations. In G. Andersen and K. Aijmer (eds.) *Pragmatics of Society*. Berlin: Walter de Gruyter. 537–67.

Stenström, A.-B., G. Andersen and I. Hasund (2002). *Trends in Teenage Talk*. Amsterdam: John Benjamins.

Stubbe, M. and J. Holmes (1995). *You know, eh* and other "exasperating expressions": An analysis of social and stylistic variation in the use of pragmatic devices in a sample of New Zealand English. *Language and Communication* 15: 63–88.

Sunagawa, Y., S. Komada, M. Shimoda, M. Suzuki, S. Tsutsui, A. Hasunuma, A. Bekes, and J. Morimoto (1998). *Nihongo Bunkei Jiten (Japanese Grammar Dictionary)*. Tokyo: Kurosio Publishers.

Svartvik, J. and R. Quirk (eds.) (1980). *A Corpus of English Conversation*. Lund, Sweden: Lund University Press.

Sweetser, E. (1988). Grammaticalization and semantic bleaching. In S. Axmaker, A. Jaisser and H. Singmaster (eds.) *Proceedings of the Fourteenth Annual Meeting of the Berkeley Linguistic Society*. Berkeley, CA: Berkeley Linguistic Society. 389–405.

Tagliamonte, S. (2012). *Variationist Sociolinguistics: Change, Observation, Interpretation*. Oxford: Wiley-Blackwell.

Tagliamonte, S. (2013). *Roots of English: Exploring the History of Dialects*. Cambridge: Cambridge University Press.

References

Tagliamonte, S. (2016). Antecedents of innovation: Exploring general extenders in conservative dialects. In H. Pichler (ed.) *Discourse-Pragmatic Variation and Change in English*. Cambridge: Cambridge University Press. 115–38.

Tagliamonte, S. and D. Denis (2010). The stuff of change: General extenders in Toronto, Canada. *Journal of English Linguistics* 38: 335–68.

Takimoto, M. (2009). The effects of input-based tasks on the development of learners' pragmatic proficiency. *Applied Linguistics* 30: 1–25.

Tannen, D. (1986). Introducing constructed dialogue in Greek and American conversational and literary narratives. In F. Coulmas (ed.) *Direct and Indirect Speech*. Berlin: Mouton. 311–22.

Tarski, A. (1935/1956). Der Wahrheitsbegriff in den formalisierten Sprachen. *Studia Philosophica* 1: 261–405; reprinted as The concept of truth in formal languages. In A. Tarski, *Logic, Semantics, Metamathematics* (translated by J. Woodger). Oxford: Clarendon Press.

Tayebi, T. and V. Parvaresh (2014). Conversational disclaimers in Persian. *Journal of Pragmatics* 62: 77–93.

Terraschke, A. (2007a). *The Use of Pragmatic Devices by German Non-Native Speakers of English*. Ph.D. dissertation, Victoria University of Wellington, New Zealand.

Terraschke, A. (2007b). Use of general extenders by German non-native speakers of English. *International Review of Applied Linguistics* 45: 141–60.

Terraschke, A. (2010). Or so, oder so, and stuff like that: General extenders in New Zealand English, German, and learner language. *Intercultural Pragmatics* 7: 449–69.

Terraschke, A. and J. Holmes (2007). "Und tralala": Vagueness and general extenders in German and New Zealand English. In J. Cutting (ed.) *Vague Language Explored*. Basingstoke, UK: Palgrave Macmillan. 198–220.

Thackeray, W. (1852). *The History of Henry Esmond, Esq*. London: Smith, Elder & Company.

Tonouchi, L. (2001). *Da Word*. Honolulu, HI: Bamboo Ridge Press.

Traugott, E. (1982). From propositional to textual and expressive meanings: Some semantic-pragmatic aspects of grammaticalization. In W. Lehman and Y. Malkiel (eds.) *Perspectives on Historical Linguistics*. Amsterdam: John Benjamins. 245–71.

Traugott, E. (1995). The role of the development of discourse markers in a theory of grammaticalization. Paper presented at *ICHL XII*, Manchester, UK.

Traugott, E. (2010). Revisiting subjectification and intersubjectification. In K. Davidse, L. Vandelotte and H. Cuyckens (eds.) *Subjectification, Intersubjectification and Grammaticalization*. Berlin: Mouton de Gruyter. 29–70.

Traugott, E. (2012). Intersubjectification and clause periphery. *English Text Construction* 5: 7–28.

Traugott, E. (2015). Toward a coherent account of grammatical constructionalization. In J. Barðdal, E. Smirnova, L. Sommerer and S. Gildea (eds.) *Diachronic Construction Grammar*. Amsterdam: John Benjamins. 51–79.

Traugott, E. (2016). On the rise of types of clause-final pragmatic markers in English. *Journal of Historical Pragmatics* 17: 26–54.

Traugott, E. and B. Heine (eds.) (1991). *Approaches to Grammaticalization*. Amsterdam: John Benjamins (2 volumes).

Traugott, E. and G. Trousdale (2013). *Constructionalization and Constructional Change*. Oxford: Oxford University Press.

Tsui, A. (1994). *English Conversation*. Oxford: Oxford University Press.
Vaughan, E., M. McCarthy and B. Clancy (2017). Vague category markers as turn-final items in Irish English. *World Englishes* 36: 208–22.
Verdonik, D. (2015). Internal variety in the use of Slovene general extenders in different spoken discourse settings. *International Journal of Corpus Linguistics* 20: 445–68.
Verschueren, J. (1999). *Understanding Pragmatics*. London: Edward Arnold.
Verschueren, J. (2000). Notes on the role of metapragmatic awareness in language use. *Pragmatics* 10: 439–56.
Vincent, D. (1983). *Les Ponctuants de la Langue*. Ph.D. dissertation, University of Montréal.
Vincent, D. and D. Sankoff (1992). Punctors: A pragmatic variable. *Language Variation and Change* 4: 205–16.
Wagner, S., A. Hesson, K. Bybel and H. Little (2015). Quantifying the referential function of general extenders in North American English. *Language in Society* 44: 705–31.
Wagner, S., A. Hesson, K. and H. Little (2016). The use of referential general extenders across registers. In H. Pichler (ed.) *Discourse-Pragmatic Variation and Change in English*. Cambridge: Cambridge University Press. 211–31.
Walsh, S., A. O'Keeffe and M. McCarthy (2008). "... post-colonialism, multiculturalism, structuralism, feminism, post-modernism and so on and so forth": A comparative analysis of vague category markers in academic discourse. In A. Ädel and R. Reppen (eds.) *Corpora and Discourse: The Challenge of Different Settings*. Amsterdam: John Benjamins. 9–29.
Ward, G. and B. Birner (1993). The semantics and pragmatics of *and everything*. *Journal of Pragmatics* 19: 205–14.
Warren, M. (2007). {/[Oh] Not a <^ Lot}: Discourse intonation and vague language. In J. Cutting (ed.) *Vague Language Explored*. Basingstoke, UK: Palgrave Macmillan. 182–97.
Watanabe, T. (2015). *Corpus-Based Study of the Use of English General Extenders spoken by Japanese Users of English across Speaking Levels and Task Types*. Ph.D. dissertation, University of Edinburgh.
Watts, R. (1989). Taking the pitcher to the "well": Native speakers' perception of their use of discourse markers in conversation. *Journal of Pragmatics* 13: 203–37.
Welsh, I. (1994). *The Acid House*. London: Jonathan Cape.
Widdowson, H. (2004). A perspective on recent trends. In A. Howatt and H. Widdowson (eds.) *A History of English Language Teaching*, 2nd edn. Oxford: Oxford University Press. 353–72.
Winter, J. and C. Norrby (2000). Set-marking tags and stuff. In J. Henderson (ed.) *Proceedings of the 1999 Conference of the Australian Linguistics Society*. www.linguistics.uwa.edu.au/research/als99/proceedings.
Youssef, V. (1993). Marking solidarity across the Trinidad speech community: The use of *an ting* in medical counseling to break down power differentials. *Discourse and Society* 4: 291–306.
Yule, G. (1996). *Pragmatics*. Oxford: Oxford University Press.
Yule, G. (2020). *The Study of Language*, 7th edn. Cambridge: Cambridge University Press.

Index

academic register, 13, 138, 179, 181
ad hoc category, 29, 39, 40, 41, 44
addressee-oriented, 42, 43, 45
adjunctive general extenders, 1
age, 126
age-grading, 129, 130
age-related variation, 127
age-specific variation, 130
American English, 144
anaphor, 6
antecedent, 6, 23
antecedent–anaphor, 36
apparent time, 129, 130, 131
approximation, 24, 47, 52, 76, 89
associative plural, 21, 202
associative plural marker, 21, 203
attention, 193
audience-design, 43
Australian English, 146
automatization, 120

backchannels, 50, 96
bracketing, 9, 56, 65, 86, 88, 90, 199
Brazilian Portuguese, 157, 176
British English, 145
business register, 13, 140

Canadian English, 146, 206
careful style, 13
casual style, 13
categorization, 22, 28, 29, 30, 35, 36, 38, 39, 40, 41, 42, 221, 228, 229
category-identifying, 6
category-marking, 37
Chinese L 1, 188
clause-final, 6
clusters, 86, 89, 94
co-construction, 9, 20, 37, 49, 72, 216
cognate, 18, 182, 183
cohesion, 24
cohesive, 6, 36, 41, 115, 204
collective affirmation, 96

collocation, 55, 102, 188
collocation requirements, 52
common ground, 46, 48, 60
complaining, 63
completion point, 212
constructed dialogue, 169
content-oriented, 42, 45
context-sensitivity, 150
contextualization cues, 52, 54
cooperative fellow speaker, 20, 47
Cooperative Principle, 45, 47
coordination, 12, 117
coordination constraints, 119
coordination tags, 1
Creole, 14
Creole marker, 14

data-elicitation, 149
debates, 211
decategorialization, 12, 116
dialectal variants, 149
direction of change, 103, 107
discourse function, 125
discourse markers, 5, 18
discourse-pragmatic features, 91
disjunctive general extenders, 1, 8
double brackets, 20, 88, 91, 140, 199
Dutch L 1, 18, 179

editing, 80
enclitic, 21, 203
English as a lingua franca (ELF), 16, 18, 178, 183, 186, 188, 192, 217
English Creoles, 151
English L 1, 177, 179, 187
evaluation, 40, 61, 62, 63
evaluative element, 8
expectation, 65, 67
expressing indifference, 73
expressive function, 8, 43
extender tags, 33, 35
extension particle, 129

235

face, 43
female speakers, 132, 134
filled pause, 80, 89, 122, 181
first language (L1), 177
fixed expressions, 100
focal referent, 21, 203
foregrounding, 92
formal speech, 3, 13
formulaic construction, 67, 165
formulaic disclaimer, 70, 71, 72, 110, 174
French, 14, 129, 166, 175, 199
French L1, 16, 178
fusion, 12, 120

gender, 128, 131
general extenders, 221, 222, 223, 224, 225, 228, 229, 230, 231, 233, 234
generic noun, 2
German, 16, 160, 175, 187, 202
German L1, 18, 177, 179, 181, 187, 189
grammatical agreement, 4, 187
grammatical markers, 12, 116
grammaticalization, 10, 11, 115, 121, 122, 130, 166, 171
Gricean maxims, 45, 47

hapaxes, 215
Hawai'i Creole English/Pidgin, 151, 153, 203
Hawaiian, 203
hedges, 7, 51, 54, 57, 58, 77, 168, 180, 216
hedging, 24
historical development, 10, 98
historical record, 10
Hong Kong English, 143
humor, 55
hyponymy, 44

iambic structure, 81
imposition, 7, 57
inference, 23
informal speech, 13
information-oriented, 133
intensifier, 8, 64, 66
interaction-oriented, 133
interjection, 74, 77
interlanguage, 186, 187
international variation, 143, 144
interpersonal, 7, 50, 53, 57
interpersonal function, 7, 8, 14, 20, 43, 45, 123, 152, 199
intersubjective, 156
intersubjectivity, ix, 7, 8, 43, 45, 46, 47, 56, 60, 62, 154, 163, 213
intertextuality, 34, 35, 40
intonation, 66

invitation, 57
Irish English, 30, 147

Jane Austen, 54, 70, 107, 109, 169
Japanese, 157, 203
Japanese L1, 17

language teaching, 16, 177, 192
Latin, 204
layering, 120
learner language, 16, 177
left-hand bracket, 9, 88, 90, 163, 183, 216
lexical bundles, 139
lexical replacement, 113, 122, 131, 146, 206
lexicalized categories, 29
lexifier language, 151
lifespan data, 131
linguistic category, 214
linguistic context, 28
linguistic variable, 126
list completers, 31, 32, 33, 211
list-completion, 6, 32, 160
list construction, 33, 212
lists, 75, 104, 211
Lithuanian, 14, 15, 159
London English, 166
long forms, 2, 13, 30, 37, 38, 40, 93, 110, 120, 139, 205

male speakers, 132, 134
maximizing, 63
mental worlds, 46
metalanguage, 76, 214
metalinguistic awareness, 76
metapragmatic awareness, 76
metapragmatics, 77
middle class, 131, 132, 134, 135, 137, 205
Middle English, 10, 98, 103, 207
minimum expectation, 70
Montreal French, 82, 136, 166, 176
morphological reanalysis, 12
morphosyntactic reanalysis, 119
multifunctionality, 5, 19, 198, 213
mutual understanding, 7

negative adjunctive form, 158
negative evaluation, 79
negative politeness, 71, 88, 164
negative politeness strategies, 7, 57
New Zealand English, 147
non-lexicalized categories, 29, 44
noticing, 193
novel constructions, 78

Index

object noun phrase, 20
Old English, 98, 207
older speakers, 13, 126, 129, 145, 206
oral punctuation marks, 9, 81, 122, 154

Parisian French, 14, 136, 166, 176, 199
participation framework, 61, 150
pejorative, 8, 61, 129, 164, 200
performance fillers, 79
Persian, 14, 173, 175, 185, 202
Persian L1, 17, 185, 190, 193
personal function, 8, 60, 199
person-oriented, 45
phonological attrition, 12, 120
phrase-final, 6
Pidgin, 203
placeholders, 80
politeness, 44
politeness function, 7
politeness strategies, 8, 45
positive politeness, 7, 48, 49, 50, 51
positive politeness strategy, 7
pragmatic awareness, 16, 17, 191, 192
pragmatic expressions, 16, 177
pragmatic fossilization, 177
pragmatic markers, 5, 7, 9, 11, 18, 20, 43, 50, 76, 81, 86, 89, 94, 116, 184, 223, 233
pragmatic shift, 122
pragmatics instruction, 17, 192
prefabricated phrase, 120
Present Day English (PDE), 98
proform, 2
pronunciation, 12
propositional information, 6
public self-image, 43
punctor, 81, 84, 122, 163, 169, 171, 181

Quality maxim, 51, 53, 67, 76, 124
Quantity maxim, 47, 48, 62, 123

rapport, 20, 123, 152
reduction, 116, 121
referential function, 6, 7, 9, 22, 35, 41, 42, 45, 57, 123, 198, 213, 234
register, 13, 137, 204
register variation, 140
relic areas, 102
reported speech, 54
request, 57, 71
restricted tags, 35, 38, 39
restrictive relative clause, 40
right periphery, 202, 216
right-hand bracket, 9, 88, 90, 163, 183
Russian, 159

Scottish English, 148
second language (L2), 177
second language learners, 8
self-repair, 80
semantic bleaching, 11, 123
semantic features, 24, 25
set expanders, 86
set-marking, 6, 22, 23, 24, 25, 26, 27, 28, 36, 37, 42, 81
set-marking tags, 22
short forms, 2, 13, 30, 36, 93, 110, 120, 205
Singaporean English, 143
SKT-construction, 3, 115
SKT tags, 38, 39
social class, 13, 134, 135, 211
social cohesion, 5
social differentiation, 13
social marker, 12, 136, 143
social marking, 125, 199, 200
social parameters, 12
social variable, 126
social variation, 125
sociolinguistic variation, 166
solidarity, 7, 48, 51, 123, 152
Spanish, 158, 187
Spanish L 1, 187
speaker uncertainty, 54
speaker-oriented, 42, 60, 62
specific extenders, 2, 40, 41, 61, 63, 101, 105, 108, 203, 204, 207
speech style, 9
spoken language, 137
stance, 60, 61, 74, 77, 78, 86
study abroad, 187
subject noun phrase, 20, 202, 203, 211
subjective, 62, 73, 163
subjective function, 174, 199
subjectivity, vi, 46, 56, 60, 61, 62, 71, 72, 232
superstrate, 151, 153
Swedish, 82, 171, 175, 190
Swedish L 1, 19, 179, 183
syntactic structure, 4
syntactically optional, 21, 202

tag, 22, 25, 31
terminating tags, 24
text, defined, 79
textual cohesion, 5
textual function, 6, 9, 20, 79, 90, 92, 171, 190, 199, 213
textual monitors, 80
three-partedness, 31, 38
tone unit, 3, 36, 93, 120
tonic stress, 153
topic, 92

238   Index

topic shift, 95
transfer, 185, 192
transfer from L 1, 182
translation, 159
translation equivalents, 15, 156, 161, 187
Trinidad Creole, 14, 51, 152
turn construction, 93
turn management, 96
turn taking, 9, 96
turn-completion, 6
turn-final items, 96
turn yielding, 93, 94
type of person, 23

unrestricted tag, 36
upper class, 211
utterance position, 20, 200
utterance-final position, 14, 20, 164, 200
utterance-final tags, 24

vague category, 27
vague category identifier, 27
vague category markers, 18, 30
vague category marking, 38
vague language, 15, 79, 178, 190
vague tags, 27
variable tags, 26
variational pragmatics, 143
variationist studies, 125

word order, 14, 202
word-finding difficulty, 80
working class, 131, 132, 134, 135, 137, 205
written language, 137

younger speakers, 13, 126, 129, 145, 206

Printed in the United States
by Baker & Taylor Publisher Services